THE VOYAGE OF PEDRO ALVARES CABRAL TO BRAZIL AND INDIA

THE VOYAGE OF PEDRO ALVARES CABRAL TO BRAZIL AND INDIA

FROM
CONTEMPORARY DOCUMENTS AND NARRATIVES

TRANSLATED
WITH INTRODUCTION AND NOTES
BY
WILLIAM BROOKS GREENLEE

GYAN

Published by

Gyan Publishing House
5, Ansari Road
Daryaganj, New Delhi-110002
Phone: 011-47034999, 9811692060
E-mail: books@gyanbooks.com

Distribution Network
gyanbooks.com
India, USA, Canada, UK, Australia, France

ISBN : 978-81-212-4557-9 (HB)
First Published, 1938

2nd Impression 2020

Printed at: Gyan Press, Delhi.

The book at your disposal is the edition of an old book originally published long back. The Text quality of this book may not be at par as compared to our other books but many readers approached us to reprint this important book so that it could satiate their hunger. We request all the readers of this book to help us to improve its quality by providing the necessary text of those pages which are not properly visible. Your valuable support in this case will be highly appreciated and acknowledged and our future readers will be benefitted immensely.

THE VOYAGE OF PEDRO ÁLVARES CABRAL TO BRAZIL AND INDIA

FROM
CONTEMPORARY DOCUMENTS AND NARRATIVES

TRANSLATED
WITH INTRODUCTION AND NOTES
BY

WILLIAM BROOKS GREENLEE

LONDON
PRINTED FOR THE HAKLUYT SOCIETY
MCMXXXVIII

COUNCIL
OF
THE HAKLUYT SOCIETY
1937

CONTENTS

INTRODUCTION

DOCUMENTS

MAPS AND ILLUSTRATIONS

PREFACE

THE voyage of Pedro Álvares Cabral has usually been thought of only in connexion with the discovery of Brazil. It is the purpose of this volume, therefore, to consider the voyage as a whole, including the influences which preceded it and the results which followed. With this general view in mind the voyage appears of greater importance, and some light is thrown on the question of the westward diversion of Cabral's fleet during which Brazil was visited.

I have outlined in the introduction the events relating to the voyage. An opportunity has thus been afforded for interpretation. This survey has been followed by more detailed discussions of special subjects. The conclusions reached express my opinions and may not be final. Few of the contemporary sources which I have here translated have hitherto been available in English. These translations are perhaps more literal than would seem necessary, because an endeavour has been made to retain so far as possible the spirit of the times and to ensure accuracy, though sometimes at the sacrifice of more modern usage.

The names of places in the texts have usually been retained in their original forms but have been given their English equivalents elsewhere. The names of persons, however, have not been translated, except in a few instances.

The sources used in the preparation of this volume have been chiefly from my own collection, supplemented by the resources of the Newberry Library of Chicago and particularly of its Edward E. Ayer Collection.

Acknowledgement is due to the works of the historians Antonio Baião, Jaime Cortesão, Duarte Leite, Henrique Lopes de Mendoça, C. Malheiro Dias, Luciano Pereira da Silva, and particularly to their contributions in the *História da Colonização Portuguesa do Brasil*, and to the works of Joaquim Bensaude, A. Fontoura da Costa, and to others whose writings I have consulted.

For courtesies in the collection of material from Italian archives I wish to thank the librarians of the Biblioteca

Nazionale Marciana, the Archivio di Stato di Venezia, the Biblioteca Medicea Laurenziana, and the Vatican libraries. I take this opportunity also to express my obligation to Dr. Alfred Métraux of the Musée Trocadéro, and to M. Charles de la Roncière of the Bibliothèque Nationale in Paris, to the Rev. Georg Schurhammer, S.J., of the Gregorian College in Rome, and to Dr. Pierce Butler of the University of Chicago, for encouragement and suggestions.

To Sir William Foster, President of the Hakluyt Society, and to Professor Edgar Prestage, of the Council, I am especially indebted for friendly assistance and advice, and to Mr. Edward Lynam, the Hon. Secretary, for many kindnesses and for seeing this volume through the press.

W. B. GREENLEE

CHICAGO, *January 1937*

INTRODUCTION

THE VOYAGE

FROM a very early period the desire of Europeans for the luxuries of the East, especially for spices and drugs, developed a lucrative commerce in those commodities. The period of the Crusades coincided with a renewed demand for them in Europe, and as this trade developed it centred in Venice, which secured its cargoes from the ports of Egypt and the Levant and distributed them throughout Europe.[1] The fall of Constantinople in 1453 and the closing of the Persian Gulf routes by the Turks restricted the spice trade to the routes of the Red Sea and gave the Arabs and Egyptians practically a monopoly.[2] During the latter half of the fifteenth century they exacted a large revenue in the form of taxes and presents from the caravans of Indian products which came continually to the ports of Egypt and Syria from the head of the Red Sea, or from Jidda and Mecca in Arabia, over which they had control.

At this time Venice had become the richest state in Europe, partly through her geographical position and partly through the avoidance of costly wars, but chiefly because of her commerce in oriental commodities. Her most lucrative trade was in spices, which had become almost a necessity throughout Europe for perfumes, for condiments, and for flavouring wines. The incense gums were needed for religious ceremonies, and for medical purposes the drugs could hardly be dispensed with. The profit which Venice obtained notwithstanding the tremendous intermediate costs was known in Lisbon, and since Portugal was a poor country the people and their king were willing to make any sacrifice in order to secure this wealth.

[1] The search for spices was one of the greatest impelling forces in medieval discovery. To it was due the discovery of America, and the rounding of the Cape of Good Hope, to obtain a sea route to India and the East Indies. It was lure of spices which, at a later date, sent English and Dutch fleets to the East, and was the cause of the beginning of their colonial empires in Asia.

[2] The Portuguese, however, had begun to affect the trade of Alexandria in a small way before Cabral reached India. The importation of ivory and Ashanti pepper from Guinea and the cultivation of sugar in Madeira and São Thomé had taken some of the trade from Egypt.

Although Portugal was one of the smallest nations in Europe, there were many reasons for her being the only one which could secure the monopoly of the Eastern trade at the beginning of the sixteenth century. Her geographical position isolated her to a large extent from the rest of the Iberian peninsula and developed a people which differed in many respects from their neighbours. A frugal life and the struggles against their enemies caused them to be hardy and courageous. The position of Portugal on the shores of the Atlantic developed able sailors and an interest in matters pertaining to the sea. When these people broke away from the loose federation of Spanish states in the twelfth century they began a struggle to maintain their isolation, which built up a strong feeling of nationalism. The relations with the English Crusaders who paused on their way to the Holy Land, the wars for the expulsion of the Moors, and the prominence of the religious orders of knighthood, all tended to inculcate in the Portuguese people the ideas of chivalry and a desire for the conversion or destruction of the infidels. With the powerful Spanish kingdom to the north and east it was but natural that they should look to the sea to the west and south for their development. Portugal had no political aspirations in Europe, and made few alliances. She sought only to retain her independence. England had been her friend since the days of the expulsion of the Moors; France could not be relied upon, but friendly relations were maintained with that country to prevent aggression and to protect Portugal from her real danger, the ambition of Spain. But Portugal and Spain were then closely allied.

The capture of Ceuta, the stepping-stone to Spain from North Africa, in 1415, marked a new era in Portuguese history. There was then opened to the people of Portugal a vista of future territorial expansion in Morocco, an outlet for their religious zeal, and perhaps also an opportunity to reach Prester John, the Christian King of Abyssinia beyond the desert, who might aid Christendom, and incidentally the Portuguese, in driving the Moors from North Africa. The plans for expansion, both religious and commercial, were developed by Prince Henry the Navigator, the Governor of the Order of Christ. His efforts to conquer Morocco showed that it would be difficult and costly. His energies and the resources of his Order were then diverted to exploration towards the south along the African coast, to reach the countries from whence, he had learned, came gold, ivory, slaves, and pepper across the Sahara.

The little caravels which were sent out from Lagos crept slowly down the coast of Africa, past Cape Non and Cape Bojador, past the desert coasts, until they found a country rich with tropical vegetation. Prince Henry spent the greater part of his life in carrying out his plans for voyages along the African coast and into the Atlantic, where he rediscovered the Azores and Madeiras, and in developing the barren soil of Algarve with African slaves. He was, above all, guided by his faith and his opposition to the growing power of Islam, but he also sought the commercial development of his country. He hoped to reach Prester John by rounding Africa, and to secure his aid, but the voyage was long and difficult and the resources at his command were inadequate. He never found Prester John, although an ambassador of that potentate visited him in Lisbon.[1] He initiated Portuguese trade in West Africa, the colonization of the Azores, and the cultivation of sugar in Madeira. Henry obtained a bull from Pope Nicolas IV in 1454 granting to Portugal, and more specifically to the Order of Christ, authority to trade and spiritual jurisdiction along the west coast of Africa, *usque ad Indos*. This bull was confirmed from time to time by others of a similar nature.

After the death of Prince Henry in 1460 less consideration was given to African discoveries, for King Afonso 'the African' was more concerned with conquests in Morocco. It was Afonso's son, John II, both as prince and as king, who saw the possibilities of the circumnavigation of Africa to secure for Portugal the wealth of the East.[2]

To John II the acquisition of the trade in spices by means of this route became a fixed aim. The visionary proposal of

[1] For the relations between Abyssinia and Europe during the fifteenth and sixteenth centuries, see Charles de la Roncière, *La Découverte de l'Afrique au moyen âge* (Cairo, 1924–7).

[2] Neither John II nor his successor, Dom Manuel, had discovery in mind when they sent their fleets to the East. Their purpose was to obtain great riches from India for immediate gain.

Columbus to reach far-off Cathay by a western route did not appeal to him. The discovery of America was at first a shock, not because of the new land which was found, but because it gave to Spain the right to navigate the Atlantic, which Portugal had come to feel was her own. The outcome, however, of the Spanish discoveries was not without political and commercial benefit to Portugal, for the papal bulls of 1493 gave her a sphere of influence in Indian seas to which she could not previously lay claim. The Treaty of Tordesillas in 1494 between Portugal and Spain was in fact a triumph for the Portuguese ruler. The moving of the line of demarcation from one hundred leagues to three hundred and seventy leagues to the westward of the Cape Verde Islands was a definite gain. While John knew from the map of Ptolemy that this change would deprive him of part of Cathay, he also knew that it would enable him to navigate freely in the South Atlantic on the way to India.

John II had three definite aims: peace in Portugal and the aggrandizement of the House of Aviz through the marriage of his only son with a princess of Castile, the continuation of the policy of religious and commercial expansion in Africa, and the attainment of the all-sea trade route to the Indies. The first objective was almost reached through the marriage of his son, Afonso, with Dona Isabel, eldest daughter of Ferdinand and Isabella. But Afonso met an untimely death in 1491. Towards the second objective John II continued the work of his father. The third of his aims came nearer to realization. During John's reign the African discoveries were pushed farther and farther to the south. A fort and factory were established on the Guinea coast at São Jorge da Mina by Diogo de Azambuja in 1482. Diogo Cão discovered the Congo, and in 1488 Bartolomeu Dias, who had been sent to reach Prester John and India, rounded the Cape of Good Hope.[1] Dias did not reach India or even Prester John, but he demonstrated that this voyage was feasible, and he discovered fourteen hundred miles of previously unknown coast. Because of affairs at home and poor health John did nothing further regarding the voyage to India. Perhaps

[1] For the history of these voyages along the coast of West Africa, see Edgar Prestage, *The Portuguese Pioneers* (London, 1933).

he felt that it would be unwise to do so during the negotiations with Spain which developed after the discovery of America and also that the resources of his country were insufficient. But his mind was fixed on this enterprise and, had he lived, a fleet would shortly have gone to India in the ships he had begun to build. John II died the 25th of October 1495, and was succeeded by Dom Manuel, then twenty-six years of age. Credit for the future success of the Portuguese in reaching India is due to John II, 'the Perfect'; his successor Dom Manuel, 'the Fortunate', but carried out his plans.

With peace assured with Spain, Dom Manuel lost no time in preparing for a new expedition to India under the command of Vasco da Gama.[1] Dias had learned during his voyage along the African coast that the sailing conditions were difficult and that the Portuguese caravels were not entirely satisfactory because they had not the carrying capacity or the sailing qualities for so long a voyage. The Guinea calms, the violent local storms, and the constant watchfulness necessary to avoid shoals he believed could be avoided by taking a route farther from shore. Here steadier winds might be anticipated, and now that the coastline was known a course could be steered with greater certainty. Dias advised da Gama to take this new route, and he recommended for his voyage square-rigged ships with a broad beam and of small draft to enter the shallow harbours of the coast, instead of lateen-rigged caravels. Two ships, the *São Raphael* and the *São Gabriel*, each of about 120 tons, were completed. Another smaller ship, the *Berrio*, of 50 tons, purchased from a rich merchant, Ayres Correia, the future factor of Cabral's fleet, was placed under the command of Nicoláu Coelho. With a store-ship of 200 tons, which was later to be abandoned, the fleet was complete. When, on the 29th of August 1499, da Gama returned he was accorded many honours.

[1] 'In the month of December 1495 [Dom Manuel] held a council at Monte Mor ho Novo in which some were of the opinion that they should not continue farther in this voyage beyond what had already been discovered, because it would cause much envy of all kings and republics as well as the Sultan of Babylonia and also those kings and lords of India; because they would have to undergo great labour and expense to the kingdom; and because the pacific trade of Guinea and the honourable conquest of places in Africa sufficed to gain merchandise and profit of rent to the kingdom and exercise for its nobility. But the king voted with those who believed to the contrary. (Damião de Goes, *Chronica de D. Manoel*, part 1, ch. 23.)

The dream of King John had become a reality. India had been reached, and the Portuguese were also encouraged, because the Indian people were understood to be Christians, who would undoubtedly prefer to trade directly with Europeans rather than with infidels. Vasco da Gama had not brought back a rich cargo from India but he had reached Calicut, the goal of his predecessor, Bartolomeu Dias, and had visited ports along the coast of Africa which, though they were not destined to be of great commercial value to Portugal in the future, provided convenient stopping-places on the route to India. He had traversed the South Atlantic for the first time and had obtained valuable information for future navigation and map-making, and he had brought with him interpreters and Arab pilots.[1] Da Gama had met several of the native rulers on his voyage, had returned with samples of the commodities for which trade was desired, and had secured information regarding trade conditions in the East. The Portuguese may have previously had some idea of the cost of spices on the Malabar coast, but these were ascertained more exactly by da Gama, and it was realized what enormous profits the Portuguese could derive from this trade. He had learned also the value of Portuguese artillery on shipboard in encounters with the Arab and Indian fleets, for guns like those of the Portuguese had never before been seen in Eastern seas.

The voyage of Vasco da Gama may be considered one of reconnaissance and the last and culminating voyage of those begun by Prince Henry. That of Bartolomeu Dias which preceded it had almost attained its goal, and, in the discovery of the sea route to India, Dias deserves at least equal credit. The voyages which followed were for commerce and conquest.

To the Portuguese people da Gama's voyage was accomplished by the will of God, who had destined them for the control of the East, and, regardless of obstacles, they must continue. But there were those who in council still debated the practical obstacles. Although Portugal had increased her wealth with the gold from Mina on the Guinea coast, she was still poor and the possibilities of loss were great. With a population

[1] From the standpoint of discovery da Gama's voyage was of importance because of his voyage on the South Atlantic and because he visited a portion of the coast of South Africa hitherto unknown. From this standpoint the voyage of Cabral was of greater value.

estimated at 1,100,000[1] they proposed to throw down the gauntlet to the Arab traders, who for centuries had held the monopoly of the Eastern seas; they were to encounter many millions of intelligent Asiatics who had been led to believe that the Portuguese were corsairs; and they were to lose many lives through shipwreck, disease, and battle. These were questions which they might well pause to consider; but Dom Manuel did not hesitate and quickly decided to continue. It was not entirely a matter of greed for wealth. It was also an expression of that courage which the Portuguese had shown in their defeat of the Moors, in the defence of their frontiers against Castile, and in their voyages on the Atlantic. There existed, too, much zeal for the conversion of the heathen and for the guidance of the Christians, whom da Gama thought he had found in Calicut, to the true Catholic Faith.

Preparations were made at once for assembling a new fleet to sail the following March. The desire of the Portuguese to hasten these preparations was partly to prevent the Arabs from arming for defence and still further inciting the Hindus against them. Soon the shipyards and arsenals were busy making ready one of the largest and certainly the most imposing fleet which had hitherto sailed the high seas of the Atlantic. Provisions and supplies for twelve hundred men for a year and a half must be provided, and a cargo with which to trade. The selection of the officers and crew was made with great care. There was no difficulty in securing them. They were to go with pay and not subject to the reward of the king as were those of da Gama. The captains were chosen to impress the rulers of India with the greatness of Portugal, and for this reason members of noble families commanded many of the ships. There went also Franciscan friars and clergy, some of whom were to remain in India. The cargo was in the charge of a factor with assistants, for a factory was to be permanently established at Calicut. The chief command of this new fleet

[1] This is the estimate made by Costa Lobo, who believes that Lisbon at this time had a population of 50,000 (*Historia da Sociedade em Portugal no seculo XV*, Lisbon, 1903, p. 32). Other estimates give Portugal a larger population, some as high as 2,500,000.

The populations of other European states at the beginning of the sixteenth century are estimated as follows: France, 16,000,000; Spain, 7,000,000; Venice (with possessions), 1,700,000; Naples, 2,000,000; Milan, 1,250,000; Papal States, 2,000,000; Florence, 700,000. (C. P. Higby, *History of Europe, 1492–1815*, Boston, 1927, ch. i.)

was given to Pedro Álvares Cabral, a young nobleman who belonged to an old though not one of the most prominent families in Portugal. The selection met with general approval.

On the 8th of March 1500 the fleet of thirteen vessels was assembled in the Tagus, some three miles below Lisbon, near the small hermitage of Restello, where the monastery of the Jeronimos now stands. Some of these were the 'round' ships of the period, so called because of their wide bulging sails, others were the lateen-rigged caravels, or perhaps a combination of the two types called *caravelas redondas*. One of these ships belonged to Bartolomeo Marchioni, a Florentine, and to other Italian merchants, another to a Portuguese nobleman, but all the rest had been provided at the expense of the Crown. Some of the best navigators and pilots of the day accompanied the fleet, among them the veteran Bartolomeu Dias, who had first rounded the Cape, Pero Escolar, João de Sá, and Nicoláu Coelho, who had gone with Vasco da Gama, and many others.

Before their departure pontifical mass was said with great solemnity.[1] The king was there, and gave his last instructions orally to the young commander and presented him with a banner carrying the royal arms. The ships were decked with many coloured flags. Musicians with their bagpipes, fifes, drums, and horns added to the gaiety. The people, both those who were to sail and those on shore, were dressed as for a fête. All Lisbon had come to see them off and to wish them good fortune, for this was the first commercial fleet to sail for India. The way had been found, and it was this voyage which was to bring back a rich reward in jewels and spices and pave the way for even greater wealth to follow. On the following day, Monday the 9th of March, the fleet left the mouth of the Tagus and departed from the Bay of Cascaes. All sails were set, and on them was displayed the red cross of the Order of Christ, for

[1] Bishop Dom Diogo Ortiz, who officiated, was, besides his prominence as a prelate, one of three experts, including Masters José Vizinho and Rodrigo, who possessed sound astronomical knowledge both theoretical and practical, obtained largely from their master, Zacuto (Fontoura da Costa, *A Marinharia dos Descobrimentos*, Lisbon, 1934, p. 87). De Barros states that Dom Diogo Ortiz, then Bishop of Ceuta, Master Joseph, and Master Rodrigo were the three cosmographers to whom the proposal made by Columbus was submitted when he insisted on a hearing. According to this author, Dom João II considered Columbus a man who talked a great deal, boasted of his abilities, and had fantastic ideas about his island of Cipango; hence he gave little credit to his words. (Dec. 1, vol. iii, ch. xi.)

Cabral's fleet also went to bring the true Faith to the people of India.[1] The voyage thus begun was to be the longest in history up to this time.

The fleet sailed with the steady north-east trade wind and a favourable current over a course well known to the pilots, who had followed it many times to the coast of Guinea. On the following Saturday, the 14th, they passed in sight of the Canary Islands and on Sunday the 22nd they reached São Nicolau of the Cape Verde Islands. No stop was made here, since it was not felt that supplies were needed. At daybreak the next morning the ship of Vasco de Ataíde was missing. The fleet searched for it for two days, but it was not found. Caminha, our most reliable authority, states that the weather was clear, although other authorities have claimed that there was a storm. This ship probably did not return to Lisbon, but the contemporary writers are at variance on this point. The fleet then continued its course, taking advantage of the north-east trade winds, and, in the hope of rounding the doldrums and the south-east trades, steered somewhat to the west of south. As the ships proceeded, the currents carried them farther west. We do not know the exact course followed, but apparently the equator was crossed at about the thirtieth meridian. The fleet then resumed its route to the south-south-west and followed the coast of Brazil at a distance because of better sailing conditions until Tuesday the 21st of April, when signs of land were encountered. The fleet continued its course, and Mount Pascoal on the coast of Brazil was sighted the next day.

The question why Cabral steered to the westward after leaving the Cape Verde Islands has been much discussed and various theories have been advanced. These and the claims for the discovery of Brazil prior to Cabral's voyage will be

[1] The conversion of the heathen was not only the desire of Dom Manuel, but it was an obligation imposed by the Pope. The bulls of 1493, granted by Alexander VI as the head of the Church, had given spheres of influence over non-Christian countries with the implied duty of bringing them under the guidance of Rome. This was shown in the bull *Ineffabilis et summi* addressed to Dom Manuel in June 1497. In it the Pope granted the request of the king and permitted him to possess the lands conquered from the infidels, provided no other Christian kings had rights to them, and prohibited all other rulers from molesting him. At the end he requested him to endeavour to establish the dominion of the Christian religion in the lands which he might conquer. This may explain the religious tone of the king's letter to the Zamorin of Calicut. (*Alguns Documentos da Torre do Tombo*, Lisbon, 1892, p. 90.)

presented elsewhere in this volume. The evidence seems to indicate that the Brazilian coast had not previously been visited and that the westerly course was taken chiefly for purposes of navigation.

Soon after land was discovered the fleet cast anchor. On Thursday the 23rd of April, the smaller vessels went directly towards shore and a landing was made. This was probably the first time the Portuguese had set foot on American soil within their sphere. On the shore they encountered strange people with bodies painted and tattooed, and decorated with coverings of brilliant feathers. Their appearance and customs were entirely unlike any that the Portuguese had seen before. The new land was named *Terra da Vera Cruz*. That night there was a storm, and the next day the fleet proceeded to the north to seek a safe harbour. This was found within a reef and was named *Porto Seguro*.

The fleet remained here until the 2nd of May, trading with the natives and replenishing its supply of water and wood. No effort was made to explore the coast, and it was not learned whether it was an island or the mainland. Cabral sent back to Portugal a supply-ship under the command of Gaspar de Lemos, carrying letters to inform the king of the new discovery. Two of these letters have been preserved, one written by Pedro Vaz de Caminha, who tells of what occurred while they were on shore, and another, which is of a more scientific nature, by Master John, an astronomer. This supply-ship probably returned directly to Lisbon and did not follow the coast, as claimed by the Portuguese historian Gaspar Corrêa. There is no record of the date of its arrival in Portugal.

When Cabral's fleet left the coast of Brazil it took its course to the Cape of Good Hope, with the evident intention of making a stop at São Bras. This sea had never been sailed previously, and this voyage from Brazil to the African coast may have been longer than any which had hitherto been made without sighting land. The fleet continued with light winds, and a comet was seen on the 12th of May which was in view for ten days. This was to the crew an ill omen. On the 24th they apparently entered the high-pressure area of the South Atlantic which has since become noted for bad weather. Here a storm suddenly overtook them, and four of the fleet sank. The seven remaining ships, with torn sails and at the mercy of the elements for many days, became separated into three divisions, two of three ships each, and one alone. Cabral's ship with two others, passing the Cape of Good Hope, and ascertaining their position through indication of land, turned to the north. A landing was made near the Ilhas Primeiras, located north of Sofala on the East African coast. Here two Moorish ships, belonging to a cousin of the King of Malindi, who had so cordially welcomed da Gama, were encountered. The Moors, fearing capture, ran their ships ashore and threw overboard some gold which they carried before it was realized that Cabral was a friend. The other three ships joined Cabral at Mozambique on the 20th of July. The remaining ship which had lost company during the storm was commanded by Diogo Dias. This lost its way and, sailing too far beyond the Cape and then turning north, sighted Madagascar, which had probably not been previously visited by Europeans.

The main fleet remained at Mozambique for ten days repairing the damage which it had suffered during the storm. They found the king of that place well disposed, because he feared the Portuguese guns, which da Gama had caused him to respect. Water and other supplies were secured here, and a pilot was obtained to guide them past the islands and shoals along the coast. They reached Kilwa on the 26th. This was the principal city of East Africa and one of considerable wealth. Here Afonso Furtado went on shore to negotiate a treaty with the king. Furtado had been appointed as factor to go with Bartolomeu and Diogo Dias to Sofala, but he evidently sailed on the flagship and was thus saved from the misfortunes which overcame their ships. Arrangements were made for Cabral and the king to meet in boats at sea. Here a letter from Dom Manuel was presented. The king, however, was suspicious of the intention of the Portuguese and resented the enmity shown towards his religion. Kilwa occupied an independent position on the East African coast, and derived a large revenue from the traders who came to Sofala and to other ports under its control. There was no reason, therefore, for welcoming the Portuguese, who could but be rivals in the trade which these Arabs enjoyed, and the attitude of superiority assumed by the Europeans caused additional hostility. Kilwa, like Mombasa, had nothing to gain from the advent of the Europeans and much to lose. While Cabral was received in an ostentatious and apparently friendly manner, ill feeling towards the Portuguese became increasingly apparent. Without being able to make a treaty Cabral decided to continue his voyage. No stop was made at Mombasa, because of the treachery which had been displayed there towards da Gama and because of the warfare existing between that city and Malindi. Malindi was reached on the 2nd of August. They were received here in a most friendly manner, and a meeting was arranged between the king and Cabral in boats before the city, as had been done at Kilwa. Gifts were exchanged, and a letter from Dom Manuel was presented to the king. The King of Malindi was the only Arab ruler with whom the Portuguese were on friendly terms during this voyage. It is apparent that the friendship on the part of the Arabs was not disinterested. One cannot but note the difference in the attitude shown by the Portuguese towards the Arab merchants of Malindi and their king, where they had a common interest, and that shown towards the Arab infidels whom they encountered on the sea. At Malindi other pilots were secured and the fleet proceeded to India. Land was reached at Anjediva, an island frequented by ships to obtain supplies when on their way to Calicut. Here the ships were careened and painted, and preparations were made for meeting the Zamorin of Calicut. Cabral's instructions provided that Arab ships should be captured if found at sea or at places other than friendly ports. He therefore hoped that some might be encountered at Anjediva, but in this he was disappointed.

Leaving Anjediva, the fleet of six ships anchored before Calicut on the 13th of September. All were gaily decked with banners, and a salute was fired. Merchants came to visit them, but Cabral, in accordance with his instructions, could not open negotiations until after certain prescribed preliminaries had been fulfilled. The most explicit of these pertained to the securing of hostages for those who went on shore. Several days elapsed before Cabral could land. The lengthy details of the negotiations regarding the obtaining of these hostages, which are given by the historians, are perhaps intended to absolve Cabral from any accusation of timidity, and to show that he was only obeying the instructions formulated for his guidance. Some of the details of what followed at Calicut are given in the narratives which are included in this volume. They tell of the meeting of Cabral and his officers with the Zamorin, of the antagonism shown by the Arab merchants, and of the conclusion of an agreement after a long delay. To please the Zamorin an Indian ship was captured, without provocation, so as to obtain for him a coveted elephant. Because of the opposition of their Arab competitors it was impossible for the Portuguese to secure adequate cargo, and only two of the ships, probably the largest ones, were loaded.[1] The intrigues of the Arabs finally caused an uprising, and the small factory which the Portuguese had established on shore was stormed and all but twenty of the seventy who were there were killed or captured. Among these were the chief factor, Ayres Correia, Pedro Vaz de Caminha, and three of the Franciscan fathers. Those who escaped, although wounded, did so by swimming to the boats, which were unable to reach the shore. Cabral waited a day in the hope that an apology might be received from the Zamorin; but none came. Angered by the death of their countrymen and the loss of their property, the Portuguese took vengeance on the Arabs by seizing ten of their ships which were in the harbour. After killing most of the crews they removed the cargoes and burned the ships, together with those of the Arabs who had hidden themselves in the holds. Because it was felt that the Zamorin had had a part in the uprising and had favoured the Moors, the city of Calicut was bombarded for a whole day and great damage done. An enmity was thus caused which went down in the history of that city, and the bombardment was never forgiven by its inhabitants.

From the Portuguese point of view these acts seemed justifiable. They had come to secure the commerce of India

[1] The flagship and that of Simão de Miranda or of Sancho de Tovar. This would be done because it would be desirable for the largest vessels to return to Portugal before the change of the monsoon. The caravels and small ships could find protection in the backwaters, if necessary, and return the following season. From the commercial standpoint, therefore, the departure from Calicut was opportune, since it permitted all the ships to be loaded and to return together.

with the permission of the Pope and they felt that it was theirs by the will of God. In its acquisition they had been opposed by infidels and heathen whom they considered inferiors. The Portuguese had the crusading spirit from centuries of war with the Moslems. The intrigues of the Arabs and the vacillation of the Zamorin were treachery and an affront to the honour and prestige of their king. The riot instigated by the Arabs, and, as they believed, sanctioned by the ruler, demanded the most severe punishment which they were able to inflict. They realized also that they were few in number and that those who would come to India in the future fleets would always be at a numerical disadvantage; so that this treachery must be punished in a manner so decisive that the Portuguese would be feared and respected in the future. It was their superior artillery which would enable them to accomplish this end. A decisive blow at the chief ruler of the Malabar coast would demonstrate their superiority and win for them the friendship of the subject states whose allegiance they sought. This bombardment of Calicut was the beginning of a policy of armed aggression to secure for the Portuguese the domination of the Indian seas. It was the first step in an active warfare against the Arab merchants in India.

The attitude of the Arab traders can easily be understood. They and their ancestors had won a large part of the commerce of the Indian Ocean from Sofala to China. This had been obtained by peaceful means through the spread of their faith and in fair competition with the native merchants. When recourse was had to war, on land or sea, their methods of combat were the same. Their trade had been threatened by the Chinese, whose junks also had come from a distance, but these had little by little retreated and the meeting-point had been pushed back from Cambay, Calicut, and Ceylon to Malacca. Through Egypt and from pilgrims to Mecca they had learned of the people of Europe, and had seen some of them in the renegades who wandered occasionally to their shores. To the Arab merchants the arrival of the Portuguese by the long sea route to take from them their trade could only have been understood as the beginning of a commercial war. They had driven back the Chinese by fair means and they may have felt that the Portuguese could be similarly treated. The Portuguese, however, had no intention of sharing this trade with the Arab and Hindu merchants. They came to monopolize it, and this was shown in every act. Nor would the Arabs share trade with the Portuguese, for the Arabs were also monopolists. With arrogance and presumption the Portuguese demanded that their ships be loaded first, and that they be given every preference. The letter which Dom Manuel sent to the Zamorin, which was interpreted to him by Arabs, requested that he should exclude the Arabs from his trade. The Arabs must have realized that, while they were tolerated in friendly ports, at sea the Portuguese were to treat them and the pilgrims to Mecca as enemies to whom no quarter was to be shown. Not only was their trade at stake but their lives as well. The letters which Cabral carried to the Arab rulers also condemned their religion, although the attitude of the Mohammedans towards Christianity had usually been one of tolerance. It was not surprising then that with war openly declared against them the Arabs fought back. This was not done with arms, because they realized that here they were deficient, but with strategy. The incident at Calicut was to them but a counter-attack in war.[1]

So far as the Hindu merchants were concerned, they traded

[1] When the news of the destruction of the Arabs' ships in the harbour of Calicut reached Egypt it caused great excitement. Hostile feeling towards the Christians had been aroused by the expulsion of the Moors from Spain and had increased when Portugal had driven out the Jews, many of whom had gone to Egypt. There had been repeated threats to destroy the holy places of the Christians in Palestine. Under the pretext that captured Venetians had revealed that they had been sent on a diplomatic mission to Shah Ismail of Persia, Bayazid II of Turkey had insisted that Venetian merchants in Egypt be imprisoned. The Circassian slave Kansuh al-Ghuri was proclaimed Sultan of Egypt the 20th of April 1501. He found a depleted treasury, and at once levied heavier taxes. The threatened loss of the Indian trade added to his displeasure. At this juncture Peter Martyr, the friend of Columbus, was selected by the Spanish sovereigns to proceed to Cairo to endeavour to pacify its ruler. Pisani, the Venetian ambassador, suggested that he proceed to Venice by land to avoid the corsairs. Here he joined a Venetian embassy and sailed with them to Alexandria. The Venetians were able to placate Kansuh, and Peter Martyr alone concluded a peace in which, while giving nothing in return, he secured the safety of the Christian sites. His letter to Ferdinand and Isabella written from Alexandria in April 1502, although it contains little of political interest, gives an interesting picture of Cairo at that period (*Legatio Babilonica*, Seville, 1511). As the common interest of Venice and Egypt in the diversion of the spice trade to the Cape route became apparent, a proposal was made for the construction of a Suez Canal (R. Fulin, 'Il canale di Suez e la Rep. di Ven.', *Arch. Ven.*, vol. i, p. 175). This undertaking was not found to be practicable, so fleets were built at Suez to drive the Portuguese from the Indian seas. In the decisive naval encounter with the Egyptians which occurred off Diu in 1509, Francisco de Almeida showed that Portugal was able to protect her rights.

chiefly with their own people,[1] but for the sale of commodities needed by Europe and the Mohammedan world they relied on the foreign Arabs. These spoke their languages, knew their customs and commodities, and through centuries of friendly intercourse had built up commercial relations which, in general, were satisfactory. The Hindus knew nothing of Europe and had seen few of its people. They saw little difference between the European commodities which the Portuguese brought them and those which came from Mohammedan sources. To the Hindus the arrival of da Gama and Cabral was but the coming of new merchants to buy their wares, and so long as they conformed to their customs they were welcome. That they were Christians did not exclude them, because in Malabar there were many Christians as well as Jews who lived there as an inferior caste. The attitude of the Indian rulers towards the Portuguese, therefore, was friendly. They were mystified by the arrival of da Gama and Cabral. These strangers had come by a route they could not understand. They did not speak their language, and the Arab merchants did what they could to belittle and malign them. Had there been a Portuguese interpreter on Cabral's fleet who could speak Malayālam fluently, the relations of the chief captain with the Zamorin would have been much closer. As it was, every move was watched with mutual suspicion. Cabral's attitude seemed unnecessarily belligerent, and in his treatment of the Zamorin there was an air of condescension. The Zamorin knew the Arab traders and believed much that they told him. He did not know these new foreigners, and was not sure that they had not come to dispossess him of his kingdom. He was also led to believe that the Portuguese were not as strong as they claimed and that he would gain more through taking the property which they left on shore than he could in future trade.[2]

[1] Hindu craft engaged in the coastal carrying trade. Their ships carried on extensive commerce with Ormuz, with Aden and the ports of East Africa. They had even reached the Cape of Good Hope prior to 1457, as shown on the celebrated map of Fra Mauro. To the east they reached Bengal, Burma, and Malacca. Though their relations with Siam, Indo-China, and Java had dwindled, communications still existed between the people of Ceylon and their Buddhist co-religionists in those parts.

[2] For the attitude of the Hindus towards the Portuguese, as well as much information of interest regarding the people of Malabar at the time of Cabral's voyage, see K. M. Panikkar, *Malabar and the Portuguese* (Bombay, 1929).

The true story of the events which led to the massacre at Calicut will never be known. The Zamorin may not have been able to control the mob which attacked the Portuguese factory. After it occurred he probably could not have called Cabral back, to apologize, without making a definite break with the Arab merchants and placing himself in the power of these new foreigners, whom he did not understand or trust. The Zamorin was not greatly concerned with the burning of the Arab ships. The bombardment of his city, however, he must have felt was unwarranted and a vital affront to himself and to his people. The rage which Cabral felt because of the massacre was equalled by that of the Zamorin at the damage done to his city. The bombardment of Calicut was a turning-point in the history of the Portuguese in India. The people of Calicut never trusted the Portuguese again nor could they be trusted by them.

Unable to do further damage at Calicut, Cabral's fleet sailed for Cochin, which was reached on the 24th of December. Dom Manuel had heard through Gaspar da Gama that another port lay farther along the coast, but he was not sure of its value. In his instructions Cabral had orders to proceed there in case he was unable to secure satisfactory treatment at Calicut. When Cabral arrived at Cochin he learned that the king of that city was aware of the treatment he had received at Calicut. This knowledge had spread as well along the coast of India. The Zamorin of Calicut, as overlord of the smaller kingdoms of the coast of Malabar, including Cochin, was much feared and hated, so that when word was received of the damage done to his city it was welcome. The rulers of these minor kingdoms felt that in the Portuguese they might have an ally who could re-establish their independence and also pay well for their products. Messengers came to Cabral from Cananore and from Quilon, in Travancore, inviting him to trade at those ports. Cabral replied that he would do so at some future time. The relations with the King of Cochin were amicable. Spices were taken on here and at Cranganore, a town on the backwaters inland from Cochin, during the two weeks that the Portuguese stayed there.[1] The

[1] This portion of the coast of Malabar has a low shore covered with coco-nut palms. Behind this is a long lagoon, into which several small rivers flow from the steep ghats behind. During both monsoons the rains or evaporation keep the atmosphere in a

smaller ships of the fleet took their cargoes at Cranganore; the larger ones, which had already been laden at Calicut, probably remained at Cochin, because Cabral, in spite of the apparent friendly attitude of the king, would hardly have taken the risk of having his whole fleet in the backwaters at the king's mercy.

Meanwhile the Zamorin of Calicut had hurriedly assembled a fleet of some eighty ships, many of them large, to intercept the return of Cabral. The King of Cochin offered the latter his aid, but it was not accepted because the Portuguese felt that with their artillery they could defeat even this number. On second thought, however, they decided to return at once to Portugal. With them went two Christians from Cranganore, and, on account of their unexpected departure, the Portuguese took two hostages home with them. The Portuguese in the factory which had been established on shore were deserted. On the return voyage a stop was made at Cananore, where the king insisted on furnishing whatever cargo they might need. He offered to sell this on credit until the next voyage, but Cabral still had money for its purchase. Taking with him an ambassador from this king, Cabral crossed to the African shore. On the way he detained a ship from Cambay. Cabral, as has been said, carried instructions which required him to capture Moorish ships at sea whenever possible, to secure loot, part of which was to go to the king and the remainder to be divided among the members of the fleet. The ship was richly laden, and it was with evident regret that it was released when it was ascertained that it was an Indian ship and did not belong to the Arabs. As the fleet approached the opposite shore the pilots advised caution, but the Spanish captain, Sancho de Tovar, insisted on taking the lead, and his ship ran aground. Because it could not be got off, it was deserted and burned, and only those on board were saved. Unable to call at Malindi, the fleet

condition of great humidity which favours the cultivation of pepper, ginger, and other spices. There are two inlets to these backwaters, one at the north, formerly the mouth of the Peragār which at the time of Cabral's visit was almost silted up; the other, as then, is at Cochin. In earlier days when the Romans visited this coast it was the former inlet which was used to reach Muziris, later known as Kodungalur, the Cranganore of the Portuguese. Here an extensive trade had been carried on for many centuries. Its location on the backwaters made it a desirable harbour for the protection of ships during the monsoon. It was here also that a Christian settlement had existed since early days, and also a settlement of black and of white Jews.

then proceeded to Mozambique to take in supplies and to put the ships in order for the long voyage around the Cape. Sancho de Tovar was here given command of a caravel and instructed to proceed to Sofala to investigate conditions there. This was probably the first time Sofala had been visited by Europeans in modern times. No landing was made, and Sancho de Tovar continued his voyage to Portugal. Another caravel, belonging to Italian merchants, the *Anunciada*, since it had been found to be the fastest, was placed under the command of Nicoláu Coelho and sent ahead of the others to advise the king of the results of the voyage. This arrived at Lisbon on the eve of Saint John's Day, the 23rd of June 1501, nearly a month before the other ships of the fleet. After leaving Mozambique on the homeward journey, another vessel, that of Pedro de Ataíde, became separated from the fleet. This went to São Bras, apparently with the idea that Cabral might stop there to wait for it. Here a note was left for the benefit of later ships, telling of what had occurred in India. This note was subsequently found by João da Nova, who departed from Portugal in four small ships three months before Cabral's first ship returned. Cabral's flagship and that of Simão de Miranda, both heavily laden, continued alone on their homeward voyage.

Before the ships became separated it had evidently been arranged that they should stop at Beseguiche, a harbour near Cape Verde, after their long voyage from the Cape. Here they could secure wood, water, and fresh fish, the sick could be cared for, and the ships put in order for their return to Lisbon. Diogo Dias seems to have arrived first, after a voyage from the Gulf of Aden which was almost miraculous. He was found there by Nicoláu Coelho in the *Anunciada*. While these two vessels were apparently awaiting the arrival of the flagship for instructions, the three ships of Amerigo Vespucci arrived. These left Lisbon on the 13th of June on a voyage to Brazil to explore the coast which Cabral had found, and for trade. Vespucci took advantage of this encounter to send a letter to Florence telling of what he had learned regarding the voyage of Cabral. His fleet evidently continued its voyage before the arrival of the ships of Cabral and Simão de Miranda. When these ships reached Beseguiche, Cabral sent the *Anunciada* to Lisbon and with it the remaining crew of the caravel of Diogo Dias. The three vessels then remained until the arrival of Sancho de Tovar from Sofala and of Pedro de Ataíde. Shortly after these reached Beseguiche, the two large ships departed for Lisbon and were soon followed by those of Sancho de Tovar, Pedro de Ataíde, and Diogo Dias. Cabral and Simão de Miranda probably arrived at Lisbon on the 21st of July 1501, Sancho de Tovar and Pedro de Ataíde on the 25th, and Diogo Dias on the 27th.

The return of Cabral's fleet had been awaited for weeks, not only by the people of Portugal but by those in other parts of Europe, and particularly by the merchants of Venice. When on the 23rd of June 1501 the *Anunciada* sailed up the Tagus and anchored at Belem, the news spread rapidly and people hurried to inquire for relatives or friends and to learn the results of the voyage. There was great sadness because of the loss of five ships at sea with all on board and of the death of many others through sickness or in the massacre at Calicut. The commercial results of the voyage were gratifying because, while Cabral's ships had not all returned laden with spices, a sufficient number would soon arrive to show that future trade with India was possible by the all-sea route and that Portugal might look forward to more fortunate voyages.

Letters were immediately sent to other cities as soon as couriers were available. Bartolomeo Marchioni was eager to inform his friends in Florence of the success of his venture and wrote them three days after the *Anunciada* arrived. At the same time, and possibly by the same messenger, the Venetian emissary Giovanni Matteo Cretico, called 'Il Cretico', and the Cremonese merchant Giovanni Francesco de Affaitadi, wrote to Venice concerning its commercial results.

Castanheda tells us that Cabral had sailed with three objectives in mind: to make peace and friendship with the King of Calicut, to establish a factory in that city, and to instruct the Christians of India. Cabral, in fact, so antagonized the Zamorin of Calicut that no factory could be left there, and he found that the people were idolaters and not Christians, as da Gama had supposed. All of the Franciscan fathers who went to instruct them and who survived the massacre returned with the fleet. Even though a portion of Brazil within the Portuguese sphere was discovered and Madagascar was probably first visited, these at the time were popularly considered as hardly more than incidents of the voyage. They were believed to be valuable only as places where wood and water could be obtained. The fact that Sofala, celebrated for its gold, was first visited by a Portuguese ship during Cabral's voyage seemed of greater importance. The voyage was of evident value to the cartographers. Da Gama had brought back much of interest for them, but further information was sought and seems to have been obtained by members of Cabral's fleet.[1] It is possible that a map was made during this voyage which is now lost, but which formed the basis for much that is given in the Cantino map of 1502.

The loss of ships had been great. Of thirteen which departed from Lisbon but five returned from India with cargo, six were lost at sea, and two returned empty. The large loss of property was partly compensated for by the profits, but the loss of life during the voyage because of shipwreck and disease shed a gloom over the nation. There was thus reason for the king and the people to be disappointed. But the losses and the inability of Cabral to attain his objectives were not his fault; they were his misfortune. His achievements, as viewed at that time, consisted in the establishment of friendly relations with two minor kingdoms on the Malabar coast, Cochin and Cananore, where spices could be obtained in the future, in the establishment of a factory at the former place, the first permanent factory in India, in finding an early Christian settlement at Cranganore,[2] in visiting Sofala, and in ascertaining a practical sea route to the Cape.

[1] In the letter said to have been written by Dom Manuel to King Ferdinand in 1505 there is a statement that the Portuguese king had a map showing Cabral's voyage. The Cantino map shows a Portuguese standard at Sofala as well as at Mozambique, Kilwa, and Malindi. Since Vasco da Gama did not visit Sofala, this flag probably indicates that the map was made, in part, from information obtained during the voyage of Cabral.

[2] It was during the voyage of Cabral that the Portuguese had the first authentic information regarding the Christians in India. That Christians were to be found there had been known previously in Europe through the writings of Marco Polo and of Friar Jordanus, Marignolli, and others, but accurate knowledge regarding them had not hitherto been available. During Cabral's voyage, Cochin and Cranganore were visited for the first time by the Portuguese, and at the latter place Christian and Jewish settlements were found. They were not known either to Pedro da Covilhan or to Vasco da Gama, neither of whom went south of Calicut.

In Europe the voyage of Cabral added greatly to the prestige and credit of Portugal. What Portugal gained in securing the spice trade of India was chiefly a loss to Venice.[1] In that city the return of Vasco da Gama had been known, but its full import was not realized. It was received by the people, then distraught with many problems, as news of interest, but they wished to believe that this new-found route, because of the long and dangerous voyage, the loss of life by disease, and the antagonism of the Arab traders, could not work to their disadvantage. When, however, news reached Venice through the letter of Il Cretico that Cabral's fleet had succeeded in bringing back a cargo, consternation spread among its merchants, to whom the monopoly of the trade in spices was an important source of income, and among the people because it touched their daily lives. From Venice the spices had been distributed through Europe by her galleys to Flanders or to Aigues-Mortes for the markets in France, or by land to the cities and fairs beyond the Alps. The news of the return of Cabral's fleet was, therefore, a matter of general concern to the rest of Europe, since the opening of this trade route might mean the shifting of the market for spices and drugs from Venice to Lisbon.[2]

[1] 'Before the Portuguese discoveries about half of the galleys which left Venice each year went to the Levant. In the return cargo of these nine or ten galleys spices formed the largest item, and in the last years of the fifteenth century they brought back about 3,500,000 English pounds of spices a year, of which about 2,500,000 pounds came from Alexandria, and of which forty to fifty per cent. was pepper. The commercial effects of the discovery of the Cape route to India were first felt in the Levant in 1502. In the four years 1502–5 the Venetians imported on an average not more than 1,000,000 pounds of spices a year. The first large cargoes arrived in Portugal in 1503, and in the four years 1503–6 the Portuguese imported an average of about 2,300,000 pounds a year, of which eighty-eight per cent. was pepper. The average yearly import of the two countries combined was at this time, therefore, a little less than the total Venetian imports before the discoveries—a comparison which suggests that for the first few years at least the Portuguese were more successful in disorganizing the Alexandrian spice market than in supplying the needs of Europe.' (F. C. Lane, 'Venetian Shipping during the Commercial Revolution', in *Am. Hist. Rev.*, Jan. 1933, vol. xxxviii, pp. 226–9.)

[2] The all-sea route really changed the sources from which Venice could secure the Indian spices and drugs from the Levant and Egypt to Portugal. Venice could still secure these commodities at Lisbon; but so could other nations, and her monopoly no longer existed. Although the trade in the commodities of the East was of great importance to Venice in the year 1500, there were other sources of wealth in her industries, which included silk goods, gold brocade, silverware, leather goods, wax candles in which incense gums of the Orient were used, and glassware from Murano, including mirrors and glass beads.

After four centuries, the voyage of Pedro Álvares Cabral occupies an even more important place in history than it did at that time. In the discovery of Brazil for Portugal Cabral added to his native land a country which has exceeded in area, wealth, and opportunity that of Portugal itself, to which, though politically independent, it is still tied by bonds of kinship and affection. It is true that the Portuguese would have discovered America in the course of their voyages to India, probably within a decade, had Columbus not crossed the Atlantic, but this does not lessen the importance of the voyage of Cabral as the first chapter in the history of Brazil.

In the long voyage to the Cape of Good Hope Cabral's fleet covered seas never before navigated and determined the practical course for sailing ships to the Cape which is still followed. The discovery of Madagascar, though considered of little importance at the time, brought that island to the attention of Europe, which had hitherto been unaware of its existence except in a most mythical way. The attack on the Arab ships at Calicut began a war to expel the Arabian Moors from Indian seas. During Cabral's voyage the advantage was clearly seen of a policy of taking the part of the petty rulers against their overlords in order to obtain favourable trade conditions and a basis for domination. This policy, continued by da Gama during his second voyage, was definitely formulated by Francisco de Almeida and put into execution by Afonso de Albuquerque. During Cabral's voyage the system of establishing fortified factories where merchandise could be accumulated was begun, and thus the delay of the fleet until purchases could be made was obviated. These policies of controlling the seas, of developing friendly relations with the petty rulers, and of establishing factories rather than undertaking territorial conquests, were continued during the Portuguese period. They were subsequently followed by the English and the Dutch in the seventeenth century.

The attainment of the commerce with India by sea, commenced during the voyage of Cabral, was the result of a number of conditions which were particularly fortunate. Perhaps in no other period of the world's history could this have been accomplished with equal success. The discoveries along the west coast of Africa, confirmed by bulls of the Church, gave to Portugal a prior claim to the route by way of the Cape. The discovery of America led to a division of the whole non-Christian world between Spain and Portugal, a division which was confirmed by the Pope and in general accepted by the nations of Europe. The close bonds between the crowns of Spain and Portugal favoured the aims of Portugal. In East Africa and in India the petty jealousies and the weakness of the native rulers made the arrival of the Portuguese at this time opportune.

When the Portuguese entered Eastern waters the relations between Egypt, Persia, Venice, and Portugal were complex. Politically Venice, Egypt, and Persia had much in common because of the danger threatened to their several interests by the aspirations of Turkey, and Venice for this reason sought Portuguese aid. From that standpoint also, both Venice and Persia were glad to see a European power in Indian seas.

The superiority of Portuguese ships, the practical experience of their navigators, and the greater efficiency of their artillery made the future control of the Indian seas possible. The lower cost of transportation enabled the Portuguese to overbid the Arab merchants for spices. It also enabled them to bring, to the East, European commodities not hitherto available there. The elimination of intermediate expense decreased the flow of precious metals to the East. The development of better trade conditions, the establishment of factories, and the encouragement of the proper cultivation of saleable spices rapidly developed a Portuguese monopoly in India.

Cabral's voyage is of importance not only because of its position in the history of geography but because of its influence on the history and economics of the period. Few voyages have been of greater importance to posterity and few have been less appreciated in their time. This voyage was the beginning of the commercial relations between Europe and the East by an all-sea route. The diversion of the commerce of India from the Red Sea route to that by way of the Atlantic was one of the chief causes for the decline of the prosperity of Venice and for the fall of the Mamelukes of Egypt. It was also responsible for the development of Portugal from an unimportant state to a nation which for a few years was one of the richest in Europe.[1]

After the departure of Cabral's fleet plans were made for future expeditions. These were to be sent to India each year in March. On the 5th of March 1501 João da Nova departed with a fleet of four vessels. In this expedition Italian merchants participated. On Cabral's return preparations were also immediately made for another and larger fleet for India. Cabral was at first selected as its commander, but was superseded by da Gama. The rapid development of the trade with India, the driving out of competitive Arab traders, the establishment of factories and forts, the ultimate Portuguese monopoly of European commerce in Eastern seas, and the religious conversions of natives belong to the history of the Portuguese in the East during the hundred years which followed.[2]

THE SOURCES

A complete narrative of Cabral's voyage cannot be obtained from a single source; it is therefore necessary to bring together many documents to reconstruct the story. Cabral himself does not seem to have made any written report. The only original records of this voyage which now exist in Portugal are Cabral's letter of appointment, portions of his instructions, and two letters, one from Pedro Vaz de Caminha and the other from Master John, which were sent back from Brazil after its discovery.[3]

[1] The Portuguese court, from the simple austerity of John II, became more like that which later existed in France under Louis XIV. 'The epoch of D. Manuel, which may perhaps be considered the most brilliant in the life of Portugal, had been an interrupted series of splendours and magnificence in which the luxury and waste practised by the sovereign extended to all classes of society, causing the court to become one of the most ostentatious in Europe' (A. Danvila, *Don Cristobal de Moura*, Madrid, 1900, pp. 33, 34). The court became austere again under John III.

[2] Later voyages brought spices to Portugal in increasing quantities. Not only were the needs of Europe satisfied, but the warehouses in Lisbon were bulging with an oversupply. Recourse was then had to a policy of the restriction of production. This was most satisfactorily employed in the Moluccas, where the cultivation of cloves was confined to the small island of Amboyna. When the Dutch and English disputed the monopoly of the Spanish and Portuguese in the East Indies at the beginning of the seventeenth century, it was the spice trade of the Moluccas which they sought.

[3] The preservation of these letters is probably due to the fact that they do not contain information regarding the navigation to India. The logs and charts of the pilots and the routine letters of other members of the fleet would be deposited in the India House, where they may have been destroyed soon after Cabral's return because of the policy of secrecy which was maintained. If preserved they may have been lost during the earthquake of 1755. They do not seem to have been known to the historians of the

To complete our knowledge of the voyage, material must be found elsewhere.

Of first importance is a letter which Dom Manuel wrote to Ferdinand and Isabella immediately after the return of the fleet, in which he tells them what occurred during the whole voyage. The original of this letter probably does not exist, but there are copies in Portuguese, in Spanish, and in Italian.

As has been previously stated, there was great interest in Italy when Cabral's fleet returned. The reports which were sent there from Lisbon after the fleet arrived therefore contain information, particularly of a commercial nature, not to be found in Portuguese sources. Few of the original documents which came to Italy are now in existence. Some are available either in manuscript copies or in printed form; others are to be found in the celebrated diaries which were kept in Venice, especially in those of Marino Sanuto and Girolamo Priuli. Those which came to Venice were chiefly in the form of letters from diplomatic representatives and from merchants; they tell not only of the cargo which was brought back but also of many incidents of the voyage, though no Venetians seem to have gone in Cabral's fleet, and their information was not always reliable.[1] Besides letters there also came to Venice the only complete account of the whole voyage by one who participated in it. This was originally written in Portuguese, but translated into Italian. The name of the Portuguese author is not known, so for identification it is referred to as the 'Anonymous Narrative'. This account, the letter of Giovanni Matteo Cretico, who was in diplomatic service, and of Giovanni Francesco de Affaitadi, a merchant, as well as of others relating to this period, appeared in a small volume which was printed in Vicenza in 1507 with the title *Paesi Nouamente retrouati Et Nouo Mondo da Alberico Vesputio intitulato*. This is one of

sixteenth century, who give little information regarding the landing in Brazil which is not contained in Caminha's letter. Indications of the records and charts of the pilots are shown on the world maps of Cantino, Canerio, and Hamy. The *Esmeraldo de Situ Orbis* and later *roteiros* are excellent coast pilots, but do not give the ocean passages.

[1] The Venetian merchants, through their relations with the Arabs, and because Europeans went occasionally to India as traders or renegades, knew something of the products and customs of the East. Their chief interest, therefore, was in what cargoes Cabral's ships were able to bring to Lisbon.

the first printed collections of voyages[1] and owes its origin at this particular time largely to the interest which Cabral's voyage aroused in Italy and elsewhere. This interest continued in other parts of Europe even more than in Portugal because of the dissemination of accounts of the voyage, particularly those in this collection, which within twenty years had been translated and published in Latin, French, German, and Spanish. Because of a policy of secrecy in Portugal there was little popular knowledge of subsequent Portuguese voyages, except in the commercial world. This added to the public interest in that of Cabral. In the literature of Europe during the first half of the sixteenth century the voyages of Cabral and of Varthema to the East acquired prominence similar to those of Columbus and Vespucci to the West. It is also of interest that *Paesi* is the first of a series of collections of voyages which were the pattern for that of Richard Hakluyt and his successors.

Another document of less importance found in Italy is a letter which appeared in printed form at Rome in 1505 purporting to have been written by Dom Manuel to King Ferdinand. The genuineness of this letter is questionable, but it is the earliest printed account of Cabral's voyage which is extant.

There should also be mentioned a report made by the Venetian Ca' Masser, who was sent to Lisbon in 1506 to investigate secretly the growing trade of the Portuguese in the East. While this report deals chiefly with the later voyages, an account of that of Cabral is also given as obtained from the popular knowledge at that time.

The Florentine merchants residing in Lisbon also sent letters home. Two were sent by Bartolomeo Marchioni, the most important of these foreign residents and one who was financially interested in the expedition. Another letter, written by Amerigo Vespucci to Lorenzo Pier Francesco de' Medici, gives an account of the voyage obtained from members of the fleet whom he met near Cape Verde on their return voyage. These

[1] It will probably never be known when and by whom the first collection of voyages was printed. The oldest now extant seems to be that containing the voyages of Marco Polo, Nicolò de Conti, and Hieronimo de San Stefano, which was printed in Lisbon in 1502. The *Libretto* published at Venice in 1504 can hardly be considered a collection of voyages; it is rather the account of several voyages. *Paesi* is often considered the first collection because it is the best known and because it inspired Grynaeus and Ramusio to make theirs, which are more famous.

Florentine accounts are to be found in a manuscript collection of voyages now in the Riccardiana Library in Florence which were copied by Piero Vagliente with the evident intention of publication.

The material from Indian sources adds something to our knowledge of the voyage. The account of Priest Joseph published in *Paesi* gives a description of Malabar and of the Christian settlements there. Corroborating this and giving additional insight into the Syrian Church, as well as telling of the arrival of Cabral's fleet, is a letter written by four bishops to the head of their Church in Mesopotamia. From the standpoint of the Arabs further information can be obtained from the history of Zain al-Dīn, who wrote early in the seventeenth century.

After the contemporary accounts of Cabral's voyage appeared, nearly fifty years intervened before it was again seriously mentioned. The first quarter of the sixteenth century was an outstanding period in Portuguese history, but the people were too occupied with accumulating and spending the wealth which was coming from the Indies to write its history. About the middle of the century, however, there appeared the works of three prominent historians whose object was to glorify the exploits of their countrymen. These historians sought out the sources available in their time both in Portugal and in India, and they add details regarding the voyage of Cabral not to be found elsewhere. Of these, Fernão Lopes de Castanheda, whose history was the first to appear in print, wrote in Portugal but spent many years in India. His work was soon followed by those of João de Barros and Damião de Goes, neither of whom had been to the East. These historians, although covering the same period, supplement one another, and because their points of view are different each presents a different interpretation. Castanheda, after being in intimate touch with Indian affairs, writes from practical experience; de Barros, with his literary background and his position in the Casa de Mina, views the voyage as a scholar; and Damião de Goes, the diplomat, interprets it in a broader manner and with more human interest. The ecclesiastics, Bishop Jeronymo Osorio and the Jesuit father Giovanni Pietro Maffei, who wrote somewhat later, owe much to their predecessors, but they also consulted original sources.

The work of the historian Gaspar Corrêa, who was contemporaneous with those above mentioned, was not accessible in print until the nineteenth century. Corrêa did not have access to the records in Portugal, but wrote voluminously about the early voyages after a long residence in India. Unfortunately he is not always accurate in his account of Cabral's voyage and confuses it with those of others which followed.

THE LIFE OF PEDRO ÁLVARES CABRAL

Pedro Álvares Cabral was probably born in the year 1467, at Belmonte, about twelve miles from the present town of Covilhan; the exact date is not known.[1] He was thus two years older than Dom Manuel, and was thirty-two years of age when he was selected in 1499 as chief captain of the fleet which was to go to India the following year. At an early age he went to the court of John II as a *moço fidalgo*, since this was the custom

[1] While claims have been made that the known ancestors of Pedro Álvares Cabral extend back to an early period, the family does not appear to have held a position of importance until the fourteenth century. When John of Castile entered Portugal during the time of Dom Fernando and the Master of Aviz, Álvaro Gil Cabral, governor of the castle of Guarda on the Portuguese border, was one of the few noblemen who, resisting all attempts of bribery, was loyal to the Crown. When John I ascended the throne this loyalty was rewarded by the addition of the governorship of the castle of Belmonte.

A daughter of Álvaro Gil Cabral, Brites Álvares Cabral, was the mother of Gonçalo Velho. It was Gonçalo Velho who was sent by Prince Henry on several voyages some seven hundred miles to the west and rediscovered the Azores, already known through their being indicated on earlier Italian charts. He was a commander of the Order of Christ. The family thus included two discoverers who occupy important places in history.

In this rough frontier country the family lived for many generations, having, as significant coat of arms, two purple goats on a field of silver. The purple colour was an indication of loyalty, the goats represented the family name.

The father of Pedro Álvares Cabral was Fernão Cabral, who married Izabel de Gouvêa in 1464. Fernão Cabral was known as 'the Giant of Beira'. He belonged to the council of John II and occupied an important position as a chief magistrate in Beira. His wife had inherited valuable lands in her own right, some of which had previously belonged to the Cabral family. Izabel de Gouvêa died in 1483 and Fernão Cabral in 1493. By his will, published at Belmonte the 6th of May 1494, his property was to be divided by lot among nine of the eleven children, two of the daughters having been provided for previously in their dowries. João Fernandes Cabral, the eldest son, remained at Belmonte.

For the genealogy of the Cabral family see Ayres de Sá (*Frei Gonçalo Velho*, Lisbon, 1899, 1900, 2 vols.) and Visconde Sanches de Baêna (*O Descobridor do Brazil, Pedro Alvares Cabral*, Acad. das Sciencias de Lisboa, Lisbon, 1897). Unfortunately these two authors do not always agree.

among the young nobility of his day.[1] Here he studied the humanities which were taught at that period. On the death of John II he continued at the Court of Dom Manuel with the position of *fidalgo* of his council, and secured the habit of the Order of Christ and an annuity. There is no portrait of Cabral,[2] but as the son of the 'Giant of Beira' he may have inherited his father's physique.[3] He was the second son and was therefore not obliged to retain his father's name. Before the voyage he seems to have used that of his mother, and was known as Pedro Alvares or Pedralvarez de Gouvêa.[4] Little is definitely known regarding the life of Cabral prior to this voyage. There is no record of his having been at sea previous to his voyage to India, and it is certain that he never made a voyage subsequently.

Vasco da Gama had returned from India and was received with great honour. He was made Count of Vidigueira and given an irrevocable commission to act as the chief of any future fleet to India, should he so desire.[5] But da Gama was tired. The voyage had been long and difficult, and he wished

[1] He and his brother, João Fernandes, were *moços fidalgos* on the 30th of June 1484 (*Alguns documentos*, p. 56).

[2] The portrait which usually represents Cabral was first published in *Retratos e Elogios dos Varões e Donas* (Lisbon, 1817). The editors, however, do not state from whence this was derived. In the monastery of the Jeronimos at Belem there are four medallions representing busts of early navigators which adorn four of the main columns. They have been supposed to represent Vasco da Gama and his brother Paulo, Nicoláu Coelho, and Pedro Álvares Cabral, but none of them shows any individuality.

[3] De Barros states that he was selected because 'of the presence of his person'.

[4] Cabral is given this name in a letter dated the 12th of April, 1497, in which Dom Manuel confirms to Pedro Álvares de Gouveia and to his elder brother, João Fernandes Cabral, an annuity of 13,000 reis each, and containing a statement that they had thanked Dom João II, probably as master of the Order of Santiago (Sousa Viterbo, *Trabalhos Nauticos*, Lisbon, 1898, vol. ii, p. 107). The name used in his appointment as chief commander of the fleet for India is also Pedralvarez de Gouveia.

[5] *Alvará* conceding to Dom Vasco da Gama the chief captaincy of all the ships departing for India during his lifetime, the king not being able to intervene in this matter, &c.:

'We, the King, make known to all to whom this our *alvará* may come, that in consideration of the very great and signal service which Dom Vasco da Gama of our council did to us and to our kingdoms in the discovery of India, for which reason we should give him all honour, increase and reward, and because of this, it pleases us that we grant him by this present *alvará* that of all the armadas which in his life we shall order made and shall make for the said parts of India, whether they be only for the trade in merchandise or whether it is necessary to make war with them, he may take and takes the chief captaincy of these, so that in the said armadas he has to go in person, and in them to serve us, and when he thus wishes to take the said captaincy, we may not place in them nor appoint another chief captain save him, because of his honour, and we confide in him that he will know very well our service; it pleases us

leisure to recuperate. It was da Gama's wish and that of the king that the leader of the next expedition to the East should be a man of a different type, who might be able to change to friendship the hostility which the native rulers had shown towards the Portuguese during the previous voyage. Perhaps da Gama had in mind also that after a more sucessful voyage by Cabral he himself might again return to show the Zamorin the true position of his country. At this time da Gama and Cabral were friends, and da Gama is said to have suggested Cabral's name for this office.

There were other reasons which induced Dom Manuel to select Cabral as chief captain of the Indian fleet. He had undoubtedly known him well at court. The standing of the Cabral family, their unquestioned loyalty to the Crown, the personal appearance of Cabral, and the ability which he had shown at court and in the council were important factors. Two of his brothers, João Fernandes Cabral and Luiz Álvares Cabral, were members of the council of Dom Manuel in 1499, and may have had some influence in this selection before the return of da Gama. The fact that Cabral was a collateral descendant of Gonçalo Velho, the honoured navigator to the Azores, may also have added a sentimental reason. The conditions which existed at court in those days are not recorded, but we know that there was much intrigue and jealousy. Cabral may have belonged to a faction which aided his choice. The selection of the chief captain for this fleet required great care. Cabral, therefore, must have been a man who was not only acceptable to Vasco da Gama and to the king but who also had the confidence of the people of Portugal and the respect of those who went with him.

Cabral went to India as the representative of the Portuguese king, with full power to act in any emergency. He fulfilled his

that we grant and we in fact grant this reward and privilege as is said. Furthermore, we order to be given to him this our *alvará* by us signed, which we order shall be in every way kept and guarded, as in it is contained our reward, without impediment or any embargo which might be placed upon it. And it pleases us, and we wish that it be as valid as a letter by us signed and sealed with our seal, and passed by our Chancellery, in spite of our ordinance, even though it may not be passed by the officers of the Chancellery. Done.' Torre do Tombo, maço 4, cartas missivas No. 36, published by S. de Baêna, op. cit., pp. 98–9; also in A. C. T. de Aragão, *Vasco da Gama* (Lisbon, 1898), pp. 221–2. The date given by Viterbo (*Trab. Naut.*, vol. ii, p. 199) is the 2nd of October 1501.

obligation under difficult circumstances in a dignified and conscientious manner. In his treatment of the Indians of Brazil he showed a humanitarian and sympathetic attitude, and there is no suggestion that they might be used as slaves. The instructions which he carried were intended to cover whatever conditions might arise. During the voyage along the east coast of Africa he followed these closely and when he used his own judgement there is nothing to criticize. The instructions for his conduct in India were based on the assumption that the Zamorin of Calicut was a Christian and on this account should be friendly. When Cabral found that this was not the case he was obliged to formulate new policies.[1] He may be criticized for the temerity which was shown regarding the securing of hostages, but suspicion was the attitude in Europe in his time. He realized that treachery might be expected from the Moorish traders and that they would do everything possible to make his relations with the Zamorin difficult. He was far from home with a small fleet and with little knowledge of the local conditions. His cruelty and intolerance may similarly be condoned. The preparation of the treaty was entrusted to the chief factor, Cabral being precluded from participating in the negotiation because of his lack of knowledge of either Arabic or Malayālam. An older and more experienced man might have been able to counteract the intrigues of the Moors. Cabral's youth and inexperience were his most serious handicaps. The seizure of the Moorish ship at Calicut was against his best judgement, and here he deferred to the experience of Ayres Correia, in whom he had great confidence. The destruction of the Moorish ships and the bombardment of Calicut were decisive steps which may seem unduly severe punishment for what was possibly an unauthorized riot; but Cabral was ill and this decision was urged by his council.

One of the duties assigned to Cabral was to impress the rulers in the East with the importance and wealth of his country. He seems to have had this much in his thoughts, but his method of

[1] Cabral had the religious mission of the fleet much at heart. He carried with him an image of Our Lady of Hope (*Nossa Senhora de Esperança*), which still exists. This image was placed in a chapel near Belmonte after Cabral's return, in care of the Franciscans (Ayres de Sá, op. cit., vol. ii, p. 489). It is shown in *História da Colonização Portuguesa do Brasil* (vol. ii, p. 25)

showing it was not always fitting. The ceremony with which he received the two natives in Brazil seems somewhat out of place, and the removal of the ships' silverware to his temporary lodgings when he landed in Calicut must have seemed strange to a people unaccustomed to its use. During the greater part of the voyage Cabral remained on board his ship, and the real work and the negotiations with the native rulers were carried out by the factors.

The voyage met with many disasters and losses in men and ships; yet no Portuguese historian places any blame on Cabral. He was certainly not responsible for the loss of the ship of Vasco de Ataíde near the Cape Verde Islands, nor for the sinking of the four ships during the storms in the South Atlantic; neither can he be blamed for the straying of the ship of Diogo Dias, nor, according to the accounts of the later chronicles, for the insubordination of Sancho de Tovar, which caused the loss of his ship and cargo. Had Cabral not lost these ships on the voyage and had he returned with a rich cargo from the East his voyage would have a more prominent place in history.

On the return of the fleet Cabral was well received. Because of the losses, less enthusiasm was aroused than that which followed the voyage of da Gama. That he was not blamed, however, is shown by the fact that he was appointed at once to command the new fleet, which was being assembled as quickly as possible to sail the following year. For eight months Cabral worked to complete these preparations, but at the last moment he was superseded by Vasco da Gama. Various reasons for this change have been given by the historians. Castanheda states that on Cabral's return the king determined to send a large armada to Calicut to avenge the massacre. Cabral was at first selected to command this fleet, but 'for some just reasons it was given to Vasco da Gama'. De Goes states that Cabral was offended and refused the position because the five ships of Vicente Sodré were excluded from his command. Corrêa tells us that it was the queen who insisted that Vasco da Gama be given the chief captaincy. We know that there was an active feud between the partisans of da Gama and those of Cabral, and that Cabral left the court never to return. Whether Cabral committed some act which offended the king, or whether da Gama finally persuaded Dom Manuel to live up to his agreement and thus caused the enmity of Cabral, we do not know; but there certainly existed a hostility between the two captains which so annoyed the king that on one occasion, when it was discussed in his presence, a partisan of da Gama was banished to Arzila for life.[1]

Cabral did not again participate in public affairs but retired to his small estate at Jardim, near Santarem. He seems to have had some other interests as well, because in a long document dated the 17th of December 1509 reference is made to a controversy with Antão Gonçalvez regarding an exchange of property. This states that Cabral was then living in Santarem.[2] Another document in the same year refers to military service which was expected of Cabral and his retainers, the exact nature of which is not disclosed. In 1518, or perhaps before, he was made *cavalheiro do Conselho*.[3]

About two years after his return from India Cabral married Dona Izabel de Castro, who was related to some of the best families in Portugal, and through her received some addition to his income. She was descended from Dom Fernando of Portugal and Henry of Castile. Her father was Dom Fernando de Noronha, and her mother, Dona Constança de Castro, was a sister of Afonso de Albuquerque. Prior to her departure from court with her husband, she was a lady-in-waiting to Queen Maria, and she continued to retain her standing at court while

[1] Afonso de Albuquerque had taken to India three of his nephews, the sons of his sister, Constança. All of these had died, so she was left only her daughter, the wife of Pedro Álvares Cabral. On the 2nd of December 1514 the great Albuquerque besought the king in a letter from Calicut to forgive Cabral his offence and reinstate him at court. In this letter he tells the king of Cabral's loyalty, of the experience he had had, of his honesty, and of his trustworthiness in anything which might be confided to him. While his uncle admits his guilt, he asks the king to forgive him as a true cavalier and *fidalgo* (Torre do Tombo, *Corpo Chron.*, part i, maço 17, doc. I, published in *Cartas de Afonso de Albuquerque*, vol. i, p. 253 et seq.). There is no indication in this letter as to the nature of Cabral's offence. There was nothing connected with his voyage to India which would justify his expulsion from court, and we can only conclude that it was some act of a personal nature in which Vasco da Gama was also involved. The strong feeling which existed between the factions of Cabral and da Gama at court was unfortunate, but it seems to have reacted against both of them. Da Gama, too, was to incur the displeasure of Dom Manuel, and did not sail again to India until 1524, after the death of that monarch.

[2] Chancellaria de Dom Manuel, vol. xxxvi, p. 40 (Ayres de Sá, op. cit., vol. i, pp. 300–4).

[3] There also exist two receipts, both dated the 4th of April 1502, in which he is called *fidalgo* of the house of the king (*Alguns Doc.*, p. 132).

in seclusion. Cabral had six children: Antonio Cabral, who died in 1521, unmarried; Fernão Álvares Cabral, through whom the line descended; Constança de Castro e Noronha; Guiomar de Castro, who died when prioress in the Convent of the Rose in Lisbon; and Izabel and Leonor, who became nuns.

That Pedro Álvares Cabral died prior to 1520 is known through three letters registered in the *Chancellaria* of Dom Manuel. These letters concede annuities to Fernão Álvares Cabral, Antonio Cabral, and Izabel de Castro, sons and wife of Pedro Álvares Cabral, 'whom may God pardon'. The letter referring to the eldest son is dated Evora, the 5th of November 1520, indicating that his father had died a short time before, although he was alive in 1518.[1] Cabral was buried with his wife and one child in a chapel of the small church of the Convento de Graça, now the Asylo de São Antonio, in Santarem.[2] The grave was opened in 1882 to verify the remains. The resting-place of the discoverer of Brazil has no adequate memorial, nor can it be readily seen by the public.

Pedro Álvares Cabral appeared in history only for a few months and there are few discoverers about whom we know so little. From a position of comparative unimportance at the Portuguese court he was selected to fill one of the greatest moment in the history of his country. Since the Portuguese people had expected too much from it, the voyage was not regarded as a success, and this view has perhaps been adopted

[1] 'Dom Manuel, &c. To whomsoever this our letter shall come we make known that, having regard for the many services which we have received and which we hope to receive in the future from Fernã dAlurž Cabrall, our *moço fidalgo*, son of P[o] dAllrž Cabrall, whom may God pardon [*que D[s] perdoe*] and wishing to show him grace and favour, we hold it for good and it pleases us that he receive and hold from us an annuity from the 1st of January coming, of the year 1521 thenceforth and as long as it shall be our wish, 20,000 reis each year, wherefore we order the Comptrollers of our Exchequer that they shall record it in our books and give concerning it each year a letter to a place where there may be good payment, and for his protection and our remembrance, we order this our letter given by us signed and sealed with our pendant seal. Given in our city of Evora on the 5th day of the month of November. Jorge Frž did it. The year of 1520.'

Torre do Tombo, Chanc. of Dom Manuel, bk. 39, p. 60; Sousa Viterbo, op. cit., vol. ii, p. 140; and Fr. Gonçalo Velho, op. cit., vol. i, pp. 449–50.

[2] The tablet has the following inscription: 'Here lies Pedralvarez Cabral and Dona Isabel de Castro, his wife, to whom this chapel belongs and to all her descendants. After the death of her husband she was *camareira mór* of the Infante Dona Maria, daughter of the King Dom João, our Lord, the third of that name.'

by historians. In the light of its results, however, it stands out as one of the greatest of Portuguese voyages, though it is the voyage rather than the commander which merits our attention.

THE DISCOVERY OF BRAZIL

(a) *Theories for the Westward Diversion*

During the voyage of Cabral's fleet to India the course was diverted to the westward of a southerly course after leaving the Cape Verde Islands, and because of this diversion the mainland of South America was reached. While this course may have seemed justified at the time for better navigation and was probably advised by da Gama, no reason for it is given in any of the contemporary accounts of the voyage or by any of the reliable historians of the period, with the exception of João de Barros, who simply states that the fleet went westward to avoid the Guinea calms. Many of the subsequent voyages to India followed this route, some because a landing was desired on the coast of Brazil to secure wood and water and additional supplies, and others because this course, though longer, had the advantage of better sailing conditions and because the destination could be reached more quickly.

In the three centuries which followed the discovery of America the science of navigation developed steadily, but the narratives of voyages were considered chiefly as matter of record or of popular interest. Ramusio, Hakluyt, and others assembled the accounts of these voyages and incorporated them in their celebrated collections. It was not until towards the beginning of the nineteenth century that a serious study of these documents and narratives was undertaken. Two factors contributed to the better knowledge of early voyages and navigation. One was a renewed interest in the voyages of discovery, particularly in those to America, and the discovery and critical examination of documents and maps relating to them; the other was the scientific discovery of the great ocean currents chiefly through the studies of the English geographer George Rennell, and of Alexander von Humboldt. It was at this time that Muñoz found the valuable documents relating to the early Spanish voyages to America which were later published by Navarrete, and that the accounts of the voyages of Vespucci and others were first questioned and controversies started which have continued to the present day. During this period attention was given to the voyage of Cabral, and the question arose as to why his course took him westward. Humboldt answers this in his *Examen Critique* with the positive statement that this occurred because the currents caused the fleet to deviate towards the west of its intended course. The authority of Humboldt and his brilliance as a scientist and critic caused this solution to remain unquestioned in the popular mind until comparatively recent years, but it was not entirely satisfactory. The importance of the voyage of Cabral in the history of Brazil brought about a discussion of this problem by several historians of that country in 1854 under the patronage of Dom Pedro II. This produced a series of studies which were published in the *Revista do Instituto Histórico e Geográphico Brasileiro*; yet the answer was not found. The question as to why Cabral went to the westward and so discovered Brazil has resulted in the formation of two schools, one of which claims that the voyage was made intentionally owing to previous knowledge of this shore, and the other that Brazil was discovered by chance. The former theory supposes that the land was revisited during this voyage, the latter that a real discovery was made. The uncertainty as to the motives for Cabral's westward diversion still exists, and has been accentuated by prominence given recently to a statement by a contemporary cosmographer, Duarte Pacheco Pereira, who claimed in his *Esmeraldo de situ orbis* that the King of Portugal had sent him to discover land to the west in the year 1498, two years prior to the landfall of Cabral.

The various theories for the westward diversion of the fleet commanded by Cabral may be summarized as follows:

I. Fortuitous.
   - *a.* That the fleet lost its bearings in the vicinity of the Cape Verde Islands, and went westward.
   - *b.* That it drifted westward because of the ocean currents.

II. Intentional because of prior discovery.
- *a.* To revisit land previously known, supposed to be indicated on a map made by Andrea Bianco prior to 1448.
- *b.* To revisit land to the westward, supposed to be shown on a map of 'Bisagudo' referred to in the letter of Master John.
- *c.* To claim officially for Portugal this land, which was believed to have been visited by Duarte Pacheco Pereira in 1498, as interpreted from passages in his *Esmeraldo de Situ Orbis*.
- *d.* To substantiate the claim that land had been found there during the reign of John II.

III. Intentional, for discovery.
- *a.* To ascertain what land, if any, existed within the Portuguese sphere to the east of the line of demarcation established by the Treaty of Tordesillas 370 leagues to the west of the Cape Verde Islands.
- *b.* To determine if the South American continent ended in this parallel, so that a course could thus be taken to India.

IV. Intentional, for reasons of navigation.
- *a.* To endeavour to round the Guinea calms, as asserted by de Barros.
- *b.* To take advantage of the favourable north-east trade winds and thus take a somewhat longer course westward for better navigation to the Cape, with the hope, perhaps, of discovering a western end of the equatorial calms, and rounding the south-east trades.

Let us examine these suggestions in detail.

I. *a.* One of the earliest theories advanced was that the fleet had lost its way while searching for the ship of Vasco de Ataíde. This theory was suggested in an ambiguous way by Antonio Galvão,[1] who here repeats a popular tradition but without historical basis. As a matter of fact there went with the fleet the best navigators of that period, who were able to locate the approximate positions of the ships on their charts at

[1] Antonio Galvão, *The Discoveries of the World in the Year 1555* (Hakluyt Society, 1862, vol. xxx), pp. 95–6.

any time, except for the influence of the ocean currents, which were not then known to exist.

I. *b*. Humboldt, in his critical studies of the early voyages to America, believed that he had solved the question from a scientific standpoint. Benjamin Franklin had discovered the Gulf Stream, and George Rennell the Agulhas Current. These had led to further investigations which showed that there also existed westward currents in the Atlantic, in the course followed by Cabral's fleet. While realizing the superiority of the Portuguese navigators, Humboldt pointed out that as they did not then have means for determining longitude at sea, these currents caused the diversion. Humboldt was acquainted with the contemporary documents, with the letter written by Dom Manuel in 1501, with that of Caminha, and with the Portuguese histories, and he agreed with them that Cabral reached the Brazilian coast by chance. He says, 'Pedro Alvarez Cabral, whom Manuel sent on the track of Vasco da Gama to the Indies, wishing to avoid the calms of the Gulf of Guinea (de Barros) . . . landed unexpectedly on the shores of Brazil. . . . The intimate knowledge which we have to-day of the multiplicity of these currents or pelagic streams of different temperatures which traverse the great longitudinal valley of the Atlantic offers an easy explanation for the extraordinary drift towards the west which the little squadron of Cabral experienced.'[1] The desire on the part of Cabral's pilots to attempt to round the Guinea calms by taking a westward course seems plausible, and the westward drift of the ocean to the north and south of the 'doldrums' is uncontestable.[2] While both of these explanations may have had an influence on the diversion they do not explain entirely the route followed by Cabral.

II. *a*. In the year 1894 Mr. Yule Oldham announced that he had discovered on a chart made by Andrea Bianco in 1448 indications of an extensive land of a shape roughly similar to that of South America, located to the south-west of the Cape Verde Islands. On this was a legend in two lines which he read, 'Authentic island is distant 1,500 miles to the west.'[3] This

[1] *Examen Critique*, pp. 102 et seq.

[2] The navigators and pilots on Cabral's fleet were unaware of the extent of this westward diversion, as is shown on the Cantino map, where Brazil is placed to the east of its true position.

[3] *Geographical Journal*, Nov. 1894, vol. iv, p. 364.

map was also examined in the Marciana Library by Sig. Carlo Errera, who corroborated, in the following year, the finding of Mr. Yule Oldham, but read the distance 500 miles instead of 1,500.[1] The question was further discussed by Mr. J. Batalha-Reis in 1897, who concluded that 'somebody had certainly seen an island and perhaps landed on it', located south-west of Cape Verde, probably at a distance of 1,500 miles.[2] There is no reference elsewhere, however, to this discovery having been made. Andrea Bianco helped Fra Mauro in the drawing of his celebrated map of the known world in 1457, and although Fra Mauro was most exact in placing on this map all available information which was known in his day, this land to the west is not shown. From the time of Aristotle and Ptolemy land was supposed to occupy at least half of the globe. While on later maps this exaggerated land area was usually represented by an hypothetical antarctic continent, it might easily on this map have been shown as land to the west. The theory of this early discovery does not seem to have been proven, and there is no indication that Cabral had any knowledge of it.

II. *b*. In the letter which Master John sent back to Dom Manuel from Brazil in 1500 he states, 'Your Highness should order a *mappa mundi* to be brought which Pero Vaaz Bisagudo has, and on it Your Highness will be able to see the location of this land. That *mappa mundi*, however, does not show whether this land is inhabited or not. It is an old *mappa mundi*, and there Your Highness will also find la Mina marked.' This map was thus known in Portugal at the time of Cabral's departure.[3] He calls it a *mappa antiga*, which is but a relative term. Carto-

[1] 'Della carta di Andrea Bianco del 1448 e di una supposta scoperta del Brasile nel 1447', in *Memorie della Società geografica italiana* (Rome, 1895), vol. v, pt. i, pp. 202–25.

[2] 'The Supposed Discovery of South America before 1448, and the Critical Methods of the Historians of Geographical Discovery', in *Geographical Journal*, Feb. 1897, vol. ix, pp. 185–210. Photographic facsimiles of this map are given by Mr. Yule Oldham and by Professor Theobald Fischer, *Sammlung mittelalterlicher Welt- und Seekarten itallenischen Ursprungs* (Venice, 1886).

[3] Da Costa believes that the reference of Master John to the map of Bisagudo shows that this map had the latitudes marked, that is, had a meridian drawn on it graduated in degrees, since only thus could Dom Manuel verify the situation of this land which Master John indicated was 17 degrees south. The oldest known Portuguese map showing America is that of Cantino of 1502. The first marine map known which shows a meridian with these conditions is that of the Portuguese cartographer Pedro Reinel, which seems to have been made at Lisbon between 1502 and 1505. Fontoura da Costa, *A Marinharia dos Descobrimentos* (Lisbon, 1935), p. 194.

graphers had made charts of the Atlantic on which several mythical islands in the Atlantic were indicated. It may have been to one of these that Master John referred. It has been suggested that such a map, and perhaps this one, had been used during the discussions prior to the signing of the Treaty of Tordesillas in 1494. A map of this sort would naturally show the Portuguese factory at Mina, on the Guinea coast, which was then important for the shipment of gold, ivory, and slaves. Batalha-Reis identifies the owner of this map as Pero Vaz de Cunha, called the Bisagudo, who was sent in 1488 by John II to build a fortress in the Senegal. There is no reference to this map of Bisagudo except in this letter, and it is difficult to believe, in the absence of other evidence, that the map referred to indicated a prior discovery of Brazil.

II. *c.* One of the most celebrated men in Portugal during this period was Duarte Pacheco Pereira. He was born in Lisbon about the middle of the fifteenth century, of a good family. He went to sea early and during the fourteen years of the reign of John II he was one of the captains in his confidence. With Diogo de Azambuja, Bartholomeu Dias, Diogo Cão, and others he explored the coast of Africa. He was a witness to and signed for Portugal the Treaty of Tordesillas in the capacity of a cosmographer. Pereira probably did not go to India with Cabral.[1] In 1505 he began to write a book for the king which was to serve as a pilot of the African coast. This was probably completed between that date and 1520, a period during which he remained on shore. To this book he gave the title *Esmeraldo de Situ Orbis*. The latter portion of the title had been used by Pomponius Mela for his famous work. In chapter ii of the first book he states that Dom Manuel had sent him to America in 1498 for the purpose of discovery. This statement, which

[1] Duarte Pacheco Pereira is not mentioned by any contemporary author as having been with Cabral's fleet. It was not until nearly fifty years later, when he became a national hero, that his name was associated with it. It was then stated by Castanheda and de Barros that a man by that name went in the caravel of Pedro de Ataíde when it sought the elephant for the Zamorin. On the other hand Vespucci states that no mathematicians or cosmographers went with Cabral. The prominence of Duarte Pacheco in these fields must have been known to all members of the fleet, and had he gone with it he would probably have been mentioned by contemporary writers. Master John and Pero Escolar gave the latitude of Porto Seguro as 17°, while Duarte Pacheco locates it as 18°, the position assigned to it in 1501 and 1504.

has given rise to the theory that Brazil was discovered at that time and thus prior to the voyage of Cabral, is as follows:

'And in addition to what is said, experience, which is the mother of things, enlightens us and withdraws us from all doubt; and consequently, Happy Prince, we have known and seen, how in the third year of your reign of the year of Our Lord of 1498, whither Your Highness sent us to discover the western part, passing beyond the greatness of the ocean sea, where is found and navigated so great a *terra firma*, with many and large islands adjacent to it, which extends to seventy degrees of latitude from the equinoctial line against the arctic pole, and although it may be somewhat distant, it is greatly peopled;[1] and on the other side of the same equinoctial circle it goes beyond to twenty-eight and one-half degrees of latitude against the antarctic pole[2] and it expands so much its greatness and extends to such great distance that of one part or of the other was not seen or known the end and finish of it; by which, according to the order which it carries, it is certain that it goes in a circle by all the roundness; so that we have learned that from the shores and coast of the sea of these kingdoms of Portugal, and from the promontory of Finis-terre and from whatever other place of Europe, and of Africa and of Asia, traversing beyond all the ocean directly to the West, where the west is according to the order of nautical art, a distance of thirty-six degrees which would be six hundred and forty-eight leagues of journey, counting eighteen leagues to a degree, and there are some places still farther away, this land is found in the navigation by the ships of Your Highness, and, by your order and licence, by

[1] This statement shows that when this was written the North American coast-line was recognized by some geographers as distinct from that of Cathay. The northern extremity noted as about 4° within the Arctic Circle had been known for about 500 years and settlements established there. That the Norsemen had made settlements in Greenland became a matter of interest to the Portuguese before the end of the fifteenth century.

[2] By coincidence the mouth of the Amazon is not only located on the equator but also the fiftieth meridian passes through it. Harrisse (*The Diplomatic History of America*, London, 1897, vol. ii) gives the position of the line of demarcation on early maps in the following longitudes:

Cantino, 1502 . . .	42° 30′
Oviedo, 1545 . . .	45° 17′
Ferrer, 1495 . . .	45° 37′
Enciso, 1518 . . .	45° 38′
Badajoz Experts, 1524 . .	46° 36′
Ribeiro, 1529 . . .	49° 45′

In claiming the location of the shore where the line of demarcation crosses Brazil, therefore, Duarte Pacheco Pereira but claimed for Portugal an arbitrary but very definite northern boundary which was beyond question within the Portuguese sphere. The southern boundary on the coast as defined by this line passing through the mouth of the Amazon would be approximately 28½° south.

those of your vassals and citizens; and going along this aforementioned coast from the same equinoctial circle beyond, for twenty-eight degrees of latitude against the antarctic pole, there is found in it much and fine brazil with many other things with which the ships come greatly loaded to these kingdoms.'

In chapter iii he also says:

'... and other ancient cosmographers who went to the same land for many years and other persons who have known that this is true information, have divided it in three notable parts. And in the third part which Your Highness sent to discover beyond the ocean, as it was an unknown thing to them, they do not speak of.'

Pereira does not here state that he went to Brazil in 1498, although he mentions the discovery of the coast of Brazil and refers to its having been explored for a distance of 28½° south. It must be remembered that the *Esmeraldo* was written subsequent to 1505, when the Brazilian coast was well known through the third voyage of Vespucci.

The voyages to America for the year 1498 are somewhat obscure. Harrisse mentions those of Vespucci, Cabot, Thirkill, Coronel, and Columbus.[1] It is possible that there were others and that this voyage of the Portuguese to America was clandestine and that there are no records. The best-known voyage to America in 1498 was the third voyage of Columbus. This sailed from San Lucar on the 30th of May of that year. Becoming frightened in the equatorial calms, or wishing to return to Hispañola more quickly, Columbus steered northward and after discovering the north coast of South America reached that island. He did not return immediately, but a fleet of five vessels left for Spain soon after his arrival, so that there was ample time for word to reach Lisbon before Cabral sailed. This voyage raises several questions. It was partly financed with money set aside by Ferdinand and Isabella for the celebration of the wedding of Dom Manuel.[2] It sailed from the Portuguese islands of Cape Verde towards the equator and it proceeded over seas hitherto unexplored, where islands or mainland within the Portuguese sphere might be found. It is possible that it was a joint expedition sent by Spain and Portugal for the

[1] *The Discovery of North America* (London, 1892), pp. 675–6.
[2] William H. Prescott, *Ferdinand and Isabella*, part ii, ch. 8.

location of the line of demarcation. This determination as provided for in the treaty had been deferred from time to time. If the voyage had been made to the west for this purpose, Pereira, a cosmographer who had signed the Treaty of Tordesillas for Portugal, would naturally have been chosen to accompany it. Had Pereira gone on any of the known voyages of 1498 he would not have visited Brazil. These references in the *Esmeraldo* do not seem to have any relation to the voyage of Cabral.

II. *d.* When Columbus presented the plan for his voyage to John II it was refused by the junta of cosmographers, not because of doubt that Cathay could be reached by navigating to the west but because it was felt that India and its spices could be attained by the African sea route with greater certainty and the way was shorter. John II and his advisers probably knew more than Columbus about the Atlantic. They had learned all that was known of indications of land to the west from those to whom they had granted permission for its discovery. They also had able navigators who could make this voyage without acceding to such exorbitant demands as those made by Columbus.

Unfortunately few records of the early navigations now remain. This is partly due to the neglect in their preservation in the Torre do Tombo,[1] to their having been withdrawn for official use and not returned because of the changing location of the court,[2] but chiefly because of a policy of secrecy which it was felt necessary to maintain.[3] Not only have almost all the early records disappeared but also many of the chronicles. Even the writings of the historians of the sixteenth century were under such strict supervision that they cannot always be trusted. The policy of secrecy had existed since the first voyages of Prince Henry. It was due to two causes: first, to prevent other nations from learning of the discoveries and, second, because the voyages and trade were considered a royal monopoly and could be engaged in only at the will of the king, who usually received part of the profits. Except for the navigation of the Norsemen to Greenland and of the

[1] Some of them may have survived in the India House, where they would have been destroyed in 1755.

[2] Pedro A. d'Azevedo and Antonio Baião, *O Archivo da Torre do Tombo* (Lisbon, 1905).

[3] See Jaime Cortesão in *Lusitania* (Lisbon, 1924), fasc. 1.

Spaniards to the Canary Islands, the Portuguese had claimed all but the coastal navigation of the Atlantic. It became not only the hope but the belief of John II that islands and probably mainland existed to the west. We have indications of this in the concession given to Fernão Domingues do Arco of Madeira in 1484, who evidently intended to explore in that direction. It is evidenced also in a similar project approved in 1486 in favour of Fernão Dulmo of Terceira, and of Dulmo and João Afonso do Estreito in 1487.[1] There are further indications that other voyages were planned, but there is no record that any discoveries were made in America. When the line of demarcation was fixed by the bulls of 1493 John used every effort to have this extended farther west. While he sought chiefly to secure sea room for his ships to India he also sought an added area to the west where he believed or knew that land was to be found. There is no evidence that such a land had been discovered by the Portuguese beyond the Atlantic during John's reign, and those who make this claim do so with the belief that the documents which existed to prove it have disappeared.

If the Brazilian coast had been previously visited, or was even believed to exist, it is reasonable to suppose that a small fleet similar to that which was later sent with Amerigo Vespucci would have gone there not only to claim officially that portion within the Portuguese sphere, but also to continue the discovery along the shore to the north, where mainland had been touched by Columbus in 1498, and to go south to ascertain if land existed there as well.

The belief that Cabral's fleet was diverted to the westward to revisit Brazil while on its voyage to India is open to several objections.

Cabral did not immediately take possession for the king, and no effort was made for further discovery. On the contrary, the ceremony during which the royal arms were raised took place during a mass which was said just before the fleet departed, and it was not felt necessary for either the ship of Gaspar de Lemos or the main fleet to ascertain whether this new shore was an

[1] For a discussion of these voyages see Edgar Prestage, *The Portuguese Pioneers* (London, 1933), ch. xi, and C. E. Nowell, 'The Discovery of Brazil—Accidental or Intentional?', in *Hisp. Am. Hist. Rev.*, Aug. 1936; also Jaime Cortesão, 'The Pre-Columbian Discovery of America', *Geographical Journal*, Jan. 1937.

island or mainland. It is hard to understand why it was decided to send a ship back to Portugal to advise the king of this discovery if the fleet had been diverted to revisit a land already known to exist. It is also strange that, if this shore had been previously visited, there was no knowledge among the members of Cabral's fleet of the natives and of the parrots which they were so interested in finding there.

There is no contemporary account of his voyage either by a Portuguese or an Italian author which does not state that Cabral made this discovery. There is, furthermore, no historian until recent years who has questioned it. Duarte Pacheco Pereira himself, while he does not mention Cabral in this connexion, does not definitely state that he visited the Brazilian coast.

Dom Manuel had no reason for maintaining secrecy regarding this or any prior voyage, particularly at a time when the thrones of Portugal and Castile were almost united.

Pedro Vaz de Caminha states that Cabral's fleet found it, and he says further, 'and God who brought us here did not do so without reason'. Caminha would not have written this to the king had he believed that this land had previously been visited.

While Master John does not mention the discovery of Brazil, the wording of his letter gives no indication that he believed that it had previously been visited. He says, 'Yesterday we almost understood by signs that this was an island and that there were four.'

The land was named Vera Cruz by Cabral. This name was changed to Santa Cruz by the king. Had the land been visited earlier, a name would already have been chosen for it and the king would not merely have modified that given to it by Cabral.

The Cantino map of 1502, which may be considered the copy of one which was official, states that this coast was discovered by the Portuguese in 1500.[1]

Perhaps the strongest proof is that the King of Portugal

[1] 'The *vera cruz* ✠ so named, which pedraluares cabrall, *fidalgo* of the house of the King of Portugal found; and he discovered it going as chief captain of 14 ships which the said king sent to Caliqut. And on the outward voyage he came upon this land, which land is believed to be mainland, in which there are many people, men and women, whom they describe as going nude as when they were born. They are more white than brown and have very long hair. This land was discovered in the era of 1500.'

himself wrote a letter in 1501 to his cousin and mother-in-law, Queen Isabella, and to his father-in-law, King Ferdinand, with both of whom he was on very friendly terms, in which he states that this land had been discovered by Cabral.

In view of this contemporary evidence and of the fact that no documents have been discovered which were not known at that time, it would seem that more conclusive proof must be produced by those who challenge the discovery of Brazil by Cabral.

III. *a.* At the commencement of the reign of Dom Manuel the best astronomers, mathematicians, and navigators in Europe were in Portugal. Many of the scientists were Jews who had been driven from Spain. They found asylum at Lisbon, where they were glad to aid the Portuguese king because they were bitterly resentful of the treatment which their race had received from Ferdinand and Isabella. There were also in Portugal Florentine merchants who, through their commercial and banking relations, knew of the aspirations of the Spanish to obtain wealth in their newly found islands to the west. The results of the voyage of Columbus, during which the north coast of South America had been reached and pearls had been found, were undoubtedly known in Lisbon at the time of the departure of Cabral's fleet. The Portuguese were also aware that other voyages were being made by the Spaniards to this coast. They, in all probability, had obtained maps and sailing directions of the Spanish voyages to America and had undoubtedly during the eight years which followed the first voyage of Columbus sent representatives on some of them. It was opportune at this particular time to ascertain whether land existed within the Portuguese sphere, and to anticipate any Spanish voyages to lands which might be theirs. While Cabral's fleet was destined for India, there was a possibility of combining in this voyage a westward divergence from the Cape Verde Islands for this purpose. By following the route commenced by Columbus in his third voyage, it might proceed farther to the west than had da Gama in his voyage to the Cape. By this route some of the Portuguese sphere to the west might thus become known. The junta of cosmographers who planned Cabral's voyage might well have felt that by taking advantage of the north-east trade winds and, if possible, by rounding the calms, this divergence for discovery could be made without delaying the arrival in India. This might also be a safer and more practical route.[1]

The belief that Cabral's fleet went to the south-west with the hope of discovery has added weight since in the same year Gaspar Corte-Real went to the north-west on a similar mission. The presence in the fleet of the astronomer, Master John, might thus be accounted for.

III. *b.* The theory that Cabral's fleet was diverted westward to reach India in that direction has nothing to commend it. There are no indications of such an intent and neither at this time nor later was there any desire on the part of Portugal to encroach, from this direction, on the Spanish rights as defined in the Treaty of Tordesillas.

IV. *a.* The theory suggested by de Barros, which is the only one advanced by any authoritative writer during the sixteenth century, was that the fleet steered to the westward to endeavour to round the equatorial calms.[2] These bend to the south-east before reaching the African coast south of Guinea. The Portuguese voyages to Mina were favoured by the strong Guinea current on their outward voyage, but on their return they were opposed by it. They thus had experience with this calm belt, which hemmed in their course to the south and made further voyages along the coast more difficult. Da Gama had crossed it at some distance from the African coast. Columbus on his third voyage, after steering to the south-west from the Cape Verde Islands, had entered it and describes the terrific heat and discomfort of the tropical seas in words which

[1] For the winds and currents of the South Atlantic and the modern passages for sailing ships, see Rear-Admiral Boyle T. Somerville, *Ocean Passages for the World—Winds and Currents* (London, 1933); A. G. Finlay, *Directory for the Navigation of the South Atlantic Ocean* (10th ed., London, 1920); and the meteorological charts for the Atlantic Ocean published periodically by the Hydrographer of the Admiralty.

[2] 'In order to avoid the land of Guinea, where the calms would impede his course, he sailed far off from land to be sure to double the Cape of Good Hope. And when he had been a month on that long voyage he saw on the second day of the octave of Easter, which was the 24th of April, that there was another coast of mainland which, according to the estimation of the pilots, appeared to be distant to the west of the coast of Guinea 450 leagues and in the height of the antarctic pole to the south ten degrees. Regarding this land the men were so firm in the belief that there was not any mainland west of all the coast of Africa that most of the pilots affirmed that it was a large island such as Terceiras and those which were found by Christovão Colom, which belong to Castile and which the Castilians commonly call Antilhas.' De Barros (Dec. I, bk. v, ch. 2).

must have been exaggerated.[1] While Cabral's fleet would wish to avoid these calms, it is doubtful whether this was the only reason for the diversion.

IV. *b*. There were several ships in the fleet. These had a length of about three times their beam. They were clumsy and carried large sails which could not easily be adjusted to the wind. Since the fleet had to be kept together its speed was determined by the poorest sailer. The route for this reason seems to have been taken with the north-west trade winds after leaving the island of São Nicolau, following the suggestion of da Gama and the experience of Columbus. When the region of the equatorial calms was reached the course was taken to the south. Beyond these calms the prevailing wind was from the south-east, the direction which they were to take to the Cape. It was evidently not felt desirable to sail against this wind with the ships but to continue the course somewhat to the west for better sailing in the hope that light favourable winds might be found to carry them to the Cape, as da Gama had suggested. This course would take them along the Brazilian shore. The south-east trade-wind area extends in an approximate oval from the Cape of Good Hope to Cape Saint Roque in Brazil. The uniformity of this wind, like that of the north-east trade, was well known to da Gama. On his outward voyage he had sailed against it from the equatorial calms to the Cape, and he had found that this head wind had made the sailing slow and caused discomfort to the crew. In da Gama's suggestion for the route to be followed by Cabral's fleet, therefore, a westward diversion was advised, not only with the belief that the Guinea calms might be rounded but even more so that the south-east trade wind might also be avoided. The rounding of this contrary wind area in the hope of finding more favourable winds to the west may have been the chief reason for Cabral's course. The voyage as far as Brazil was the correct course to the Cape.[2]

[1] The equatorial calms lie between the north-east and south-east trade winds. They are narrowest in February and March particularly between 28° and 33° west. The most favourable time for crossing the 'doldrums' also is between December and June, when the passage for sailing vessels will be less interrupted by calms, squalls, and variable winds than at other times. (Somerville, op. cit., p. 32.)

[2] According to Somerville the present route for sailing ships from the English Channel to the Cape of Good Hope is the same as that to Rio de Janeiro. The Cape Verde Islands should be sighted and passed to the westward, as the winds are stronger

Unfortunately Cabral does not seem to have sailed far enough to the south after leaving the Brazilian coast to obtain the benefit of the westerly winds. This error was evidently recognized, for subsequent voyages took their course eastward in the parallel of the Tristão da Cunha Islands. They thus avoided the high pressure area to the north which was so disastrous to Cabral's fleet.

It must not be forgotten that the fleet was destined for India. It was large for the time and carried a valuable cargo. The course to be followed, therefore, was the one which it was believed would ensure the most favourable winds and the greatest safety irrespective of any hopes of rounding the calms or discovery. The discovery of Brazil according to this theory was accidental.

From the foregoing it seems probable that Cabral's fleet was the first to reach the shores of Brazil under the Portuguese flag. The westward diversion of the fleet, during which Brazil was visited, seems to have been made not for one but for several reasons. The chief motive was to follow the most practicable and safest route to the Cape of Good Hope.

(b) *Claims for the Prior Discovery of Brazil*

The theories that Brazil had been visited by Europeans prior to the voyage of Cabral may be divided into two classes: those claiming that the voyage had been made by navigators in early times who did not return, and those made in the fifteenth century by others who brought back word of discoveries. To the former class belong those theories which are based on Biblical references, on allusions by classical writers, or on evidences to be found on the South American continent. A discussion of these belongs to a field which is not within the scope of this volume.[1] In the second class are the theories based on indications in the charts of Andrea Bianco and Pero Vaz Bisagudo, on the belief that voyages had been made during the

on that side. The equator should be crossed as far west as possible so that there may be less interval of doldrum to cross. 'Having crossed the equator as recommended, a vessel should stand across the south-east trade wind on the port tack, even should the vessel fall off to W. by S., for the wind will draw more to the eastward as the vessel advances, and finally to East at the southern limit of the trade' (op. cit., p. 443).

[1] See Paul Gaffarel, *Histoire de la découverte de l'Amérique* (Paris, 1892), vol. i, and Candido Costa, *As Duas Americas* (Lisbon, 1900).

reign of John II and that Duarte Pacheco Pereira had visited Brazil in 1498. These have already been discussed as reasons for the diversion of Cabral's fleet to the westward. There remain to be mentioned other claims, probably unknown to Cabral, which have been seriously advocated for the prior discovery of Brazil. These include the Spanish voyages, the voyage of Jean Cousin, and the statements of three persons which, it is believed, indicate that Brazil was previously known.

Columbus visited Trinidad and probably the coast of Pária in 1498, and may be considered the first European to visit the South American continent. The discovery of the mainland during his third voyage was disputed by the Spanish Crown in a celebrated trial during which testimony was taken in 1513 and 1515 by the Spanish *Fiscal* and Diego Columbus, the son of the great admiral.[1] The question was not settled at that time; but, in view of the evidence there produced and the research of subsequent historians, it is almost certain that he did so. After this discovery Columbus returned to Hispañola, where he remained until his return to Spain in chains. Word was sent back to Spain, however, that pearls had been found along the South American coast. This news caused other fleets to be sent to Pária to seek these new riches and to make further discoveries. The advantage of following a more southerly route from the Cape Verde Islands and thus to take advantage of the north-east trade winds had been apparent during the voyage of Columbus, so this course seems to have been chosen. It has been claimed that during these voyages the coast of Brazil was followed until Venezuela was reached, and that it was thus discovered prior to the voyage of Cabral. Five Spanish fleets may have sailed during the year 1499, under the commands of Alonzo de Ojeda (who it is said was accompanied by Amerigo Vespucci as a merchant and by Juan de la Cosa as pilot), Cristobal Guerra, Vicente Yañez Pinzon (who had gone with Columbus on his first voyage), and Diego de Lepe. Some believe that there should be added the name of Alonso Vellez de Mendoza. The information which remains concerning these voyages is confused and conflicting. Much of it is to be found

[1] F. de Navarrete, *Collección de los Viajes y Descubrimientos* (2nd ed., Madrid, 1880), vol. iii, pp. 541–628.

in the *probanzas* above mentioned. Ojeda there claims that on his voyage he first sighted land 200 leagues (Vespucci says 300) before reaching Pária and would thus have visited the coast of Brazil in 1499. The accounts of this voyage by Ojeda and Vespucci have caused much controversy which is too involved to be adequately given here, but it is reasonably certain that Brazil was not visited by them at this time. The references to other Spanish voyages are chiefly given in the *probanzas* and cannot be considered confirmed, because of lack of sufficient corroborating evidence. The voyage of Vicente Yañez Pinzon, however, has documentary support in its favour. In his testimony given in 1513 Pinzon states that he discovered 'from the Cape of Consolacion which is in the part of Portugal and is now called Cape S. Agustines' and that he discovered the whole coast to the west and north-west as far as the mouth of the Drago. In an agreement signed by Ferdinand and Isabella at Granada the 5th of September 1501[1] his discoveries on the South American mainland were recognized as from the places which he had designated as Santa Maria de la Consolacion and Rostro Hermosa, along the coast to the north-west, past the large river which he called Santa Maria de la Mar-dulce, and all the land as far as the Cape of San Vicente. In this document he is named as royal captain and governor of these lands from the first-named place to the river of Santa Maria de la Mar-dulce and the islands in the mouth of that river.[2]

In the same year Angelo Trevisan, the secretary of the Venetian ambassador to Spain, had access to the papers of Peter Martyr relating to the voyages to America. After the departure of Martyr for Egypt on the 14th of September, Trevisan sent copies of these in Italian translation to his former employer, Domenico Malipiero, at Venice.[3] These accounts of the Spanish voyages were printed in 1504 in a collection known as the *Libretto de tutta la navigatione de Re de Spagna*[4] and subsequently reprinted in the *Paesi* of 1507. Among them was an

[1] *Collección de Documentos Inéditos* (Madrid, 1878), vol. xxx, pp. 535–42.

[2] These names are not shown on the map of Juan de la Cosa.

[3] Copies of these letters are now in the Sneyd Collection at Newcastle-upon-Tyne.

[4] Two copies of the *Libretto* are extant, one in the John Carter Brown Library and the other in the Marciana. The former was reproduced in facsimile and edited by Lawrence C. Wroth (Paris, 1930), and the latter with facsimile and translation by J. B Thacher in his *Christopher Columbus* (New York, 1903), vol. ii, pp. 439–514.

account of the voyage of Pinzon which was sent to Venice in December 1501. All of this was unknown to Peter Martyr, who included this account of Pinzon's voyage in the first edition of his First Decade in 1511 and also in the complete Decades in 1516, both of which were in Latin. In the *Libretto* the statement is made that Pinzon's fleet of four caravels departed from Palos on the 18th of November 1499, and after taking their course south-west from the Cape Verde Islands came in sight of land on the 20th of January 1500. It then continued along the coast for 600 leagues, passing a gulf of fresh water. The coast of Pária was reached, and on the 3rd of June the fleet departed for Hispañola.

The account of the voyage, as given by Peter Martyr in the Seville edition of 1511 and in that of Alcalá of 1516, agrees substantially with that in the *Libretto*, but it states that the first landing was on the 26th of January. Further evidence that the Pinzon brothers visited the shore of Brazil is indicated on the map of Juan de la Cosa. This map, which is dated 1500 (though there is evidence that the only copy now known was drawn not earlier than 1508[1]), might provide proof that Cape São Agostinho was reached by Pinzon and the coast followed to the north-west as far as the coast of Venezuela. It was in fact originally drawn expressly for this voyage, for on it are prominently shown three Spanish flags along the shore, two caravels, apparently those of the Pinzon brothers, and an inscription opposite Cape São Agostinho stating that it had been discovered by Vicente Yañez in 1499. The coast shows some resemblance to that of Brazil, and there is an indication of the mouth of the Amazon. The map does not show Vespucci's voyage of 1501 or Cabral's voyage to India, although an island appears to the east of Brazil with the inscription 'island discovered for Portugal'. This map, therefore, contains information collected after the return of Gaspar de Lemos and Pinzon in the autumn of 1500 but before Vespucci reached Portugal in 1501. The voyage of the Pinzons in 1499 along the Brazilian shore was accepted by the early Spanish historians. These Spanish voyages were discussed during the nineteenth century by Navarrete, Humboldt, Varnhagen, Harrisse, Vignaud, and

[1] Nunn, George E., *The Mappemonde of Juan de la Cosa* (Jenkintown, 1934).

others, and while no agreement was reached, the general opinion has been that the voyages of Pinzon and Lepe, at least, followed this shore. In 1921 Professor Duarte Leite made a critical and unprejudiced examination of these Spanish voyages which was published in chapter iii of the *História da Colonização Portuguesa do Brasil* with the title 'The False Precursors of Álvares Cabral'. In 1931 he further discussed the questions involved in his *Descobridores do Brasil.* As a result of his studies Professor Leite concludes that 'In 1499 Hojeda did not cross the equator nor bring to view the Orinoco; Pinzon was not in the Amazon in 1500, and was farther north, not passing beyond Cape Orange; Diego de Lepe and Vellez de Mendoza visited only the greatest of rivers when the splendours of history had already displayed it in the sixteenth century.' The claims of these Spaniards to the discovery of the Brazilian coast are according to this author false, and were made either for personal ends or to exclude the Portuguese from possessions on the South American continent. Professor Leite takes up each voyage in succession, and with a full knowledge of the sources and of subsequent criticisms challenges the claims that Brazil had been visited by the Spaniards before the voyage of Cabral. He asserts that these voyages may have been made to the vicinity of Trinidad, but it was the Orinoco and not the Amazon whose fresh waters extended far into the sea. The descriptions of the natives and of the positions of the north star are not correct in these narratives. The distances are greatly exaggerated, and the landmarks given by Pinzon and other navigators in the authentic contemporary documents may with greater reason be located on the coast of Venezuela. The map of Juan de la Cosa according to this criticism cannot be considered to be based upon authentic information regarding Brazil, and either the original map has been altered or a copy made on which the claims of Pinzon were inserted and the line of demarcation shown to the east of Cape São Agostinho. If these claims of Pinzon were fictitious the map was altered or redrawn after 1500; indeed not earlier, as we know from other evidence, than 1508. While these claims have not been accepted by all historians, there has been no adequate attempt as yet to refute them. In view of the present knowledge of the early

Spanish voyages there is thus a probability that Pedro Álvares Cabral was not only the first Portuguese but also the first European to visit the shores of Brazil.

Many French historians believe that Brazil was discovered by a navigator from Dieppe prior to the voyage of Cabral. The claim for this discovery is based on a tradition prevalent in Dieppe that a certain Jean Cousin was selected by some prominent merchants of that city to go on a voyage of exploration. He accepted this offer, and set sail in the year 1488. In order to avoid the storms and the sand-banks along the African coast he decided to take a course well out to sea. Arriving at the latitude of the Azores he was carried to the west by an ocean current. This took him to an unknown land at the mouth of an immense river. He claimed possession of this land and, instead of returning directly to Dieppe, went to the south-east, that is, towards South Africa. He discovered Cape Agulhas, and, after noting the coast, returned, arriving home in 1499.

The Normans undoubtedly visited the Brazilian coast during the first few years of the sixteenth century. They were not welcomed by the Portuguese, and they are seldom mentioned by them during this period. Nevertheless, they were not deterred from making these voyages by the fact that the world had been divided between Spain and Portugal, for had not Francis I made the statement: 'Je voudrais bien qu'on me montrât l'article du testament d'Adam qui partage le Nouveau-Monde entre mes frères, l'Empereur Charles Quint et le roi de Portugal, en m'excluant de la succession'?

There is no proof of this voyage, and the author who suggests it, Desmarquets, is not considered reliable. Unfortunately the public records at Dieppe were destroyed by the English in 1694, so that the question can never be settled. While this voyage may have been made, it seems more probably that the tradition regarding it was derived from the account of some voyage subsequent to that of Cabral, possibly that of de Gonneville. If it took place it would not have been sufficiently well known in Portugal to have influenced Cabral on his voyage.[1]

It has been asserted that in a will signed before a notary on the 3rd of May 1580, in the presence of a judge and witnesses,

[1] See the works of La Roncière, Gaffarel, d'Avezac, Heulhard, and Anthiaume.

one João Ramalho stated that he had been in Brazil since 1490, ninety years before.[1] This statement has caused some to believe that Ramalho had arrived in Brazil on a clandestine voyage prior to that of Cabral and had later taken up his residence in São Paulo. There seems to have been a man by that name in Brazil as early as 1532, when Martim Afonso de Sousa states that he lent him signal services. This João Ramalho was associated with Antonio Rodrigues. Both of them married Indian wives and had considerable influence with the natives. Father Simão de Vasconcellos in his *Chronica da Companhia de Jesus* (bk. i, No. 77) states that he was a man 'infamous for grave crimes and at that time excommunicated'. He is similarly mentioned by Ulric Schmidel and others. The date of the arrival of João Ramalho has given rise to much discussion, particularly in São Paulo. It has also been suggested that he might have been one of the convicts left by Cabral. It is more probable that he arrived in Brazil with one of the later fleets.

Another claim to a knowledge of Brazil prior to Cabral's voyage has been based on a document recently found by Jordão de Freitas in the Torre do Tombo, dated the 12th of July 1537. In evidence produced at a trial the following statement was made:

'They hope to prove that in the year 1531 (or 1532), in the said month, the ship and people who it is said belonged to the author went to *Fernambuquo*, a port of Brazil, where was a castle and fortress made by El Rey, our lord, and his Portuguese vassals thirty years ago and more. In the said port the said castle was made, and the port was inhabited by the Portuguese who had their dwelling-houses there forty and more years ago [*Tinham ay suas casas de Morada Avya Quarenta Anos e Mais*]. And at the time when it is said that the ship of the author arrived there, there was in the said castle a factory [*Castelo feitoria*] of the said lord and of many Portuguese merchants who had much merchandise there, as well from Portugal for trading as that which they obtained from the land, namely, brazil-wood, cottons, animal skins of different colours, parrots and monkeys and oils and slaves and much other Portuguese merchandise of great value. And they also had much artillery of copper and iron and powder and lances and *bestas espinguardes* and other offensive and

[1] See Candido Costa, op. cit., pp. 221–4. Also various articles in *Rev. Inst. Hist. e Geog. Brasiliero*.

defensive arms for their protection and against their enemies.' (*Lusitania*, ix, p. 322.)

Another claim is that indicated in a letter written to Dom Manuel by Estevão Frois, a Portuguese, in 1514. In this he says that he was held in a Spanish prison at Hispañola after a voyage to Northern Brazil, and asks for intervention by the king. In the course of the letter he states that the Spaniards were unwilling to accept his proof that the Portuguese had possessed Brazil for twenty years and more.[1]

These claims are probably based on the reports of the early French and Portuguese voyages made to Brazil as private enterprises during the thirty years which followed that of Cabral.[2]

THE DISCOVERY OF MADAGASCAR

During the voyage of Cabral's fleet to India the ship of Diogo Dias became separated and, losing its bearings, went too far to the east. When a northern course was taken the coast of Madagascar was encountered, and a landing was made at its northern extremity. This was the first known visit to this island by Europeans in modern times. The Anonymous Narrative, the letter of King Manuel, and most of the subsequent historians state that this ship reached the African mainland somewhat to the north of Malindi, and after an almost miraculous voyage returned to Lisbon. Corrêa, alone, tells of the discovery of Madagascar. While Corrêa cannot be relied on for the early voyages to India, in this case the information which he gives seems to be correct. After describing the storm in the South Atlantic and the voyage of the other ships around the Cape to Mozambique, Corrêa continues:

[1] See *Hist. da Colon. Port. do Brazil*, vol. i, pp. xxxiii–xlix, where a facsimile and a modern translation of the letter are given.

[2] These were undertaken by private French traders in search of brazil-wood, parrots, and monkeys, or by the 'New Christians' or converted Jews from Portugal. 'And the King of Portugal leased the lands which were discovered for him [in Brazil] to certain New Christians and they are obliged each year to send six small ships and to discover each year three hundred leagues farther and to build a fortress in the land discovered and to remain there three years, and the first year they are to pay nothing and the second one-sixth and the third one-fourth, and they agree to carry enough brazil-wood and slaves, and perhaps they will find here other profitable things.' See the letter of Piero Rondinelli written from Seville the 3rd of October 1502 (*Raccolta di Documenti e Studi . . . della R. Commissione Colombiana*, part iii, vol. ii, pp. 120–1. From Riccardiana Library MS. 1910).

'Except Diogo Dias, who, not knowing where he was going, did not arrive at land as soon as he should, and went on the other side of the island of Sam Laurenço. And because they saw it on his day,[1] they gave his name to it. And when they arrived at it, thinking that it was the coast of Moçambique, they ran along it, keeping a sharp lookout, seeking Moçambique, until they came to the end of the island, which was turning back so that the wind was on the other side, which was against them. On this account they then knew that it was an island and that they erred. Then they went to the island and cast anchor in a good port which made a harbour, protected from the winds of the sea. And lowering a boat they went on shore, where they found a spring of very good water. There were no people, and there were very good fish. He then sent there a convict whom he carried, because the king sent convicts in all the ships to thus adventure in doubtful lands; and the king ordered that they should be pardoned in the event of death or life. This one went inland and found some villages of straw houses, and the people were black and nude. He spoke with them by signs, without any of them doing him any harm. And he returned to the ship. And with him came some of those people, who sold chickens and yams [*inhames*] and fruit from bushes, good to eat. And these they exchanged for knives and axes and things of iron, little painted beads and caps and small looking-glasses. Our people did very well there for several days, but because the crew began to fall ill of fever and died, on this account they departed and went with a side wind as much as they could, to take the coast of Moçambique, and they reached the coast beyond Melinde. And they ran along the coast seeking Moçambique by the signs which the pilot carried in the instructions. And they went so far that they passed Cacotorá and went as far as the Cape of Guardafú, since they did not know where they were. And they continued along the shore within the strait until they arrived at the city of Barbora.'

No historian who mentions the voyage of Diogo Dias states that he stopped at any of the ports of East Africa south of Mogadishu. His destination was Sofala, but because he became separated from the fleet he sought Mozambique, which seems to have been the appointed meeting-place. It must be remembered that Dias did not have an Arab pilot. He undoubtedly knew of the difficult sailing along the coast, and with the feeling that the main fleet had preceded him he may have hoped to join it

[1] The 10th of August.

before it crossed to India with the favourable monsoon. Bartholomeu and Diogo Dias had instructions independent of those carried by Cabral, and the cargo which they carried was for trade with the people of the coast of Africa. The contents of these instructions are not known, but they may have directed that these two ships should proceed north along the coast before they returned, for discovery. In this case Diogo Dias was but following his instructions. The discovery of Madagascar seems not only probable but was a necessary result of the course taken, for had not Madagascar intervened either Mozambique or Malindi would have been reached. In subsequent voyages to India the route to the east of Madagascar was sometimes used and a landing made at the northern point for messages and supplies as at São Bras and Mozambique. At this period the Portuguese were not interested in colonizing; they wished only to purchase commodities raised by others. Madagascar had little to offer in this respect, so its discovery was not considered a matter of great importance. No other claim is made by Portuguese navigators for the discovery of the island prior to 1506, and no other author accounts for its name.[1]

[1] Madagascar was visited by the Arab and Hindu navigators in early times and was known to the Greeks, who may also have been there. During the first centuries of our era there was an Indonesian or Khmer migration, the results of which are still evident in the natives of the eastern shore. It was mentioned by Marco Polo, who probably confused it with Zanzibar, but it was not definitely located and described until the coming of the Portuguese in the sixteenth century. It is shown on the Cantino and Canerio maps, which are supposed to have utilized a map brought back with Cabral's fleet. On these maps it has the shape of a rectangle. This configuration continued on most of the maps of the island until the middle of the eighteenth century, although that of the celebrated Portuguese geographer Pedro Reinel shows it more exactly. Madagascar does not appear on the map of Juan de la Cosa.

For further data regarding the early history of Madagascar and the names applied to it, see A. Grandidier, *Histoire de la Géographie de Madagascar* (Paris, 1885); G. Ferrand, 'Le K'ouen-louen', in *Journal Asiatique*, 1919, vol. xiii; M. Bittner, *Die topographischen Capitel des Indischen Seespiegels Mohît*, with thirty maps by W. Tomaschek (Vienna, 1897).

DOCUMENTS

LETTER OF PEDRO VAZ DE CAMINHA TO KING MANUEL

WRITTEN FROM PORTO SEGURO OF VERA CRUZ THE 1ST OF MAY 1500

BEFORE Cabral's fleet departed from the new land which had been found to the west, Pedro Vaz de Caminha wrote a letter to the King of Portugal in which he related what happened during its sojourn there. This letter is the first and by far the most important document which has come down to us describing the discovery of that country. It has sometimes been called the first page in the history of Brazil. In this letter Caminha carefully wrote down each day what appeared to him to be new and curious, as well as almost every act of the members of the fleet in their dealings with the inhabitants. It is very important as the first account of the natives of that country. Later investigations have shown nothing to discredit the narrative from the standpoint of ethnology, and few subsequent writers have given us a better idea of the customs of the people inhabiting the coast of Brazil.

Unfortunately Caminha devotes but little space to that portion of the voyage prior to the arrival in Brazil regarding which there has been such uncertainty. When land was sighted, however, he is most minute in his descriptions. Because he recorded the events as they occurred, there can be no question as to their correctness so far as Caminha knew them.

The letter was addressed to the king, and may thus be considered an official document, although written in the easy style of a narrative. It may have been written either because of instructions from the king before Cabral began his voyage or by Caminha of his own volition, since his personal interest in writing is shown at the end of the letter, where he asks a favour from the king. Both his position and family gave him the right to address a letter to Dom Manuel.

Master John states that Ayres Correia wrote a letter. As chief factor, Correia would have little about which to write to the king from Brazil, and it is possible that this letter, written by Caminha, was the one referred to as having been written by his superior. The authenticity of this letter cannot be questioned, although it does not seem to have been known to all sixteenth-century writers.

Pedro Vaz de Caminha was the son of Vasco Fernandes de Caminha, a cavalier of the household of the Duke of Guimarães and *mestre da balança da moeda* in the district of Oporto. He inherited this position from his father,[1] and after his death in India it was given to his nephews, Rodrigo de Osouro and Pedro Vaz.[2] The office was one of honour and responsibility and was held by the family under four sovereigns, from Afonso V to John III. Caminha's career indicated that he was a man who was more interested in trade than in politics or navigation. He had a good education for the time, but apparently had not studied Latin. When the fleet of da Gama returned to Lisbon with the report of the riches and splendour of India, Caminha accepted the position of writer in the fleet which was to follow under the command of Pedro Álvares Cabral. He was to go to Calicut, where he was to take part in the commercial activities at the factory to be established there. Caminha sailed in Cabral's flagship with Ayres Correia, the chief factor, in company with other writers. He was killed in the massacre at Calicut in December 1500.

The chroniclers, Damião de Goes and Fernão Lopes de Castanheda, are the only authors of this period who mention Pedro Vaz de Caminha, and they refer to him only as a writer at the factory in Calicut. Our knowledge of Caminha is obtained, therefore, almost entirely from his own statements, and the only document we have is this letter.

The manuscript[3] was found by the Spanish historian Juan

[1] By a royal letter of Afonso V dated the 8th of March 1476, Pedro Vaz de Caminha was named *mestre da balança* in the mint at Oporto on the death or resignation of his father (*Chanc. de D. Afonso V*, bk. 38, p. 99). This position was confirmed to him by Dom Manuel in 1496 (*Corpo Chron.*, parte 1ª, maço 18, no. 108).

[2] In a letter of the 3rd of December 1501, in which the king appointed Caminha's nephew, Rodrigo de Osouro, to succeed him, he says, 'Pedro Vaz de Caminha former *mestre da balança* of our city of Oporto who died in India where we sent him'. On the death of Rodrigo de Osouro, his brother, Pedro Vaz, succeeded to the position on the 17th of December 1536.

[3] The original is written on seven sheets of paper, each with four pages, twenty-seven pages in all. It is kept in the Torre do Tombo, and is classified as *Corpo Chronologico*, gaveta 8, maço 2, no. 8.

Bautista Muñoz, in the Archivo da Torre do Tombo at Lisbon prior to 1790, and was first published in 1817 by Father Manuel Aires de Casal in *Corografia Brasileira* from an inexact copy found to exist in the Real Arquivo da Marinha at Rio de Janeiro. It has been republished many times since, both in Portugal and Brazil, and has been translated into French and German. The best text is that given in *Alguns Documentos do Archivo Nacional* (Lisbon, 1892, pp. 108–21), and it is from this that the translation has been made.

SENHOR:

Although the chief captain of this your fleet, and also the other captains, are writing to Your Highness the news of the finding of this your new land which was now found in this navigation, I shall not refrain from also giving my account of this to Your Highness, as best I can, although I know less than all of the others how to relate and tell it well. Nevertheless, may Your Highness take my ignorance for good intention, and believe that I shall not set down here anything more than I saw and thought, either to beautify or to make it less attractive. I shall not give account here to Your Highness of the ship's company and its daily runs, because I shall not know how to do it, and the pilots must have this in their charge.

And therefore, Senhor, I begin what I have to relate and say that the departure from Belem, as Your Highness knows, was on Monday, the 9th of March,[1] and on Saturday, the 14th of the said month, between eight and nine o'clock, we found ourselves among the Canary Islands, nearest to Grand Canary; and there we remained all that day in a calm, in sight of them, at a distance of about three or four leagues. On Sunday, the 22nd[2] of the said month, at ten o'clock, a little more or less, we came in sight of the Cape Verde Islands, that is to say, of the

[1] The departure of the fleet from the Tagus was Monday the 9th of March 1500. All the writers of the period with the exception of Gaspar Corrêa give this date, although there is some confusion, due to the fact that the ceremony for the departure took place at Belem on the preceding day. Corrêa states that the fleet left on the 25th of March, the Day of *Nossa Senhora*. His account of the voyage, however, was largely from hearsay, and, with the belief that the fleet left on that feast-day, he assigned the corresponding date to it.

[2] Castanheda and de Goes agree with Caminha as to this date.

island of Sam Nicolao,[1] according to the assertion of Pero Escolar,[2] the pilot. On the following night, on Monday at day-break, Vasco d'Atayde with his ship was lost from the fleet[3] without there being there heavy weather or contrary winds to account for it. The captain used all diligence to find him, seeking everywhere, but he did not appear again. And so we followed our route over this sea[4] until Tuesday of the octave of Easter, which was the 21st of April, when we came upon some signs of land, being then distant from the said island, as the pilots said, some six hundred and sixty or six hundred and seventy leagues; these signs were a great quantity of long weeds, which mariners call *botelho*,[5] and others as well which they also call *rabo de asno*.[6] And on the following Wednesday, in the morning, we met with birds which they call *fura buchos*. On this day at the vesper hours we caught sight of land,[7] that is, first of a large mountain, very high and round, and of other

[1] The fleet was now in Portuguese waters. It had had a satisfactory voyage thus far with the north-east wind behind it. The distance from Lisbon to the Cape Verde Islands is 1,510 nautical miles. The fleet had therefore made an average run during the thirteen days of 116 miles a day, or at the rate of about 5 knots. This rate was made under favourable conditions, and probably was not exceeded on the voyage to Brazil.

[2] Pero Escolar had gone to India with Vasco da Gama, sailing on the *Berrio* with Nicoláu Coelho. Caminha does not identify Escolar as a pilot on Cabral's ship. Later on in the letter he states definitely that Afonso Lopez was the pilot of the chief captain.

[3] This ship was therefore in sight after ten o'clock Sunday morning and could not be seen at day-break the following morning. The fleet did not stop at São Nicolau but evidently continued its course with the north-east wind. Vasco de Ataíde's ship thus lost convoy during the night 50 to 75 miles south-west from that island.

[4] *e asy segujmos nosso caminho per este mar de lomgo*. The expression *de lomgo* is also used by Caminha when he tells of sailing *de lomgo da costa*, along the coast, after arriving at Brazil. This, therefore, has no special significance, although some writers have tried to identify it with longitude, indicating a westward course. The expression generally used at this period for longitude was 'the height east-west'. The word longitude was employed by Ptolemy because the known world of his day was longer in this direction.

[5] This is evidently an error for *botelha*, bottle, instead of *botelho*, a measure or family name.

[6] Donkey's tail.

[7] This date is correct, since Easter Sunday in the year 1500 occurred on the 19th of April. Therefore Cabral first saw Brazil on Wednesday the 22nd of April 1500. From early times the discovery has been celebrated in Brazil on the 3rd of May. An effort has been made to reconcile these two dates because of the Gregorian Calendar. According to this change the new date for the discovery of Brazil would be the 1st of May from 1583 to 1699, the 2nd of May from 1700 to 1799, the 3rd of May from 1800 to 1899, and the 4th of May from 1900 to 2099, and so on. It will thus be seen that this happy coincidence is not entirely satisfactory. Formal possession of the land was taken by Portugal on Friday the 1st of May. The following Sunday, or the 3rd of May, was the feast of the Invention of the Cross in commemoration of the discovery of the true Cross at Jerusalem by Saint Helena in 326. There is, therefore, an adequate sentimental reason why this date, the 3rd of May, should be retained. The old date, the 12th of October, is celebrated in Brazil for the discovery of America by Columbus.

lower lands to the south of it, and of flat land, with great groves of trees. To this high mountain the captain gave the name of *Monte Pascoal*,[1] and to the land, *Terra da Vera Cruz*.[2] He ordered the lead to be thrown. They found twenty-five fathoms; and at sunset, some six leagues from the land, we cast anchor in nineteen fathoms, a clean anchorage. There we remained all that night, and on Thursday morning we made sail and steered straight to the land, with the small ships going in front, in 17, 16, 15, 14, 13, 12, 10, and 9 fathoms, until half

[1] 'Mountain pertaining to Easter'. This may be considered the first land sighted in Brazil by the Portuguese. It is conical in shape, one of the highest mountains in the Province of Bahia, and is still called by its original name of Monte Pascoal, given to it by Cabral. Its summit is located 16° 53′ 20″ south latitude and 41° 44′ west longitude (or 16° 56′ 8″ and 41° 45′ by another determination). It has a height of 356 m.

[2] The name *Vera Cruz* seemed a most appropriate one both to Cabral and to the members of his fleet. For many nights they had been seeing the brilliant stars of the Southern Cross. Cabral, a knight of the Order of Christ, bore with him the banner of that Order, a red cross on a white ground, and this same emblem was displayed on the sails of the fleet. The discovery was made during the festivities of Easter, when, as one writer observes, the twelve ships were there like the twelve apostles; and in a few days, on the 3rd of May, occurred the feast of the Invention of the Cross. Easter had not yet been celebrated in a proper manner, and the members of the fleet were looking forward to the services at the cross on the following Sunday.

This land was first named by Cabral *Terra da Vera Cruz*; Caminha called it *Ilha da Vera Cruz*, and Master John simply *Vera Cruz*. In the letter sent by Dom Manuel to the Catholic Sovereigns after the return of the fleet, he refers to it as *terra de Santa Cruz*. The ecclesiastics named it *Sancta Cruz* or *Sanctae Crucis*. The official name of the newly found country may therefore be considered *Santa Cruz*. But this name lasted only a short time. During the following decade the interest of the Portuguese was focused on India, and the land of Santa Cruz was thought of only as a stopping-place for ships bound for the East, or as one where dye-wood could be obtained.

The most interesting objects which the members of Cabral's crew saw in Brazil were the brilliantly coloured macaws. It was, therefore, popularly called *terra de papagaios*, or the land of parrots. This name was first given in a letter written by the Venetian Il Cretico on the 26th of June 1501, after the return of Cabral's fleet.

The lucrative trade in brazil-wood which soon developed, particularly with Flanders, for dyeing, caused the name of Brazil to be applied to it. This brazil-wood was called by the natives *ibira-pitanga* or red wood. It is classed by botanists as genus *Caesalpinia*. Columbus had found brazil-wood in the West Indies, but it had been ignored in the search for gold. The wood had formerly come from the East, where it had been known as early as the ninth century. The name was derived from the Arabic word *bakkam*, which had become Latinized into *bresilium*. There was also another reason for this name. As early as 1351 there appeared in the Medici atlas the representation of an island designated as Brazil. This island elusively changed its location until long after South America was discovered. The coincidence of these names, the lack of interest shown by the Portuguese in the new land, and the belief in the popular mind that the country was useful only for its dye-wood, caused the name to be definitely changed from Santa Cruz, or Sancta Cruz, to Brazil, and afterwards to Brasil. The old name was still retained by the ecclesiastics for many years, and they bitterly resented the substitution of the vulgar name of Brazil for that of Sancta Cruz with all its religious significance. It was called Santa Cruz until the middle of the sixteenth century. As a fitting memory of this discovery the national flag of Brazil still shows the stars of the Southern Cross.

a league from the shore, where we all cast anchor in front of the mouth of a river. And we arrived at this anchorage at ten o'clock, more or less. And from there we caught sight of men who were going along the shore, some seven or eight, as those on the small ships said, because they arrived there first. We there launched the boats and skiffs, and immediately all the captains of the ships came to this ship of the chief captain, and there they talked.[1] And the captain sent Nicolao Coelho[2] on shore in a boat to see that river.[3] And as soon as he began to go thither men assembled on the shore, by twos and threes, so that when the boat reached the mouth of the river eighteen or twenty men were already there.[4] They were dark, and entirely naked, without anything to cover their shame. They carried in their hands bows with their arrows.[5] All came boldly towards

[1] This indicates that Caminha went on Cabral's ship, and on this account the diary sent to the king may have been kept at the suggestion either of Cabral or of Ayres Correia.

[2] Nicoláu Coelho was captain of one of the ships. He had distinguished himself for bravery during the voyage with da Gama, when he went as commander of the *Berrio*, and had been received with great honour by the king upon his return. During Cabral's voyage he headed both landing parties in Brazil and was probably the first Portuguese to set foot on Brazilian soil. His ship was the first to reach Portugal on the return voyage of the fleets of both da Gama and Cabral.

[3] The Rio Cahy. This location for the first landing-place in Brazil is ascertained by measuring back 10 leagues from Porto Seguro, which can be identified because of its harbour. It has also been assigned to the mouth of the Rio do Frade, but probably in error.

[4] I am indebted to Dr. Alfred Métraux for the following regarding these Indians:

'The Tupinamba Indians occupied almost without interruption during the sixteenth century the whole coast of Brazil, from the mouth of the Amazon River as far as Rio Grande do Sul. They were divided into a certain number of nations who all bore the name of Tupi, but the Portuguese and the French often gave them different appellations to distinguish them. The indigenes whom Cabral met were the Tupiniquin. They possessed a narrow band of the coast which extended from Camamu on the North, to the Rio São Matheus (Cricaré) on the South. They even reached as far as Espiritu Santo.

'All these Tupi tribes of the Brazilian coast spoke the same language, and their customs, as well as their material civilization, were very similar and uniform. The descriptions given of the Tupinamba at the mouth of the Amazon correspond very exactly with what other authors tell us of the Tupinamba of the Rio de Janeiro, also known under the name of Tamoio. This uniformity of the civilization of the Tupi-Guaraní of the coast proves that they had emigrated on the Atlantic littoral at a very recent date. They had preserved, until the arrival of the whites, the tradition of their migrations. They came, without doubt, from the centre of Brazil, where to-day live numerous tribes belonging to the same linguistic family of Tupi-Guaraní.'

See A. Métraux, *La Civilisation matérielle des tribus Tupi-Guaraní*, and *La Religion des Tupinamba* (Paris, 1928), in which ample bibliographies are given of the early writers on the Indians of Brazil.

[5] The bows were long and well shaped with a notch at either end for attaching a cotton cord. With the Tupiniquin, the section was oval, although other tribes of the

TUPINAMBA FEATHER BONNETS
(National Museum, Copenhagen. a and e, and d and g are inside and outside views of the same bonnets).

the boat, and Nicolao Coelho made a sign to them that they should lay down their bows, and they laid them down. He could not have any speech with them there, nor understanding which might be profitable, because of the breaking of the sea on the shore. He gave them only a red cap [*barrete*][1] and a cap [*carapuça*][2] of linen, which he was wearing on his head, and a black hat. And one of them gave him a hat of long bird feathers with a little tuft of red and grey feathers like those of a parrot.[3] And another gave him a large string of very small white beads which look like seed pearls;[4] these articles I believe the captain is sending to Your Highness.[5] And with this he returned to the ships because it was late and he could have no further speech with them on account of the sea. On the fol-

Tupinamba used different shapes. The arrows had long shafts properly feathered. Due to the scarcity of quartz and obsidian, the points were made of reed or bone. Points covered with burning cotton were sometimes used in warfare to destroy the houses of their enemies.

[1] A four-cornered hat made of soft material.

[2] A conical cap ordinarily made of blue- or rose-coloured cloth which was used by Portuguese sailors and farmers. Among Mediterranean sailors it was red, and worn by masters or pilots. These caps are still seen along the coast of Portugal.

[3] The bonnet or *acangaop* here described was worn because of the brilliant colouring of the separate feathers, which were selected to suit the wearer's taste. An illustration of one of these taken from an old print is given by Métraux. In addition to this type there were two others. These were made of short feathers interlaced with cotton thread to form a net, which made a compact covering as on the throat of a bird. In some cases small pieces of wood were used for firmer attachment, thus making the bonnet thick and heavy. One of these covered closely the head and ears and extended to the neck or shoulders; the other had a longer extension to the middle of the back. They sometimes wore short tufts of radiating feathers on the head.

The feathers for these bonnets were carefully selected for uniformity of size and colour. They were sometimes dyed. The method of attaching the feathers showed a highly developed technique.

The Tupinamba also wore diadems. These consisted of long coloured feathers attached to a band worn around the head. They were sometimes used with the caps or bonnets. Other feathers were attached to bands and worn around the neck, waist, or arms as bracelets. The so-called bustles consisted of radiating feathers of the American ostrich, the *nanduguaçu* of Brazil. These are shown in nearly all of the early pictures of the Tupinamba. The men wore diadems, bonnets, mantles, or bustles. The women contented themselves with simpler feather ornaments.

[4] *aljaveira*. The members of the fleet were on the alert to discover pearls, because just before their departure word had been brought back to Spain, and had probably reached Portugal, that these had been discovered during the third voyage of Columbus. According to Métraux, both men and women wore long strings of shells which were wound around the neck and suspended on their chests or wound about the wrists. The beads were chiefly shell, but bone, wood, and other materials were also used. They also had strings of larger beads with pendants which were worn around the neck. Similar necklaces of shells resembling seed pearls are still used by the Indians of Brazil.

[5] Dom Manuel had changed the expression *Vossa Senhoria*, which had been previously used, to *Vossa Alteza*. The title *Magestade* was not used by the Portuguese kings in the sixteenth century, since it was only applied to God.

lowing night it blew so hard from the south-east with showers that it made the ships drift, especially the flagship.

And on Friday morning, at eight o'clock, a little more or less, on the advice of the pilots, the captain ordered the anchors to be raised and to set sail. And we went northward along the coast with the boats and skiffs tied to the poop, to see whether we could find some shelter and good anchorage where we might lie, to take on water and wood, not because we were in need of them then, but to provide ourselves here. And when we set sail there were already some sixty or seventy men on the shore, sitting near the river, who had gathered there little by little. We continued along the coast and the captain ordered the small vessels to go in closer to the land, and to strike sail if they found a secure anchorage for the ships. And when we were some ten leagues along the coast from where we had raised anchor, the small vessels found a reef within which was a harbour, very good and secure [*seguro*] with a very wide entrance. And they went in and lowered their sails. And gradually the ships arrived after them, and a little before sunset they also struck sail about a league from the reef, and anchored in eleven fathoms. And by the captain's order our pilot, Affonso Lopez, who was in one of those small vessels and was an alert and dextrous man for this, straightway entered the skiff to take soundings in the harbour. And he captured two well-built natives who were in a canoe.[1] One of them was carrying a bow and six or seven arrows and many others went about on the shore with bows and arrows and they did not use them. Then, since it was already night, he took the two men to the flagship, where they were received with much pleasure and festivity.

In appearance they are dark, somewhat reddish, with good faces and good noses, well shaped.[2] They go naked, without any covering; neither do they pay more attention to concealing

[1] *almadia.* This is a Portuguese word, evidently derived from a Berber word which originally meant a ferry boat (*el maziyah*). In the narratives of Cabral's voyage it has the general meaning of any small native craft, such as the dugout, raft, bark canoe, or those of a similar nature. Because there is no exact equivalent in English, it will be retained in these translations in its original form.

[2] The earliest illustration showing the Tupinamba Indians was printed at Augsburg or Nuremberg prior to 1504. It is not, however, an accurate representation. See article by Rudolph Schuller in the *Journal de la Soc. des Américanistes*, 1924, vol. xvi, p. 111.

or exposing their shame than they do to showing their faces, and in this respect they are very innocent. Both had their lower lips bored and in them were placed pieces of white bone, the length of a handbreadth, and the thickness of a cotton spindle and as sharp as an awl at the end. They put them through the inner part of the lip, and that part which remains between the lip and the teeth is shaped like a rook in chess. And they carry it there enclosed in such a manner that it does not hurt them, nor does it embarrass them in speaking, eating, or drinking.[1] Their hair is smooth, and they were shorn, with the hair cut higher than above a comb of good size, and shaved to above the ears.[2] And one of them was wearing below the opening, from temple to temple towards the back, a sort of wig of yellow birds' feathers, which must have been the length of a *couto*,[3] very thick and very tight, and it covered the back of the head and the ears. This was glued to his hair, feather by feather, with a material as soft as wax, but it was not wax. Thus the head-dress was very round and very close and very equal, so that it was not necessary to remove it when they washed.

[1] 'They have a large hole in the lower lip which they make when they are young. They take the children and prick the hole with sharpened deer's horn. In this they insert a small piece of stone or wood and anoint it with salve, and the hole remains open. Then when the children are fully grown and fit to bear arms, they enlarge the hole and insert in it a large green stone. This stone is shaped so that the smaller end is inside the lip and the larger end outside. The result is that their lips hang down with the weight of the stones. They have also at both sides of the mouth, and in either cheek, other small stones. Some of these are of crystal and are narrow and long.' Hans Staden (transl. by Letts, p. 143). These labrets are not only mentioned by Hans Staden, who was in Brazil forty-seven years later, but by Cardim, and nearly all the early writers who visited Brazil. Perhaps the most exaggerated description is given by Vespucci in his letter addressed to Lorenzo de' Medici in 1502 (C. E. Lester, *The Life and Voyages of Americus Vespucius*, pp. 182–3).

[2] *os cabelos seus sam credios, e andavam trosquJados de trosquya alta mais que de sobre pemtem, de bem gramdura, e rapados ataa per cima das orelhas*; *tosquiar* means literally to shear. The hair was cut by a blow of one stone upon another. *Sobre pemtem* means the length cut over a barber's comb. Hair was usually removed by plucking but they also shaved with a sharp piece of quartz or with a bamboo knife.

[3] *e huum d eles trazia per baixo da solapa de fonte a fonte pera detras huna maneira de cabeleira de penas d ave amarela, que seria de compridam de huum couto. . . .* The Tupinamba shaved their hair above the forehead in a half-moon, extending from temple to temple. An illustration of this is given in Léry. The cut portion was not covered with feathers. The word *solapa* has many meanings. It here indicates the space within this crescent. Hair was allowed to grow only on the head. There were other arrangements of cutting the hair besides the half-moon in front. The meaning of the word *couto* is not clear but it may be the equivalent of the Spanish *coto*, meaning the width of the hand with the thumb extended. The method of cutting the hair as shown in illustrations of later writers indicates that the back portion of the head was also shaved to above the ears. There was thus left a portion covered with hair about the width of a handbreadth.

When they came on board, the captain, well dressed, with a very large collar of gold around his neck, was seated in a chair, with a carpet at his feet as a platform. And Sancho de Toar and Simam de Miranda and Nicolao Coelho and Aires Correa and the rest of us who were in the ship with him were seated on the floor on this carpet. Torches were lighted and they entered, and made no sign of courtesy or of speaking to the captain or to any one, but one of them caught sight of the captain's collar, and began to point with his hand towards the land and then to the collar, as though he were telling us that there was gold in the land.[1] And he also saw a silver candlestick, and in the same manner he made a sign towards the land and then towards the candlestick, as though there were silver also. They showed them a grey parrot which the captain brought here; they at once took it into their hands and pointed towards the land, as though they were found there. They showed them a sheep, but they paid no attention to it. They showed them a hen; they were almost afraid of it, and did not want to touch it; and afterwards they took it as though frightened. Then food was given them; bread and boiled fish, comfits, little cakes, honey, and dried figs. They would eat scarcely anything of that, and if they did taste some things they threw them out. Wine was brought them in a cup; they put a little to their mouths, and did not like it at all, nor did they want any more.[2] Water was brought them in a

[1] The Tupi-Guaraní were, in fact, acquainted not only with gold but with silver and copper as well, which had been obtained by successive trade with the people of the Andine plateau. Silver trinkets were found among the Guaraní Indians during the expedition of Sebastian Cabral, who went to the south of Brazil in 1526 to determine the Line of Demarcation, under the Treaty of Tordesillas, by astronomical observations. The belief that silver was to be found there gave the name to the Rio de la Plata; and later the name Argentine was applied to that country for the same reason. Silver, however, is only to be found on the Andine plateau. The migration of cultural elements from other parts of South America, particularly as related to the Tupi-Guaraní, has been carefully studied by Nordenskiöld and Métraux. These exchanges carried to other parts the cultural elements of the Tupi-Guaraní as well. The comparative rapidity of these movements is shown by the distribution of those introduced by the Europeans. Between the first relations of these peoples with those of Europe soon after Cabral's voyage and the conquest of Peru by Pizarro, the two elements which spread most rapidly were chickens and iron fish-hooks.

[2] This does not mean that they did not drink intoxicants, for Hans Staden tells us: 'The women prepare the drinks. They take the mandioca root and boil it in great pots. Afterwards they pour it into other vessels and allow it to cool a little. Then young girls sit around and chew the boiled root in their mouths, and what is chewed they set apart in a special vessel. When the boiled root is all chewed, they place it

jar;[1] they took a mouthful of it, and did not drink it; they only washed their mouths and spat it out. One of them saw some white rosary beads; he made a motion that they should give them to him, and he played much with them, and put them around his neck; and then he took them off and wrapped them around his arm. He made a sign towards the land and then to the beads and to the collar of the captain, as if to say that they would give gold for that. We interpreted this so, because we wished to, but if he meant that he would take the beads and also the collar, we did not wish to understand because we did not intend to give it to him. And afterwards he returned the beads to the one who gave them to him. And then they stretched themselves out on their backs on the carpet to sleep without taking any care to cover their privy parts, which were not circumcised, and the hair on them was well shaved and arranged. The captain ordered pillows to be put under the head of each one, and he with the head-dress took sufficient pains not to disarrange it. A mantle was thrown over them, and they permitted it and lay at rest and slept.

On Saturday morning the captain ordered sails to be set and we went to seek the entrance, which was very wide and deep, six or seven fathoms, and all the ships entered within and anchored in five or six fathoms; this anchorage inside is so large and so beautiful and so secure that more than two hundred large and small ships could lie within it.[2] And as soon as the ships were in place and anchored all the captains came to this ship of the chief captain, and from here the captain ordered Nicolao Coelho and Bartolameu Dias[3] to go on shore, and they

back again in the pot which they fill with water, mixing the water with the chewed root, after which they heat it again.

'They have special pots, half buried in the ground, which they make use of much as we use casks for wine or beer. They pour the liquid into these and close them, and the liquor ferments of itself and becomes strong. After two days they drink it until they are drunken. It is thick, but pleasant to the taste.' This method is similar to that used by the Quichua Indians of Peru in making *chicha* from maize. The Tupinamba Indians also used other intoxicants made from vegetables, maize, and fruits.

[1] This was probably an *albarrada*, the Arabic name for a jar for cooling water.

[2] This was called Porto Seguro, the present Bahia Cabrália, located in latitude 16° 21′ S. The early village built at Porto Seguro was later abandoned by the inhabitants because the site was unhealthy and it was moved farther south to the present location bearing this name.

[3] This is the same Bartolomeu Dias who, in an endeavour to reach India, had rounded the Cape of Good Hope in 1488.

took those two men, and let them go with their bows and arrows. To each of them he ordered new shirts and red hats and two rosaries of white bone beads to be given and they carried them on their arms, with rattles and bells. And he sent with them to remain there a young convict,[1] named Affonso Ribeiro, the servant of Dom Joham Tello, to stay with them, and learn their manner of living and customs; and he ordered me[2] to go with Nicolao Coelho. We went at once straight for the shore. At that place there assembled at once some two hundred men, all naked, and with bows and arrows in their hands. Those whom we were bringing made signs to them that they should draw back and put down their bows, and they put them down, and did not draw back much. It is enough to say that they put down their bows. And then those whom we brought, and the young convict with them, got out. As soon as they were out they did not stop again, nor did one wait for the other; rather they ran, each as fast as he could. And they and many others with them passed a river which flows here with sweet and abundant water which came up as far as their waists. And thus they went running on the other side of the river between some clumps of palms, where were others, and there they stopped. And there, too, the young convict went with a man who, immediately upon his leaving the boat, befriended him, and took him thither. And then they brought him back to us, and with him came the others whom we had brought. These were now naked and without caps. And then many began to arrive, and entered into the boats from the seashore, until no more could get in. And they carried water gourds and took some kegs which we brought and filled them with water and carried them to the boats. They did not actually enter the boat, but from near by, threw them in by hand and we took them, and they asked us to give them something.

[1] The fleet carried twenty convicts, or banished men, condemned to death. These were to be landed at desirable places to proselyte the natives and to learn their language. Their success was to be rewarded with pardon. Some of these convicts were of great value in this and succeeding voyages. Vasco da Gama had also carried ten or twelve convicts for the same purpose.

[2] The fact that Cabral sent Caminha, a writer, on shore with the two captains may indicate that he had been selected by the chief captain to write the account of the sojourn in Brazil although as yet it had not been decided to send word of this discovery to the king. If Caminha continued to narrate the events of the voyage his account was probably lost during the massacre at Calicut.

Nicolao Coelho had brought bells and bracelets and to some he gave a bell and to others a bracelet, so that with that inducement they almost wished to help us. They gave us some of those bows and arrows for hats and linen caps, and for whatever we were willing to give them. From thence the other two youths departed and we never saw them again.

Many of them, or perhaps the greater number of those who were there, wore those beaks of bone in their lips, and some, who were without them, had their lips pierced, and in the holes they carried wooden plugs which looked like stoppers of bottles.[1] And some of them carried three of those beaks, namely, one in the middle and two at the ends. And others were there whose bodies were quartered in colour,[2] that is, half of them in their own colour, and half in a bluish-black dye, and others quartered in checkered pattern.[3] There were among them three or four girls, very young and very pretty, with very dark hair, long over the shoulders, and their privy parts so high, so closed, and so free from hair that we felt no shame in looking at them very well. Then for the time there was no more speech or understanding with them, because their barbarity was so great that no one could either be understood or heard. We made signs for them to leave, and they did so, and went to the other side of the river. And three or four of our men left the boats and filled I do not know how many kegs of

[1] *Espelhos de boracha.* That is, the stoppers used with skin containers for wine. These wooden decorations were used by the young men. They might also have been worn to fill the openings in the face as a relaxation from the heavy stone labrets.

[2] The black paint used for the fanciful decoration of the body was derived from the fruit of the *genipapeiro.* The red colour used particularly for the face and feet was derived from the fruit of the *urucú.*

[3] The account given by the Portuguese friar Fernão Cardim, which Purchas inserts in his *Pilgrims*, vol. xvi, ed. 1906, p. 422, corroborates the description of Vaz de Caminha.

'But to make themselves gallant they use divers inventions, painting their bodies with the juice of a certaine fruite wherewith they remaine black, making in their bodies many white stroakes, after the fashion of round hose, and other kinde of garments. They emplume themselves also, making Diadems and Bracelets, and other very fine inventions, they esteeme very much all manner of fine Feathers: they let no haire grow in the parts of their body, but they pull them out, onely the head excepted, which they cut in many fashions, for some weare them long with a halfe Moone shaven before, and they say they tooke this use from Saint Thomas, and it seemeth that they had some notice of him though confusedly: others make certaine kinde of crownes and circles that they seeme Friers: the women all doe weare long haire, and ordinarily blacke, and the haire of the one and of the other is smooth: when they are angrie they let their haire grow long and the women, when they mourne, doe cut their haire, and also when their husbands goe a farre journey.'

water which we carried, and we returned to the ships. And upon seeing us thus, they made signs for us to return. We returned and they sent the convict and did not wish him to stay there with them. He carried a small basin and two or three red caps to give to their chief, if there was one. They did not care to take anything from him and thus they sent him back with everything, and then Bertolameu Dias made him return again to give those things to them, and he returned and gave them in our presence, to the one who had first befriended him. And then he came away and we took him with us. The man who befriended him was now well on in years, and was well decked with ornaments and covered with feathers stuck to his body, so that he looked pierced with arrows like Saint Sebastian.[1] Others wore caps of yellow feathers, others of red, others of green; and one of the girls was all painted from head to foot with that paint, and she was so well built and so rounded and her lack of shame was so charming, that many women of our land seeing such attractions, would be ashamed that theirs were not like hers. None of them were circumcised, but all were as we were. And, thereupon, we returned, and they went away.

In the afternoon the chief captain set out in his boat with all of us and with the other captains of the ships in their boats to amuse ourselves in the bay near the shore. But no one went on land, because the captain did not wish it, although there was no one there; only he and all landed on a large island in the bay, which is very empty at low tide, but on all sides it is surrounded by water so that no one can go to it without a boat or by swimming. There he and the rest of us had a good time for an hour and a half, and the mariners fished there, going out with a net, and they caught a few small fish. And then, since it was already night, we returned to the ships.

[1] The whole body was sometimes covered with feathers taken from the throats of birds, or small feathers, which were attached with wax or gum as described by Caminha. This custom is rather widely distributed over tropical South America. The Tupinamba formerly so prepared their dead before burial. In some cases the head only was covered with throat feathers, which were similarly attached to the hair, giving the appearance of a wig. As the feathers had great value, and they wished to use them again, they were washed with the juice of a certain root to expand them and in order to remove them from the hair. The feathers were preserved by being placed in bamboo tubes sealed with wax.

TUPINAMBA CEREMONIAL DANCE
(From Jean Léry: "Navigatio in Brasiliam Americae." in De Bry: "Americae Tertia Pars"... Frankfort, 1592.)

On Low Sunday in the morning the captain determined to go to that island to hear mass and a sermon, and he ordered all the captains to assemble in the boats and to go with him; and so it was done. He ordered a large tent to be set up on the island and within it a very well-provided altar to be placed, and there with all the rest of us he had mass said, which the father, Frei Amrique, intoned and all the other fathers and priests who were there accompanied him with the same voice. That mass, in my opinion, was heard by all with much pleasure and devotion. The captain had there with him the banner of Christ,[1] with which he left Belem, and it was kept raised on the Gospel side. After the mass was finished, the father removed his vestments, and sat down in a high chair, and we all threw ourselves down on that sand, and he preached a solemn and profitable sermon on the history of the Gospel, and at the end of it he dealt with our coming and with the discovery of this land, and referred to the sign of the Cross in obedience to which we came; which was very fitting, and which inspired much devotion.

While we were at mass and at the sermon, about the same number of people were on the shore as yesterday with their bows and arrows, who were amusing themselves and watching us; and they sat down, and when the mass was finished and we were seated for the sermon, many of them arose and blew a horn or trumpet[2] and began to leap and to dance for a while, and some of them placed themselves in two or three *almadias* which they had there. These are not made like those I have

[1] In addition to the royal standard Cabral also took with him the banner of the Order of Christ, of which he was a member. The ceremony during which this banner was presented probably also took place at Restello, which belonged to that Order. There is some confusion among historians regarding these two banners and it is sometimes stated that it was the banner of the Order of Christ which was given to Cabral by Dom Manuel. The fleet was on its way to India, where Cabral went as the representative of the king. It was but fitting, therefore, that he should take a banner with the royal arms. In fact, he had occasion to use it in this capacity when he took possession for Portugal of a house given by the King of Calicut. The fleet also went on a religious mission and the banner of the Order of Christ added significance, because it was the emblem of Prince Henry in his conflicts with the Moors. It was thus appropriately used at this time. When da Gama left on his first voyage he too was given a banner of the Order of Christ. Barros (*Asia*, Dec. 1, bk. iv, ch. i).

[2] Their trumpets were made of cylinders of hollow wood or of the leg bones of animals, often encased in wood. In warfare they used large shells which were blown through a perforated hole. Drums, flutes, whistles, and rattles were also used. In the illustrations accompanying the narratives of Hans Staden and Jean de Léry given in de Bry, the trumpets are shown with an egg-shaped enlargement at the extremity.

already seen; they are simply three logs fastened together,[1] and four or five, or all who wanted to, entered them, scarcely moving away at all from the land, but only far enough to keep their footing. After the sermon was finished the captain and all the rest proceeded to the boats with our banner displayed and we embarked, and thus we all went towards the land, to pass along it where they were, Bertolameu Dias going ahead in his skiff, at the captain's order, with a piece of timber from an *almadia* which the sea had carried to them, to give it to them. And all of us were about a stone's throw behind him. When they saw the skiff of Bertolameu Dias, all of them came at once to the water, going into it as far as they could. A sign was made to them to put down their bows, and many of them went at once to put them down on shore and others did not put them down. There was one there who spoke much to the others, telling them to go away, but they did not, in my opinion, have respect or fear of him. This one who was telling them to move carried his bow and arrows, and was painted with red paint on his breasts and shoulder blades and hips, thighs, and legs, all the way down, and the unpainted places such as the stomach and belly were of their own colour, and the paint was so red that the water did not wash away or remove it, but rather when he came out of the water he was redder. One of our men left the skiff of Bertolameu Dias and went among them, without their thinking for a moment of doing him harm; on the contrary, they gave him gourds of water and beckoned to those on the skiff to come on land. Thereupon Bertolameu Dias returned to the captain, and we came to the ships to eat, playing trumpets and pipes without troubling them further. And they again sat down on the shore and thus they remained for a while. On this island where we went to hear mass and the sermon the water ebbs a great deal and uncovers much sand and much gravel. While we were there some went to look for shell fish, but did not find them; they found some thick and short shrimps. Among them was a very large and very fat shrimp such as I had never seen before. They also found shells of

[1] These rafts are often described by later writers. They were about 6 feet long and 2 feet wide, made of four or five logs of medium size, tied together with twigs or creepers. The Indians sat on them with their legs extended, and propelled them with a small paddle.

cockles and mussels, but did not discover any whole piece. And as soon as we had eaten, all the captains came to this ship at the command of the chief captain and he went to one side with them and I was there too, and he asked all of us whether it seemed well to us to send news of the finding of this land to Your Highness by the supply ship, so that you might order it to be better reconnoitred, and learn more about it than we could now learn because we were going on our way.[1] And among the many speeches which were made regarding the matter, it was said by all or by the greater number, that it would be very well to do so; and to this they agreed. And as soon as the decision was made, he asked further whether it would be well to take here by force two of these men to send to Your Highness and to leave here in their place two convicts. In this matter they agreed that it was not necessary to take men by force, since it was the general custom that those taken away by force to another place said that everything about which they are asked was there; and that these two convicts whom we should leave would give better and far better information about the land than would be given by those carried away by us, because they are people whom no one understands nor would they learn [Portuguese] quickly enough to be able to tell it as well as those others when Your Highness sends here, and that consequently we should not attempt to take any one away from here by force nor cause any scandal, but in order to tame and pacify them all the more, we should simply leave here the two convicts when we departed. And thus it was determined, since it appeared better to all.

When this was finished the captain ordered us to go to land in our boats in order to ascertain as well as possible what the river was like, and also to divert ourselves. We all went ashore

[1] *e, tamto que comemos, vieram logo todolos capitaães a esta naao per mandado do capitam moor, com os quaaes se ele apartou, e eu na conpanhia, e preguntou asy a todos se nos parecia seer bem mandar a nova do achamento d esta terra a Vosa Alteza pelo navjo dos mantijmentos, pera a mjlhor mandar descobrjr, e saber d ela mais do que agora nos podiamos saber, por hirmos de nosa viajem* . . . (*Alguns Documentos*, p. 113). This sentence is important. It shows that Pedro Vaz de Caminha occupied a prominent place among those in the fleet as he was a member of this council. Gaspar de Lemos was evidently to return directly to Portugal with news of the discovery and it was suggested that further acquaintance with the land should be obtained on a succeeding voyage. Cabral's fleet was also to proceed at once to the East without making other discoveries along the coast. It is probable that Caminha began to write his letter on this day, Monday the 26th of April.

in our boats, armed, and the banner with us. The natives went there along the shore to the mouth of the river[1] where we were going, and before we arrived, in accordance with the instructions they had received before, they all laid down their bows and made signs for us to land. And as soon as the boats had put their bows on shore, they all went immediately to the other side of the river, which is not wider than the throw of a short staff;[2] and as soon as we disembarked some of our men crossed the river at once and went among them, and some waited and others withdrew, but the result was that we were all intermingled. They gave us some of their bows with their arrows in exchange for hats and linen caps and for anything else which we gave them. So many of our men went to the other side and mingled with them that they withdrew and went away and some went above to where others were. And then the captain had himself carried on the shoulders of two men and crossed the river and made every one return. The people who were there could not have been more than the usual number, and when the captain made all return, some of them came to him, not to recognize him for their lord, for it does not seem to me that they understand or have knowledge of this,[3] but because our people were already passing to this side of the river. There they talked and brought many bows and beads of the kind already mentioned, and trafficked in anything in such manner that many bows, arrows, and beads were brought from there to the ships. And then the captain returned to this side of the river, and many men came to its bank. There you might have seen gallants painted with black and red, and with quarterings both on their bodies and on their legs, which certainly was pleasing in appearance. There were also among them four or five young women just as naked, who were not displeasing to the eye, among whom was one with her thigh from the knee to

[1] This was the Mutary (Itacumirim) River.

[2] *jogo de manqual.*

[3] The Tupinamba did not appear to have chiefs with authority. The head of a communal house or one more proficient in warfare led in his respective sphere. There was some authority exercised by the elders but rather as advisers than as chiefs. This feeling of freedom of action was one of the reasons why Europeans had so much difficulty in making the natives work under their supervision, and it gradually led to the practical extermination of many tribes and the substitution of negroes for common labour. The apparent lack of authority among the Tupinamba was of great interest to the followers of Rousseau in the eighteenth century, who saw in their mode of government the simple life which they themselves sought.

the hip and buttock all painted with that black paint and all the rest in her own colour; another had both knees and calves and ankles so painted, and her privy parts so nude and exposed with such innocence that there was not there any shame. There was also another young woman carrying an infant boy or girl tied at her breasts by a cloth of some sort so that only its little legs showed. But the legs of the mother and the rest of her were not concealed by any cloth.

And afterwards the captain moved up along the river, which flows continuously even with the shore, and there an old man was waiting who carried in his hand the oar of an *almadia*. When the captain reached him he spoke in our presence, without any one understanding him, nor did he understand us with reference to the things he was asked about, particularly gold, for we wished to know whether they had any in this land. This old man had his lip so bored that a large thumb could be thrust through the hole, and in the opening he carried a worthless green stone[1] which closed it on the outside. And the captain made him take it out; and I do not know what devil spoke to him, but he went with it to put it in the captain's mouth. We laughed a little at this and then the captain got tired and left him; and one of our men gave him an old hat for the stone, not because it was worth anything but to show. And afterwards the captain got it, I believe to send it with the other things to Your Highness. We went along there looking at the river, which has much and very good water. Along it are many palms, not very high, in which there are many good sprouts.[2] We gathered and ate many of them. Then the captain turned towards the mouth of the river where we had disembarked, and on the other side of the river were many of them, dancing and diverting themselves before one another, without taking each other by the hand, and they did it well.[3] Then Diogo

[1] Green stones were particularly prized by the Indians of South America.

[2] *palmitos*.

[3] Like that of other Indian tribes, the dancing of the Tupinamba consisted in stamping the feet and turning to the rhythm of rattles, drums, and wind instruments. A leader used a stick as a baton to mark the time. Women participated in these dances as well as the men, particularly in the ceremonies attending cannibalism. The following description translated from Fernão Cardim is given in Purchas's *Pilgrims* (vol. xvi, pp. 427–8):

'The Fathers doe teach them from their cradles to dance and sing, and their dancings are not sundrie changes, but a continuall stamping with the feet standing still, or going round about, or stirring their bodie or their head, and they doe it all by such compasse

Dias,[1] who was revenue officer of Sacavem, crossed the river. He is an agreeable and pleasure-loving man, and he took with him one of our bagpipe players and his bagpipe,[2] and began to dance among them, taking them by the hands, and they were delighted and laughed and accompanied him very well to the sound of the pipe. After they had danced he went along the level ground, making many light turns and a remarkable leap which astonished them, and they laughed and enjoyed themselves greatly. And although he reassured and flattered them a great deal with this, they soon became sullen like wild men and went away upstream. And then the captain crossed over the river with all of us, and we went along the shore, the boats going along close to land, and we came to a large lake of sweet water which is near the seashore, because all that shore is marshy above and the water flows out in many places. And after we had crossed the river some seven or eight of the natives joined our sailors who were retiring to the boats. And they took from there a shark which Bertolameu Dias killed and brought to them and threw on the shore.[3] It suffices to say that up to this time, although they were somewhat tamed, a moment afterwards they became frightened like sparrows at a feeding-place. And no one dared to speak strongly to them for fear they might be more frightened; and everything was done to their liking in order to tame them thoroughly. To the old man with whom the captain spoke he gave a red cap; and in spite of all the talking that he did with him, and the cap which

and pleasantnesse as can be desired, at the sound of a Timbrell made after the fashion of those which the children use in Spaine with manie smal stones within or certaine seeds whereof they make also verie good beads: and so they sing dancing altogether, for they doe not one thing without the other, in such compasse and order that sometime an 100 men dancing and singing together in a row one behind the other doe end all at one stroke, as if they were altogether in one place. The singers as well men as women are much esteemed among them, in so much that if they take an enemie a good singer, and an Inventer of Verses, they therefore spare his life, and doe not eate him nor his children.'

[1] Diogo Dias was a brother of Bartolomeu Dias and commanded one of the caravels. He is called Diogo by Castanheda and Corrêa; Barros and Damião de Goes give his name as Pedro.

[2] The bagpipe formed the natural accompaniment to folk dances in Galicia and Portugal. Its use on ship-board was of value to keep up the spirits of the sailors.

[3] In other accounts a manatee is described and not a shark. Caminha apparently did not see this animal and did not believe the stories told of its unusual appearance. The method of fishing employed by the Tupinamba by shooting with arrows or catching in nets is described by Hans Staden and in other early narratives. Fish was preserved by smoking and not with salt. This preserved fish ground to flour was called *piracuí*.

he gave him, as soon as he left and began to cross the river, he immediately became more cautious and would not return again to this side of it. The other two whom the captain had on the ships, and to whom he gave what has already been mentioned, did not appear again, from which I infer that they are bestial people and of very little knowledge; and for this reason they are so timid. Yet withal they are well cared for and very clean, and in this it seems to me that they are rather like birds or wild animals, to which the air gives better feathers and better hair than to tame ones. And their bodies are so clean and so fat and so beautiful that they could not be more so; and this causes me to presume that they have no houses or dwellings in which to gather, and the air in which they are brought up makes them so. Nor indeed have we up to this time seen any houses or anything which looks like them. The captain ordered the convict, Affonso Ribeiro, to go with them again, which he did. And he went there a good distance, and in the afternoon he returned, for they had made him come and were not willing to keep him there; and they had given him bows and arrows and had not taken from him anything which was his. On the contrary, he said, one of them had taken from him some yellow beads which he was wearing and fled with them; and he complained and the others at once went after him and returned to give them back to him. And then they ordered him to go back. He said that he had not seen there among them anything but some thatched huts of green branches, and made very large, like those of Entre Doiro e Minho.[1] And thus we returned to the ships to sleep when it was already almost night.

On Monday after eating we all disembarked to take in water.[2] Then many came there, but not so many as at the other times, and now they were carrying very few bows and they kept a little apart from us, and afterwards little by little mingled with us. And they embraced us and had a good time; and some of

[1] Entre Doiro e Minho is the extreme northern province of Portugal, of which Oporto is the capital. Since Caminha resided there it was but natural that he should have made this comparison. At the mouth of the Minho is the town of Caminha, which probably gave the name to the writer's family.

[2] It was at this landing that Master John with the pilot of Cabral's ship and that of Sancho de Tovar went on shore to determine the latitude.

them soon slunk away. They gave there some bows for sheets of paper and for some worthless old cap, or for anything else. And in such a manner it came about that a good twenty or thirty of our people went with them to where many others of them were, with girls and women, and brought back many bows and caps of bird feathers, some green and some yellow, samples of which I believe the captain will send to Your Highness. And according to what those said who went there they made merry with them. On that day we saw them closer and more as we wished, for all of us were almost intermingled. And there some of them had those colours in quarters, others in halves, and others in such colours as in the tapestry of Arras,[1] and all with their lips pierced, and many with the bones in them, and some of them without bones. Some of them were carrying prickly green nut shells from trees, which in colour resembled chestnuts, excepting that they were very much smaller. And these were full of small red grains which, when crushed between the fingers, made a very red paint with which they were painted.[2] And the more they wetted themselves the redder they became. They are all shaved to above the ears, likewise their eyebrows and eyelashes. All of them have their foreheads from temple to temple painted with a black paint, which looks like a black ribbon the breadth of two fingers.

And the captain ordered that convict, Affonso Ribeiro, and two other convicts to go there among them, and likewise Diogo Dias, because he was a cheerful man, with whom they played. And he ordered the convicts to remain there that night. They all went there and mingled with them,[3] and as they said later, they went a good league and a half to a village of houses in which there must have been nine or ten dwellings,

[1] *panos darmar.* These were the *panos de ras* (Arras) or tapestries of many colours with which the walls of the palaces were adorned in winter. The tapestries of Arras, France, were the most celebrated in Europe during the fourteenth and fifteenth centuries.

[2] These seeds were obtained from the *urucú* tree, probably the *annatto* (*Bixa orellana* of the family Bixaceae), extensively found in tropical America. The pulp surrounding the seeds furnishes a dye now used for fabrics, dairy products, chocolate, and varnishes. The annatto tree has spinose capsules filled with seeds which furnish a salmon-coloured dye.

[3] The members of Cabral's fleet during their short stay in Brazil evidently did not have occasion to note customs which later writers considered of interest, among others the practice of cannibalism, the use of tobacco, and tattooing.

each of which they said was as long as the captain's ship. And they were of wood with sides of boards and covered with straw, of reasonable height, and all had one single room without any divisions. They had within many posts, and from post to post a net is tied by the ends to each post, high up, where they sleep.[1] And underneath they made their fires to warm themselves.[2] And each house had two small doors, one at one end, and another at the other. And they said that thirty or forty persons dwelt in each house, and that thus they found them.[3] And that they gave them to eat of the food which they had, namely, much manioc[4] and other roots which are in the land, that they eat.

And, as it was late, they presently made all of us return and

[1] Hammocks were used by the natives throughout tropical America. Those of the Tupinamba were made of cotton cord woven in a net and sometimes dyed. They were supported between posts or between trees and were used for sleeping in the communal houses or as places in which the elders reclined during the conferences within the stockade.

[2] The fires were for warmth and dryness and also to keep off insects and evil spirits. They served as a method of lighting as well. Several methods were employed for producing fire, all of which were by friction on wood.

[3] The villages of the Tupinamba Indians were usually built on a slight elevation conveniently located for fresh water, hunting, fishing, and the cultivation of manioc. The village was taken down and partly removed if the food-supply became difficult to obtain. They are described in other early narratives as consisting of a single or double stockade of posts tied together with twigs having narrow openings for attacking the enemy. Within this enclosure were the long rectangular communal houses arranged around a central plaza. The pictures in de Bry and Staden show that four was the usual number, but Métraux states that, while this was the rule, in the larger villages there might be more. It was in this plaza that the life of the village was centred. It was here that the cannibalistic ceremonies were performed which are so vividly described in later narratives. The houses were long and narrow, with semicircular roofs. The question of light and ventilation does not seem to have been important. These 'malocas' or houses probably had an average length of 300 feet and a width of 30 feet, but the size naturally varied with the size of the village. The framework was made of logs held together with twigs and creepers. On this framework removable mats of leaves were placed which formed the enclosure. There was a low door at either end and one or sometimes two on the side. There were no divisions within the house; each family occupied the space between two posts. The houses were occupied by from thirty to two hundred individuals. Their chief enemies, the wild tribes of the interior, whom they had driven away from the coast, lived without shelter. See the description in Purchas's *Pilgrims* (vol. xvi, pp. 423–4).

[4] *Inhame*, given here, is the Portuguese word for yam. Many species of yam are found in tropical regions, including Brazil. The chief food of the Tupinamba, however, was manioc, a root which resembles the yam but is somewhat larger, sometimes being as long as three feet and from six to nine inches in diameter. Two kinds of manioc or cassava are known, both of which are probably indigenous to South America. It was the bitter species, *Manihot utilissima*, which was used by these Indians. Because the sap of the cassava root contains hydrocyanic acid and is therefore highly poisonous it cannot be eaten raw but must be washed and heated to be safe. From the dried roots thus prepared a meal was made which was used in making a bread. When properly treated the starchy pellets of cassava form the tapioca of commerce.

did not wish any one to remain there; and also, as they said, they wished to come with us. They traded there, for bells and for other trifles of little value which we were carrying, very large and beautiful red parrots[1] and two little green ones and caps of green feathers and a cloth of feathers of many colours, woven in a very beautiful fashion.[2] All of these things Your Highness will see, because the captain will send them to you, as he says. And thereupon they came back and we returned to the ships.

On Tuesday, after eating, we landed to set a watch over the wood and to wash clothes. Some sixty or seventy men without bows or anything else were there on the shore when we reached it. As soon as we arrived they at once came to us without being frightened, and afterward many more came. There must have been a good two hundred, all without bows, and they all mingled so much with us that some of them helped us to load wood and put it in the boats, and they vied with us and derived much pleasure therefrom. And while we were taking on the wood two carpenters made a large cross from one piece of wood which was cut yesterday for this. Many of them came there to be with the carpenters; and I believe that they did this more to see the iron tools with which they were making it than to see the cross, because they have nothing of iron. And they cut their wood and boards with stones shaped like wedges put into a piece of wood, very well tied between two sticks, and in

[1] These were macaws, a name derived from the Tupi *macaúba*. They are among the argest and most magnificent of parrots, with very long tails and brilliant contrasting colouring. It was from them that the Tupinamba secured most of the feathers used for decorations. These were new to the Portuguese, although the smaller species were to be found in the Old World, and had been obtained by them in Guinea. To those on the voyage these birds seem to have been the greatest novelty found in Brazil. They are shown on many of the early maps of that country. On the Cantino map they are particularly prominent. Here other parrots are also shown on the opposite coast of Africa.

[2] This was a feather mantle. These have long been celebrated and specimens have been preserved in the principal ethnological museums. The feathers used were largely from the *guara abucu* (*Ibis rubra*), of whose feathers these Indians were particularly fond and in fact undertook long expeditions to obtain them. They were fastened around the shoulders and extended like a cape down the back, sometimes almost to the feet. The feathers were tied to the cotton string, which formed a network to hold them. According to the account of Soares de Souza (*Tratado descriptivo do Brazil em 1587*, Rio de Janeiro, 1851, p. 320), the mantles were made exclusively by the men. They were worn by the sorcerers and perhaps by others. Feather ornaments must have been the chief distinction of wealth. It was a peculiar characteristic of these Indians that they carried their decorations at their backs rather than in front. The Tupinamba did not know how to weave.

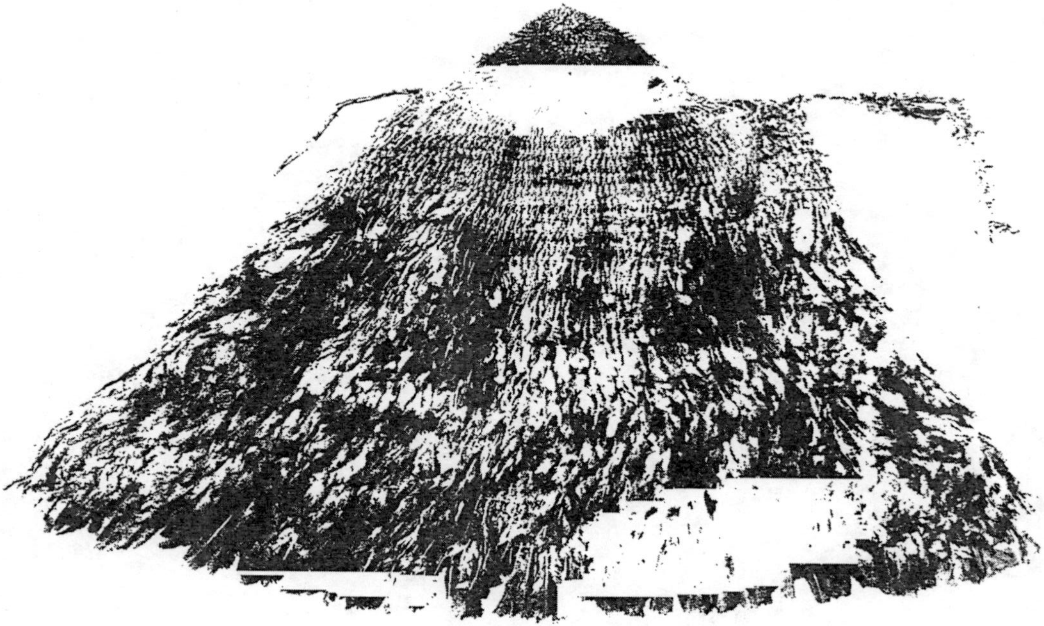

TUPINAMBA FEATHER MANTLE
(*Musée Ethnographique du Trocadéro, Paris*)

such a manner that they are strong, according to what the men said who were at their houses yesterday, for they saw them there.[1] By now they kept us so much company as almost to disturb us in what we had to do. And the captain ordered the two convicts and Diogo Dias to go to the village, and to other villages if they should hear of them, and on no account to come to sleep on the ships, even if they should order them to; and so they went. While we were in this grove cutting wood some parrots flew across these trees, some of them green, and others grey, large and small, so that it seems to me that there must be many in this land, but I did not see more than about nine or ten. We did not then see other birds except some *pombas seixas*, and they seemed to me considerably larger than those of Portugal. Some said that they saw turtle-doves, but I did not see any; but since the groves are so numerous and so large and of such infinite variety, I do not doubt that in the interior there are many birds. And towards night we returned to the ships with our wood. I believe, Senhor, that heretofore I have not given account to Your Highness of the form of their bows and arrows. The bows are black and long and the arrows long, and their tips of pointed reeds, as Your Highness will see from some which I believe the captain will send to you.[2]

On Wednesday we did not go on shore, because the captain spent the whole day in the supply ship emptying it, and had transported to the ship what each one could carry. Many of the natives came to the shore, as we saw from the ships. There must have been some three hundred, according to what Sancho de Toar said, who was there. Diogo Dias and Affonso Ribeiro, the convict, whom the captain sent yesterday to sleep there at any cost, returned when it was already night because they did not want them to sleep there, and they found green parrots and other birds which were black, almost like magpies, except that they had white beaks and short tails. And when Sancho de

[1] Hatchets were made from a very hard blue-black stone and were of different shapes. Samples of these are often found in deserted villages along the coast of Brazil. The Tupinamba were adept in shaping stone, since it was much used for adornment.

[2] The points were of the nature of bamboo. Points of bone and the teeth of animals were also used. The shafts without the point were sometimes employed in making fire. The Tupi-Guaraní Indians probably did not use poisoned arrows, neither did they use a throwing-stick, although both were used by other Indians of South America (E. Nordenskiöld, *Comparative Ethnological Studies*, vol. iii, p. 53).

Toar returned to the ship, some of them wished to go with him; but he did not want any except two proper youths. He ordered them to be well fed and cared for that night, and they ate all the food which was given them, and he ordered a bed with sheets to be made for them, as he said, and they slept and were comfortable that night. And so nothing more happened that day to write about.

On Thursday, the last of April, we ate early in the morning and went on shore for more wood and water, and when the captain was about to leave his ship Sancho de Toar arrived with his two guests, and because he had not yet eaten, cloths were laid for him and food was brought, and he ate. We seated the guests in their chairs, and they ate very well of all which was given them, especially of cold boiled ham and rice. They did not give them wine, because Sancho de Toar said that they did not drink it well. After the meal was over we all entered the boat and they with us. A sailor gave one of them a large tusk of a wild boar, well turned up. And as soon as he took it he at once put it in his lip; and because it did not fit there, they gave him a small piece of red wax. And this he applied to the back of his ornament to hold it and put it into his lip with the point turned upward, and he was as pleased with it as though he had a great jewel. And as soon as we disembarked he at once went off with it, and did not appear there again. When we landed there were probably eight or ten of the natives about, and little by little others began to come. And it seems to me that that day there came to the shore four hundred or four hundred and fifty men. Some of them carried bows and arrows and gave all for caps and for anything which we gave them. They ate with us of what we gave them. Some of them drank wine and others could not drink it, but it seems to me that if they accustomed themselves to it, they would drink it with great willingness. All were so well disposed and so well built and smart with their paints that they made a good show. They loaded as much of that wood as they could, very willingly, and carried it to the boats, and were quieter and more at ease among us than we were among them. The captain went with some of us for a short distance through this grove to a large stream of much water, which in our opinion was the same as the one which runs down to the shore, from which we took water. There we stayed for a while, drinking and amusing ourselves beside the river in this grove, which is so large and so thick and of such abundant foliage that one cannot describe it. In it there are many palms, from which we gathered many good sprouts. When we disembarked, the captain said that it would be well to go directly to the cross, which was leaning against a tree near the river, to be set up the next day, which was Friday, and that we should all kneel down and kiss it so that they might see the respect which we had for it. And thus we did. And we motioned to those ten or twelve who were there that they should do the same, and at once they all went to kiss it. They seem to me people of such innocence that, if one could understand them and they us, they would soon be Christians, because they do not have or understand any belief, as it appears. And therefore, if the convicts who are to remain here will learn their language well and understand them, I do not doubt that they will become Christians, in accordance with the pious intent of Your Highness, and that they will believe in our Holy Faith, to which may it please Our Lord to bring them. For it is certain this people is good and of pure simplicity, and there can easily be stamped upon them whatever belief we wish to give them; and furthermore, Our Lord gave them fine bodies and good faces as to good men; and He who brought us here, I believe, did not do so without purpose. And consequently, Your Highness, since you so much desire to increase the Holy Catholic Faith, ought to look after their salvation, and it will please God that, with little effort, this will be accomplished.

They do not till the soil or breed stock, nor is there ox or cow, or goat, or sheep, or hen, or any other domestic animal which is accustomed to live with men; nor do they eat anything except these manioc, of which there is much, and of the seeds and the fruits which the earth and the trees produce. Nevertheless, with this they are stronger and better fed than we are with all the wheat and vegetables which we eat.[1]

[1] The banana, sugar cane, rice, coffee, the water-melon, and onion were introduced by the whites. Banana cultivation and the domestic fowl spread with extreme rapidity over the greater part of the South American continent during the sixteenth century (Nordenskiöld, op. cit.).

While they were there that day, they continually skipped and danced with us to the sound of one of our tambours, in such a manner that they are much more our friends than we theirs. If one signed to them whether they wished to come to the ships, they at once made ready to do so, in such wise that had we wished to invite them all, they would all have come. However, we only took four or five this night to the ships, namely: the chief captain took two, and Simão de Miranda, one, whom he already had for his page, and Aires Gomes, another, also as a page. One of those whom the captain took was one of his guests whom we had brought him the first night when we arrived; to-day he came dressed in his shirt and with him his brother. These were this night very well entertained, both with food and with a bed with mattresses and sheets to tame them better.

And to-day, which is Friday, the first day of May, we went on land with our banner in the morning and disembarked up the river towards the south, where it seemed to us that it would be better to plant the cross, so that it might be better seen. And there the captain indicated where the hole should be made to plant it, and while they were making it, he with all the rest of us went to where the cross was down the river. We brought it from there with the friars and priests going ahead singing in the manner of a procession. There were already some of the natives there, about seventy or eighty, and when they saw us coming, some of them went to place themselves under it in order to help us. We crossed the river along the shore and went to place it where it was to be, which is probably a distance of two cross-bow shots from the river. While we were busy with this there came a good one hundred and fifty or more. After the cross was planted with the arms and device of Your Highness which we first nailed to it, we set up an altar at the foot of it. There the father, Frei Amrique, said mass, at which those already mentioned chanted and officiated. There were there with us some fifty or sixty natives, all kneeling as we were, and when it came to the Gospel and we all rose to our feet with hands lifted, they rose with us and lifted their hands, remaining thus until it was over. And then they again sat down as we did. And at the elevation of the Host when we knelt, they placed themselves as we were, with hands uplifted, and so quietly that

I assure Your Highness that they gave us much edification. They stayed there with us until communion was over, and after the communion the friars and priests and the captain and some of the rest of us partook of communion. Some of them, because the sun was hot, arose while we were receiving communion and others remained as they were and stayed. One of them, a man of fifty or fifty-five years, stayed there with those who remained. While we were all thus he collected those who had remained and even called others. He went about among them and talked to them, pointing with his finger to the altar, and afterwards he lifted his finger towards Heaven as though he were telling them something good, and thus we understood it. After the mass was over the father took off his outer vestment and remained in his alb, and then he mounted a chair near the altar, and there he preached to us of the Gospel and of the apostles whose day this is,[1] treating at the end of the sermon of this your holy and virtuous undertaking, which caused us more edification. Those who still remained for the sermon were looking at him, as we were doing. And the one of whom I speak called some to come there; some came and others departed. And when the sermon was over, Nicolao Coelho brought many tin crosses with crucifixes, which he still had from another voyage, and we thought it well to put one around the neck of each; for which purpose the father, Frei Amrique, seated himself at the foot of the cross, and there, one by one, he put around the neck of each his own [cross] tied to a string, first making him kiss it and raise his hands. Many came for this, and we did likewise to all. They must have been about forty or fifty. And after this was finished it was already a good hour after midday; we went to the ships to eat, and the captain took with him that same one who had pointed out to the others the altar and the sky, and his brother with him, to whom he did much honour. And he gave him a Moorish shirt, and to the other one a shirt such as the rest of us wore. And as it appears to me and to every one, these people in order to be wholly Christian lack nothing except to understand us, for whatever they saw us do, they did likewise; wherefore it appeared to all that they have no idolatry and no worship. And I well believe that,

[1] That of Saint Philip and Saint James.

if Your Highness should send here some one who would go about more at leisure among them, that all will be turned to the desire of Your Highness. And if some one should come for this purpose, a priest should not fail to come also at once to baptize them, for by that time they will already have a greater knowledge of our faith through the two convicts who are remaining here among them. Both of these also partook of communion to-day. Among all those who came to-day there was only one young woman who stayed continuously at the mass, and she was given a cloth with which to cover herself, and we put it about her; but as she sat down she did not think to spread it much to cover herself. Thus, Senhor, the innocence of this people is such, that that of Adam could not have been greater in respect to shame. Now Your Highness may see whether people who live in such innocence will be converted or not if they are taught what pertains to their salvation. When this was over we went thus in their presence to kiss the cross, took leave of them, and came to eat.

I believe, Senhor, that with these two convicts who remain here, there stay also two seamen who to-night left this ship, fleeing to shore in a skiff.[1] They have not come back and we believe that they remain here, because to-morrow, God willing, we take our departure from here.

It seems to me, Senhor, that this land from the promontory we see farthest south to another promontory which is to the north, of which we caught sight from this harbour, is so great that it will have some twenty or twenty-five leagues of coast-line. Along the shore in some places it has great banks, some of them red, some white, and the land above is quite flat and covered with great forests. From point to point the entire shore is very flat and very beautiful. As for the interior, it appeared to us from the sea very large, for, as far as eye could reach, we could see only land and forests, a land which seemed very extensive to us. Up to now we are unable to learn that there is gold or silver in it, or anything of metal or iron; nor have we seen any, but the land itself has a very good climate, as cold and temperate as that of Entre Doiro e Minho, because in the present season we found it like that. Its waters are quite endless.

[1] These may have returned, however, before the ships sailed.

So pleasing is it that if one cares to profit by it, everything will grow in it because of its waters. But the best profit which can be derived from it, it seems to me, will be to save this people, and this should be the chief seed which Your Highness should sow there. And if there were nothing more than to have here a stopping-place for this voyage to Calicut, that would suffice,[1] to say nothing of an opportunity to fulfil and do that which Your Highness so much desires, namely, the increase of our Holy Faith.

And in this manner, Senhor, I give here to Your Highness an account of what I saw in this land of yours, and if I have been somewhat lengthy you will pardon me, for the desire I had to tell you everything made me set it down thus in detail.[2] And, Senhor, since it is certain that in this charge laid upon me as in any other thing which may be for your service, Your Highness will be very faithfully served by me, I ask of you that in order to do me a special favour you order my son-in-law, Jorge Do Soiro,[3] to return from the island of Sam Thomé. This I shall take as a very great favour to me.

I kiss Your Highness's hands.

From this Porto Seguro of your island of Vera Cruz to-day,[4] Friday, the first day of May of 1500.

PERO VAAZ DE CAMINHA.

[*Superscribed*] To the King our Lord.

[*This is on the back in a contemporary hand*] Letter of Pero Vaaz de Caminha concerning the discovery of the new land which Pedro Alvarez made.

[1] This statement, repeated in the letter of Dom Manuel to the Spanish sovereigns, shows that Caminha had no knowledge of any prior discovery of this shore.

[2] Caminha could not have written this whole letter of fourteen folio pages on the 1st of May. From the wording of the letter and the exactness with which the details are recorded it must have been written as a diary and dated just before the sailing of the ship which carried it to the king.

[3] Sousa Viterbo believes that this was the Jorge de Osouro who had been exiled to the island of São Thomé, having been taken with others by force from a church where they had sought safety. They were accused of having stolen bread, wine, and chickens, and of having wounded a priest. De Osouro was pardoned by the king on the 16th of January 1496, and seems to have been sent back to São Thomé for some other reason.

[4] When Cabral first sighted land he gave it the name *terra da Vera Cruz*, but Caminha here calls it *ilha da Vera Cruz*, indicating that at the time of the departure of the ship of Gaspar de Lemos they still believed the land to be an island and so reported it. This accounts for the fact that on the map of Juan de la Cosa it is shown as an island and designated *isla descubierta por portugal*. In the instructions given for a voyage made after 1502 it is still called *Ilha da Cruz*. Cf. *Annaes Maritimas e Coloniaes* (Lisbon, 1845), pp. 279 et seq.

LETTER OF MASTER JOHN TO KING MANUEL

WRITTEN FROM VERA CRUZ
THE 1ST OF MAY 1500

ANOTHER letter which was sent to Dom Manuel before Cabral's fleet left Brazil was one which, though brief, is important for its scientific significance. It was written by a Galician astronomer, Master John. The title of Master indicates that he had been a teacher, and the degrees which he adds to his signature imply that he was a scholar. As personal physician and surgeon of Dom Manuel, his duties involved those of an astrologer, and because of this he held the position of astronomer on the fleet.

That Master John was not a popular member of the expedition is indicated by the fact that he was placed in one of the smaller ships and not in that of the chief captain. It is probable that he, like so many men of his profession at that period, was a converted Jew.[1] It would have been natural otherwise that he should be on the flagship or on the ship of Sancho de Tovar, also a Spaniard. Master John is not mentioned in any account of the voyage. As nothing further is heard of him, it is possible that he was on one of the ships lost in the South Atlantic, since Vespucci in his letter written from the Cape Verde Islands states that there were no cosmographers or mathematicians with the fleet at that time. If Master John survived the voyage and continued his vocation as physician and surgeon as well as astrologer, he may have been the Master Joham, astrologer, who was given an annuity of 12,000 reis by Dom Manuel in 1513, as indicated in a document found by Sousa Viterbo and published in his *Trabalhos Nauticos dos Portuguezes* (vol. i, p. 168). It seems improbable that there would be two men of that name, both astrologers, to whom Dom Manuel was under obligation.

[1] Master John was undoubtedly acquainted with Abraham Zacuto, one of the most celebrated astronomers of his day, who came to Portugal in 1492 when the Jews were driven from Spain. Master John may also have left Spain at the same time. For Zacuto see the works of Joaquim Bensaude and of Francisco Cantera, *Abraham Zacut* (Madrid, 1935), with bibliography.

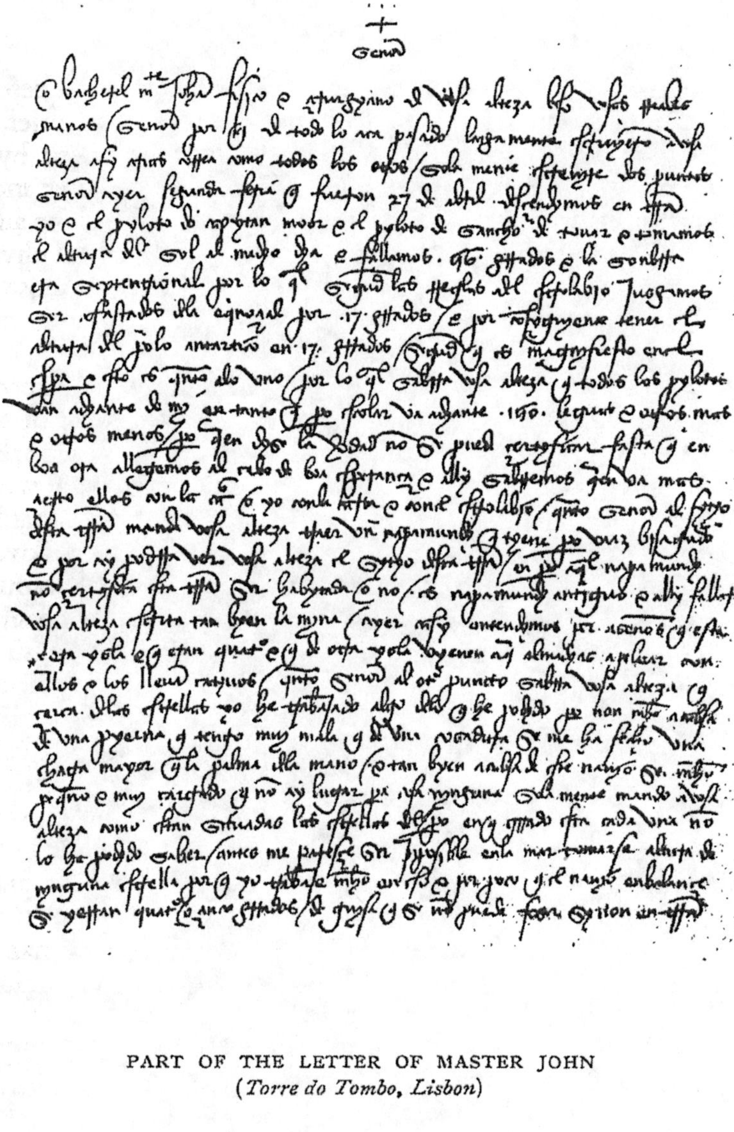

PART OF THE LETTER OF MASTER JOHN
(*Torre do Tombo, Lisbon*)

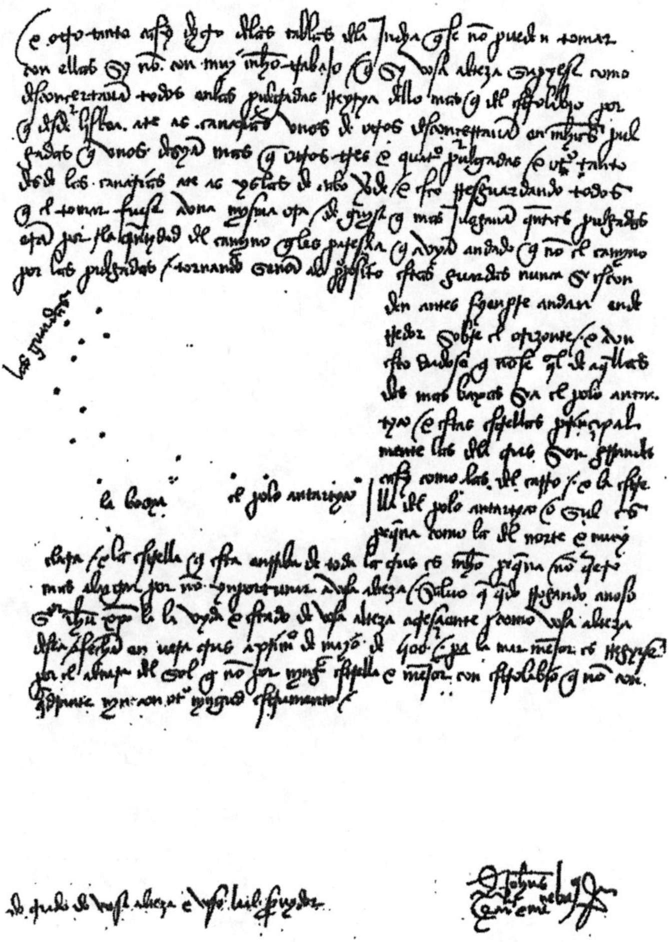

PART OF THE LETTER OF MASTER JOHN

(Torre do Tombo. Lisbon)

If these two men were identical, Master John was the translator of the *De Orbis Situ* of Pomponius Mela, a copy of which translation is in the Ajuda Library, Lisbon.

This letter and that of Caminha are the only original documents now extant in manuscript written by those who went on Cabral's fleet. The letter of Master John corroborates that of Caminha. While giving little information regarding the new land it is of importance as showing the methods used for the determination of position at sea. It has also aroused much interest because of the reference which he makes to a certain *mappa mundi* of Pero Vaz Bisagudo. This has been interpreted by some to show that Brazil had previously been discovered; but in the lack of other evidence this assumption cannot be considered to have been proved.

It had not been thought necessary to take an astronomer on previous voyages made by the Portuguese, nor were any taken on those which followed. The chief duty of Master John seems to have been to study the constellations of the southern hemisphere. His letter is the first document in which the Southern Cross is shown. Its brilliance was known to the Portuguese navigators from the time of Cadamosto and must have been noticed by the pilots and navigators who succeeded him. Sun tables had been computed after the equator had been passed by Alvaro Esteves in 1471, but a method of locating the south pole was desirable for navigation and to determine the variation of the compass. Master John probably did not ascertain its location on the voyage to Brazil. It is more reasonable to suppose that its position had been shown to the Portuguese by the Arab pilots when da Gama went to the East, and they may also have been instructed by them how it was to be located. The sketch which Master John includes in his letter is fairly accurate, both for the location of the stars and for the method used in determining the antarctic pole, although the latter is indirect.

The letter of Master John was written in Spanish, a language which the king both spoke and wrote. It was found in the Archivo Nacional da Torre do Tombo by Varnhagen (*Corpo Chron.*, parte 3, maço no. 2), who published it for the first time in *Revista do Instituto Histórico e Geográphico* of Rio de Janeiro (tomo v, 1843, p. 342) and included a facsimile of it in the first edition of his *Historia Geral do Brazil*, vol. i, p. 432. The text has been printed many times since. That used for this translation is the one published in *Alguns Documentos*, &c. (Lisbon, 1882), pp. 122–3. The reduced facsimile here given is from that shown in *Historia da Colonização Portuguesa do Brasil* (Porto, 1923, vol. ii, p. 102). In this publication there is a text by Dr. Antonio Baião and a translation into modern Portuguese by Dr. Luciano Pereira da Silva, who also gives a description of the letter. This facsimile and text were again printed by Fontoura da Costa (*Marinharia dos Descobrimentos*, p. 114).

SEÑOR:

I, the bachelor Master John, physician and surgeon of Your Highness, kiss your hands. Señor: because Arias Correa as well as all the others have written to Your Highness at length concerning all that happened here, I shall write only regarding two points. Señor: yesterday, Monday, which was the 27th of April, we went on shore, I and the pilot of the chief captain and the pilot of Sancho de Tovar; and we took the height of the sun at midday; and we found 56 degrees,[1] and the shadow was north.[2] By this, according to the rules of the astrolabe, we judged that we were 17 degrees distant from the equinoctial and consequently had the height of the antarctic pole in 17 degrees,[3]

[1] The height of the sun was taken with the astrolabe and indicated 56° on the 27th of April by the Julian Calendar. When this determination was made, Master John referred to his book of instructions for the use of the astrolabe and he found that the sun's declination at noon for that day was approximately 17° 0′. The latitude was thus 90° − 56° 0′ − 17° 0′ = 17° 0′ S. The table of declinations of the sun used was evidently that given in a manuscript similar to that shown in *Tractado da Spera do Mundo*, printed at Evora in 1517, which gives the declination for the 27th of April as 16° 54′ and the place latitude as 17° 0′. This was probably based on the work of the eminent Spanish astronomer Abraham Zacuto. Master John apparently did not use an early form of the *Regimento do Estrolabio e do Quadrante*, printed after 1509, since this shows a declination of 16° 42′, indicating a latitude of 17° 18′, a fact which Master John would have noted. A copy of the *Regimento do Estrolabio e do Quadrante* is in Munich. Facsimiles of these two treatises have been published by Joaquim Bensaude, *Histoire de la science nautique portugaise à l'époque des grandes découvertes*, vol. i, Munich, 1914, vol. ii, Geneva, 1914. For a discussion of this subject see vol. ii, ch. ii, of *Historia da Colonização Portuguesa do Brazil*.

[2] It is difficult to understand why Master John makes this statement. The shadow should have been south. See J. Bensaude, *L'Astronomie nautique au Portugal*, Berne, 1912, pp. 12, 28.

[3] The latitude of the bay of Corôa Vermelha is 16° 21′ 2″, so the determination of Master John was as accurate as could reasonably be expected.

as is manifest in the sphere.[1] And this is what concerns one point. Whence Your Highness will know that all the pilots go beyond me to such an extent that Pero Escolar exceeds me by 150 leagues, and some more and some less;[2] but which one tells the truth cannot be ascertained until in good time we arrive at the Cape of Good Hope, and there we shall known who goes more correctly, they with the chart, or I with the chart and the astrolabe.[3] As regards the situation of this

[1] *segund que es magnifiesto en el espera.* The word *el espera* may be interpreted in two ways. Either Master John means that this determination was shown in the heavens or celestial globe, or he refers to a book by that name. The word *espera* both in Spanish and Portuguese means sphere or globe. If he refers here to a book, instead, it would indicate one of several treatises on astronomy chiefly used for astrology, which had previously appeared. Most of these were based on the *Tractatus de Sphera* also known as *Sphera* or *Sphaera*. It was a small work written in a simple style by John Holywood, generally known as Sacro Bosco, an astronomical author who studied in Oxford and later taught at the University of Paris during the first half of the thirteenth century. This was based on the works of Ptolemy, particularly the *Almagest*, with the interpretations of Arabian scholars. One edition of this was translated into Portuguese but not published until some time before 1518 (facsimile by Joaquim Bensaude, *Histoire de la science nautique portugaise*, vol. i, Munich, 1914). There were other books on astronomy and astrology of a like nature and similarly named. Among these was the *Sphera Mundi* of Leopold, Duke of Austria, dating from about 1200. An edition of this was issued in Augsburg in 1489.

[2] This indicates that this coast had not been located on any previous voyage.

[3] The determination of the position of the ships at sea during Cabral's voyage could not be made with exactness. Latitude was ascertained by the height of the sun, the planets, or the stars above the horizon, but this could only be ascertained roughly. The instruments for obtaining the angle, the astrolabe and the quadrant, required a stability difficult to obtain at sea. The sun tables were not accurate. In the vicinity of the equator the difficulty of determining latitude by the position of the pole increased because the north polar star might be invisible and its location there would be judged only in relation to the guards. In 1500 Polaris was approximately 3½° from the pole. The determinations of latitude by means of solar observations were as accurate as elsewhere. The dip of the horizon had been known since early times, and refraction had been recognized by Ptolemy but was not accurately applied in 1500. The science of astronomy had progressed as far as it could without the use of the telescope. The courses of the sun, the moon, and the planets were known, but from a geocentric standpoint. Determinations were not ordinarily made closer than half of a degree.

There was no adequate means of determining longitude. While both clocks and watches were in use, the former was obviously impracticable at sea, and until the fusee was invented at Nuremberg for the latter some twenty-five years later, watches did not keep uniform time. Hour-glasses were carried on the ships, but were chiefly used for changing the ship watches. For longitude, therefore, dead reckoning was necessary, and the position was worked out on charts. The original record was made with chalk in a folding log book and changes in the course were indicated with pegs on a traverse board. The loxodromic curve was probably not understood. Knowledge of it is first accredited to Pedro Nunez (1492–1577).

The speed of the ship was often determined by the 'Dutchman's log'. Here a light object was thrown overboard from the forecastle, and the time noted until it passed an observer on the poop. The interval was learned by counting, or the repetition of some simple sentence. The log line from the stern was not used until 1521. The direction was determined by the compass, and sometimes by the winds. The variation of the

land, Señor, Your Highness should order a *mappa mundi* to be brought which Pero Vaaz Bisagudo has, and on it Your Highness will be able to see the location of this land. That *mappa mundi*, however, does not show whether this land is inhabited or not. It is an old *mappa mundi*, and there Your Highness will also find la Mina marked. Yesterday we almost understood by signs that this was an island, and that there were four, and that from another island *almadias* come here to fight with them, and they take them captive.[1]

In regard, Señor, to the other point. Your Highness will know that I have done whatever work I could concerning the stars, but not much, because of a very bad leg which I have, for a wound larger than the palm of my hand has developed from a scratch;[2] and also because this ship is very small and

compass was not understood, and constant correction had to be made astronomically. This variation had been known to the Chinese for many centuries, and probably also in Europe. It became a serious problem in the transatlantic voyages. The pilots of Columbus had noted it and believed they had found, at last, a method for determining longitude, when they found that the magnetic needle gradually approached the true north until the isogonic line of the Atlantic was reached, and its variation then gradually increased as they continued westward, but in an opposite direction. But the isogonic line did not run in all places north and south.

Terrestial globes were in use at this period, and formed part of the pilot's equipment. To mariners these were a valuable guide, and a special law was passed to prevent their being taken permanently from Portugal.

When Vasco da Gama reached the Bay of Saint Helena on his voyage to India he erected a tripod on land from which was suspended a large marine astrolabe made of wood and the latitude of that place was so determined. This could be checked with the observations made on previous voyages along the coast. It is probable that this same instrument or one similar was used by Master John and the pilots when they endeavoured to determine the latitude of the landing-place when Cabral's fleet reached Brazil. Master John, as an astrologer, had been accustomed to astronomical astrolabes of both the spherical and plane types, and had used them on land. He was not, therefore, accustomed to the use of the nautical astrolabe. Both the astrolabe and the quadrant relied on gravity for the determination of the horizon. The motion of the ship and the consequent swaying of the instrument made this exceedingly difficult. This has been avoided in later quadrants and particularly in the modern sextant, where the horizon is viewed directly and coincides with the object when the proper angle is adjusted.

The determination of the altitude made by Master John was reasonably accurate considering the type of instrument he used. He states that any error would be corrected when they reached the Cape of Good Hope, where he believed that the determination was correct. With the latitude of the Cape Verde Islands and of the Cape of Good Hope known and with the rhumb lines and distances from these points ascertained, the position of Porto Seguro could be found. This statement further shows that Cabral had intended to stop at the Cape of Good Hope, probably at the bay of São Bras as da Gama had done, and as he had suggested that Cabral should do on his voyage, but Cabral was diverted from this course by the storm.

[1] The people with whom the Tupinamba fought were even less civilized. They were the ones who had formerly occupied this coast.

[2] Although the letter is written in Spanish Master John uses several Portuguese words. Both *cosadura* and *chaga* in this sentence are Portuguese.

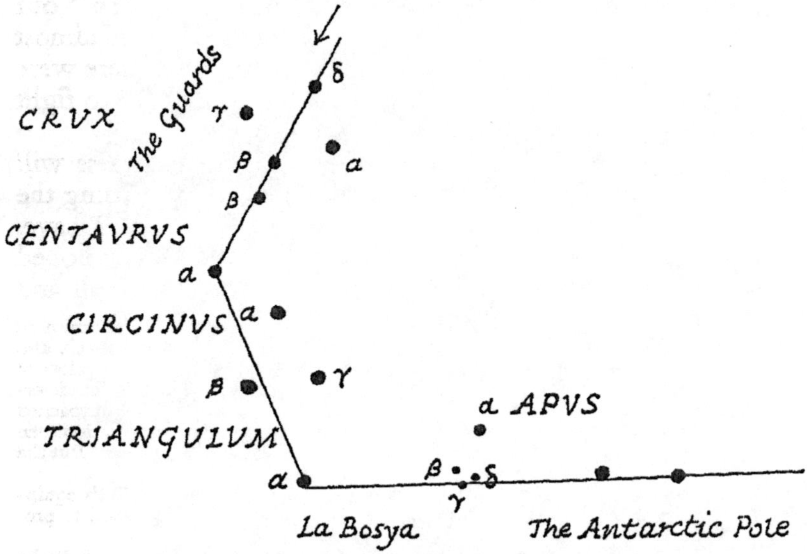

The Southern Cross
as given by Master John, with identification of the stars and the method for locating the Antarctic Pole

very heavily laden, so that there is no room for anything. I inform Your Highness only how the stars are located, but in which degree each one is, I have not been able to learn; rather it seems impossible to me to take the height of any star on the sea, for I labour much at it and, however little the ship rolls, one errs by four or five degrees, so that it cannot be done except on land. And I say almost the same thing about the India tables,[1] for it cannot be taken with them save with very much work; for if Your Highness knew how they all disagreed in the inches, you would laugh at this more than at the astrolabe, because from Lisbon to the Canaries they disagreed with one another by many inches, for some said three and four inches more than others.[2] And the same was true from the Canaries to the islands of Cape Verde; and this although all took precautions that the observation should be at the same hour, so that they judged rather how many inches there were by the length of the journey which it seemed to them they had gone, than the journey by means of the inches. Returning to the point, Señor, these guards are never hidden; rather do they always go round above the horizon, and even this is doubtful,

[1] *tablas de la India.* These were called *tavoletas* or *tabuas* of India by the Portuguese and were the *kamals* of the Arab pilots. The *kamal* was first known to the Portuguese during the voyage of da Gama and is mentioned by Sernigi and de Barros. The primitive method used in the Indian seas for determining the height of the poles when within the tropics was to extend the arm to a fixed distance and to measure the height of the star above the horizon in fingers. This led to a more accurate measure called the *kamal.* The *kamal* consists of a rectangular piece of wood of dimensions in fingers or *isba'ṡ.* At the centre of this is attached a cord having knots at determined distances. This rectangle is held vertically with the left hand in line with the right eye and the cord is grasped with the teeth. When the upper and lower edges of the rectangle correspond with the star and the horizon, respectively, the knot of the cord at the teeth designates the height of the star in *isba'ṡ.* According to Bittner the *isba'* was equivalent to 1° 42′ 50″ and 210 *isba's* equalled 360°. Two *isba's* were called a *polar,* and four *isba's,* or the equivalent of four fingers, were called a *dubbān.* The *kamal* seems to have been the forerunner of the cross-staff. Its use has continued in India until modern times. Pilots sailing north or south along the Coromandel coast had the knots placed where towns were located. Another type of *kamal* used at an early date consisted of nine rectangles or tables on a single cord, but without knots.

Da Gama had brought back samples of the *kamals* used by the Arab pilots. From these larger rectangles were made for the higher latitudes. The tables with which the stars were observed on Cabral's fleet were in *isba's.*

For the *kamal* see Luciano Pereira da Silva, 'Kamal, Tabuas da India e Tavoletas Nauticas' (*Lusitania,* Lisbon, 1924, fasc. iii) with illustration of *kamals* in the Museum für Völkerkunde, in Hamburg. See also the works of Fontoura da Costa, Bittner, and Ferrand cited elsewhere.

[2] *Pulgadas.* These were the fingers or *isba's* of the Arabs previously referred to. Four *pulgadas* would be a variation of nearly six degrees.

for I do not know which of the two lowest ones is the antarctic pole.[1] And these stars, principally those of the cross, are large, almost as those of Ursa Major [*del carro*]; and the star of the antarctic pole, or south, is small, like that of the north, and very clear,[2] and the star which is above the entire cross is very small.

In order not to trouble Your Highness, I do not wish to write further, except that I am asking Our Lord Jesus Christ to increase the life and estate of Your Highness as Your Highness desires. Done in Vera Cruz, the first day of May of 1500. At sea it is better to direct oneself by the height of the sun than by any star, and better with the astrolabe than with the quadrant or with any other instrument.

From the servant of Your Highness and your loyal servitor, Johanes *artium et medicine bachalarius.*

[*Superscribed*]

To the King our Lord.

[1] The south polar star in the year 1500 was almost exactly 180° S. latitude. The guards were not hidden at any time. At the horizon of Vera Cruz at the end of April 1500, the Southern Cross began to disappear about four o'clock in the morning. (Fontoura da Costa, op. cit., p. 114).

[2] The difficulty which Master John had in determining a star at the antarctic pole can be understood, because no star exists there which can be easily seen. The star La Bosya took the place of Polaris in the northern hemisphere. The guards α and γ Crucis, while they point almost directly to the pole, could not easily be used for its identification because of their remoteness. Master John thus uses a somewhat circuitous but surer method by following the bright stars to α Trianguli and thence to the pole by the 'Bird of Paradise', as the three small stars of Apus were called. The pole is located beyond both of the stars, one or the other of which Master John tried to identify with it.

LETTER FROM KING MANUEL TO FERDINAND AND ISABELLA

THE 29TH OF JULY 1501

A FEW days after the arrival of Cabral's flagship, Dom Manuel wrote to Ferdinand and Isabella, telling them briefly what had occurred during the voyage. In this letter there is apparently no attempt to conceal anything of importance which happened, and in general it is not contradicted by later writers. If authentic, this letter is the most authoritative account which we have of the whole voyage. It was apparently written by the king on the 27th of July, from Santarem, where he had received a report that Cabral's main fleet had arrived.[1]

The Spanish original of this letter, according to Navarrete, was formerly kept in the Archivo de la Antigua Diputación de Aragon, at Saragossa, but was destroyed on the 27th of January 1809, during the Napoleonic War.[2] A copy, however, was made by one D. Joaquin Traggia, which was published by Navarrete (*Coll. de los viages y descubrimientos*, &c., vol. iii). Another copy, in Portuguese, is preserved in the Archivio di Stato in Venice, and was first published by Professor Belgrano.[3] This is almost identical with the Spanish letter, except that it states that it was written from Lisbon on the 28th of August. A photographic reproduction was published by Eugenio do Canto in 1906 in an edition of sixty copies, and a transcription in modern spelling is given by C. Malheiro Dias (*Hist. da Col. Port. do Brasil*, vol. ii). This author is of the opinion that the Spanish text was derived from it. Dias bases his theory on the fact that there are a few small omissions in the Spanish text, which are given in the Portuguese manuscript, and that Dom Manuel was in the habit of writing to the Spanish sovereigns in Portuguese. There is a contemporary Italian translation of

[1] According to de Barros, upon the return of Vasco da Gama, Dom Manuel sent an account of that voyage to all his cities. It is probable that the king sent a similar letter after the return of Cabral's fleet not unlike the one here given, addressed to the Spanish sovereigns.

[2] For an account of the destruction of this library and also of those in Valencia in 1812, see Navarrete, op. cit., vol. i, pp. 131–7.

[3] *Bolletino della Società Geografica Italiana*, 3rd ser., vol. iii, pp. 217 et seq.

this letter dated the 29th of August 1501, which is now in the Sneyd Collection at Newcastle-on-Tyne (MS. C 59A), the first portion of which was published by G. Berchet (*Raccolta Colum-biana*, part iii, vol. ii, p. 118, Rome, 1893), who assigns it to an anonymous author. In this there are some variations from the Spanish text, but they are evidently the fault of the translator. This early Italian version helps to confirm the authenticity of the letter. An English translation of the Spanish copy has been made by J. R. McClymont (*Pedralvarez Cabral*, London, 1914). The translation which is published here is somewhat more literal, and has been made from the Spanish text and compared with the Portuguese version.[1]

[1] Another letter attributed to Dom Manuel is the first printed account of the Portuguese voyages to India now in existence. This appeared in Rome, as an octavo volume with eight unnumbered leaves, on the 23rd of October 1505 from the press of Master Johannes Besicken. It is entitled 'Copy of a letter of the King of Portugal sent to the King of Castile concerning the voyage and success of India'.

While it has not been questioned that this account was published in 1505, it is very improbable that it is a copy of a letter written by Dom Manuel to his father-in-law, King Ferdinand. It is more reasonable to suppose that the so-called letter, with an attractive title, was compiled in Rome from information obtainable in Italy, possibly with the addition of some knowledge derived from Portugal. This is indicated in several ways. In the first place Ferdinand was not then King of Castile. Also there was no occasion for Dom Manuel to write this letter. He had written almost an identical letter to Ferdinand in 1501 regarding Cabral's voyage and had seen him many times since. A third indication is shown in the fact that parts of other documents are included, taken from the letter written by Dom Manuel in 1501, the Anonymous Narrative, and the account of Priest Joseph, which were then available in Italy either in manuscript or printed form. It was printed at a time when pamphlets and broadsides took the place of newspapers. These are very rare now because it was the custom to print them only in small numbers. Their survival is usually due to their having been bound together as collections. The copy of this letter in the Marciana Library is one of a volume of seventeen pamphlets of various periods so preserved. The letter contains errors which would not have been made by Dom Manuel. For instance, the letter states that Cabral (instead of da Gama) commanded the fleet sent in 1502. While Cabral had been selected for this position, Dom Manuel had good reason to know that da Gama had superseded him. The descriptions of this voyage, and of those which followed, are inadequate and are much confused, although the news concerning them should have been the occasion for writing this letter.

Neither this letter nor copies of it are to be found in either Spain or Portugal, and there is no contemporary reference to it.

Three copies of this pamphlet are known to exist, one in the Marciana Library at Venice, discovered by Varnhagen; one in the Corsini Library at Rome, discovered by Narducci; and one in the Colombina Library at Seville, discovered by Gallardo. The copy in the Marciana Library was reprinted in 1881 by Arthur Coke Burnell. Of this only twenty-five copies were published for private circulation. Another edition from the Marciana copy was edited by Prospero Peragallo with a translation into modern Portuguese and published by the *Academia Real das Sciencias*, Lisbon, 1892, in a collection of monographs entitled *Centenario do Descobrimento da America.*

The letter is not given in translation because the portions of it referring to Cabral's voyage are almost identical with earlier documents here published.

THE LETTER WHICH THE KING, OUR LORD, WROTE TO THE KING AND QUEEN OF CASTILE, HIS KIN,[1] CONCERNING THE NEWS OF INDIA

MOST high and most excellent and most powerful Sovereigns, Father and Mother:

During these past days, after the first news arrived from India, I did not write at once to Your Majesties concerning the matters there because Pedro Alvarez Cabral, my chief captain of the fleet, which I had sent there, had not yet returned. And after his arrival I also delayed in doing so because two ships of his company had not yet come.[2] One of these he had sent to Çofalla, a gold-mine which was discovered recently, not to establish trade, but only to have true information of what was there; because of the two ships which went there for this purpose, one was lost at sea, and the other was separated from the fleet in stormy weather and did not go there. And after the aforesaid ships had arrived, and I was on the point of notifying Your Majesties, Pero Lopes de Padilha told me that you would be glad to have news of what had happened there. The following is briefly everything which took place. My aforesaid captain with thirteen ships departed from Lisboa the 9th of March of last year, and during the octave of Easter he reached a land which he newly discovered, to which he gave the name of Santa Cruz. In it he found the people nude as in the first innocence, gentle, and peaceable. It seemed that Our Lord miraculously wished it to be found, because it is very convenient and necessary for the voyage to India, because he repaired his ships and took water there.[3] And on account of the long voyage

[1] Queen Isabella of Castile was half Portuguese on her mother's side, and her grandfather was the Infante John, one of the sons of John I. It would not be strange, therefore, when listening to the story of Columbus and of his hopes for new discoveries for Spain that she would be fired with some of the spirit of adventure shown by her great-uncle, Prince Henry. Queen Isabella was a first cousin of Dom Manuel, and through his marriage to her daughter, Isabel, and, after Isabel's death, to Maria, was still more closely related to him. Ferdinand, in addition to being the father-in-law of Dom Manuel, was also related to the House of Aviz.

[2] Those of Sancho de Tovar and Pedro de Ataíde. Sancho de Tovar had gone to Sofala. From this letter it would appear that Cabral and Simão de Miranda arrived on the 21st of July 1501, Sancho de Tovar and Pedro de Ataíde on the 25th, and Diogo Dias on the 27th.

[3] The value of Brazil as expressed in the letter of Pedro Vaz de Caminha is here repeated.

which he had to make, he did not stop to obtain information about the said land; he only sent me a ship from there to notify me how he found it; and he pursued his route by way of the Cape of Good Hope. In that gulf, before arriving at it, he encountered great storms, in which, during one single day, four ships foundered together before his eyes, of which not a single person escaped. At this time, also, another of his ships disappeared, of which no news has been received up to this time.[1] And that in which he went, with the others which remained, passed through great danger. And thus he went his way to make port at the kingdom of Quiloa, which belongs to the Moors, under whose sovereignty is the said mine of Çofalla, because he carried my letters and messages for its king, to establish peace with him, and a treaty concerning purchases and trade at the said mine. And before reaching the aforesaid kingdom, he found two ships with a great quantity of gold, which he took possession of, and because they belonged to the said King of Quiloa, after doing them much honour, he let them go. He was very well received by that king, who came in person to converse with my said captain on the sea, and entered with him in his boat, and he sent him presents; and after receiving my letters and messages, he agreed to the treaty. And since the ships which were destined for that mine were among those which were lost, no trade was begun there at that time, because the merchandise which the other ships carried was not suitable for what was needed for that land.[2] And he departed from there and went to another kingdom, Melinde, for which he also was carrying my letters and messages, because its king, who likewise is a Moor, had done good deeds to Dom Vasco, who first went there to discover it. This king likewise visited him on the sea and also sent him presents, and confirmed and established peace and friendship with him, and gave him the pilots whom he needed for his voyage.[3] These kingdoms extend from the Red Sea in this direction, and in the interior

1 At the end of this letter the king states that he has just heard that the ship of Diogo Dias was not lost.

2 That is, trinkets, beads, copper, &c., for the negroes.

3 The ports of Malindi and Mombasa were the rendezvous for the pilots for India and the East African coast. See Bittner and Tomaschek, op. cit., and G. Ferrand, *L'Astronomie nautique arabe* (Paris, 1928).

they border on Gentiles, and these Gentiles border on the land of Prester John, whom they call the *abechy*.[1] In their language this means 'branded with iron', because, as a matter of fact, they do this, and they are branded with iron as a sign that they are baptized in water.[2] From there he departed for Calecut, which is seven hundred leagues beyond. This city, as I believe you must already know, is of the Gentiles who worship many things and believe that there is only one God. And it is very populous, and there are in it many Moors who, until now, always traded there in spices, because it is thus like Bruges in Flanders,[3] the principal trading place for the things of India, which come to it from outside; and in it there are only cassia-fistula and ginger. He arrived at this city five months after having departed from Lisbon. And he was very honourably received by the king, who came to a house beside the sea to speak to him, with all his lords and many other people. And there he gave him my messages and established with him my peace and concord. Concerning this agreement the aforesaid king ordered a letter written on a sheet of silver with his seal inlaid in gold, for this is the custom in his land in matters of great importance, and other letters written on leaves of trees which resemble palms, on which they ordinarily write. And from these trees and their fruit are made the following things: sugar, honey, oil, wine, water, vinegar, charcoal, and cordage for ships, and for everything else, and matting of which they make some sails for ships, and it serves them for everything which they need. And the aforesaid fruit, in addition to what is thus made of it, is their chief food, particularly at sea. After the agreement had thus been made with the said king, my factor sent on shore the entire establishment which I had ordered for the above-mentioned factory, and at once he began to trade with his merchandise and to load the ships with spices.

[1] *Coavixi* in the Spanish version.

[2] Branding in the form of a cross was practised at an early date by the Jacobites and Syrians. The Abyssinians also so branded, but not necessarily as a fire baptism. Father Álvares, who visited Abyssinia in 1520 and witnessed several baptisms, does not mention this custom in that connexion. He describes, however, branding on the forehead as a preventive from colds.

[3] Bruges, which had been the northern counterpart of Venice in the fourteenth century, while still retaining a position as a financial centre, was losing much of its commerce to Antwerp because of the gradual silting up of the river Zwyn. This could not be navigated by 1490.

In the meantime, the King of Calecut sent word to my captain that a very large and well-armed ship which had annoyed him on previous occasions, belonging to another king, his enemy, had sent word to him that it was passing before his port, without any fear of him, and he begged him to order it to be captured, enlarging on the matter, as it greatly concerned his estate and honour.

And the said captain, in view of the good treatment which he and also my factor were beginning to receive, and in order to confirm further peace and friendship, agreed to do it. And in order to show him the strength of our people in ships and artillery, he sent against it only the smallest ship which he had, with a large bombard.[1] And it overtook them within the harbour of another king,[2] his neighbour, and before his eyes and those of all his people he captured it, and brought it to Calecut with 400 bowmen and some artillery and with seven elephants, trained in warfare, on board (there these would be worth thirty thousand cruzados,[3] for they gave five thousand for only one of them), and with other merchandise of spices. This ship my captain ordered to be presented to him, and he gave it to him with everything which came in it, and he came to the shore with all his state and pomp to see it, since it was to them a very great surprise that so small a ship with so few men should take so large a ship with so many people, and to receive the message which the said captain was sending him concerning it. And the Moors, especially those of Mecca, who were there, seeing that they were in this concord and friendship, and that two ships were already loaded with spices, and seeing also the great loss which they were suffering, sought all the means that they could to put discord between my factor and the king. And they stirred up a tumult on land to hinder them; and because all the merchandise was in the hands of the Moors they hid it, and secretly sent it elsewhere. When he learned this, the aforesaid captain sent word to the King of Calecut, complaining to him and asking him to fulfil what he had agreed, which was that in twenty days he would give him merchandise with which

[1] This was the caravel *S. Pedro* of Pedro de Ataíde. The use of bombards on caravels was the invention of John II.

[2] The King of Cananore.

[3] The cruzado contained 229·5 grammes of fine gold, and was worth about 9*s.* 8*d.* (see Ravenstein, *Vasco da Gama*, p. 242).

to load the said ships, and that until they were loaded, he would not give authority to load to any others. And the king answered him that he would at once order all the merchandise which there was in the land to be given to him, and that if any ship should be loaded in his harbour without the knowledge of his officials, he gave him the authority and power to detain it until he sent his said officials, so that they might arrange to turn it over to him. As soon as the Moors learned of this, they agreed to load a ship publicly with great diligence, using still greater care in hiding the merchandise than they had previously done, and this, in order to give an excuse for an outbreak to begin, for they are powerful. And the city is of many nationalities and of extensive population, in which the king can, with difficulty, attend to the tumults of the populace. And when my factor saw that the ship was being loaded, he asked the said captain to detain it, as the king had agreed. And the said captain, fearing an outbreak, hesitated to do it; and the said factor again asked him to detain it, telling him that the chief Moors and also some Gentiles told him that if the said ship were not held they could in no way load their ships. According to what followed it appears that they were doing it in order to give rise to the said outbreak. And my captain, after hesitating many times, fearing what followed, ordered the people of that ship to be told that, because of the authority which he had for this, it should not leave; but they were not willing to agree to this. And then it was necessary to order it to be held. And he commanded his boats to bring it inside the harbour, where it surely could not leave without his permission. And as soon as the Moors saw this, since it was the end which they desired, at that very moment they came quickly with all the rest of the population, whom they had already stirred up, to attack the said factor and his house, and fought with him. And he with those few whom he had with him, defended themselves for some time, and leaving the house, rallied at the sea. And my captain, who was then ill,[1] as soon as he was told of the uprising on land, ordered all his boats to aid him, and although the sea was very rough he nevertheless gathered up some of the people.

[1] At this time Cabral was suffering from fever and ague, and was being bled by the ship's barber.

They killed the factor and with him fifty people were lost, either dead or captives. After this was done, when my captain saw that the king had not come to help and that he sent no message and was providing himself with some equipment implying war, and also had taken possession of my property which had remained on shore, he waited one day to see if he would make amends for the said matter. When he saw that he was sending him no message, fearing that he was arming himself effectively, as he afterwards did, to prevent him from taking the vengeance he could take at that time, he decided to act at once, and he took ten large ships which were in the harbour, and ordered all the people who were on them to be put to the sword, with the exception of a few who, concealing themselves, escaped death, and whom afterwards he did not wish to kill, but brought captive to me. And he ordered the said ships to be burned in front of the port, which caused great horror to the king and to the people of the land. On the ships there were three elephants which died there. In this manner he spent the entire day; and as soon as it was night, he went with all the ships, and placed himself as near land as he could in front of the city; and as soon as it was dawn, he began to fire with artillery, and bombarded it until night, especially the houses of the king. In this he did much damage, and killed many of his people, as he learned afterwards, and he killed one of the chief men who was near the king. On account of this, the king immediately departed from the city, for it seemed to him that he was not safe anywhere. And he sailed from there to another port of his, which was called Fandarene [Pandarani], which he also damaged with artillery, and killed people. And from there he sailed to the kingdom of Cochim, which is the region from which spices come, 30 leagues beyond Calecut, and on the way, he found two other ships of Calecut, which he also captured and ordered to be burned. And when he reached Cochim, after having informed the king of what had happened in Calecut, he was very well received by him, and made an agreement with him in the same manner which he had done in Calecut. Then he immediately sent my factor and certain men with him on shore, for whom they gave him honourable men as hostages, whom he brought to me; and they loaded his ships in 16 days; and the merchandise they brought to him in their boats was brought with so much greater friendliness and security that it appeared that Our Lord permitted the outbreak at Calecut in order that this other agreement might take place, which is of greater profit and security, because the harbour is much better and of much more extensive trade, since, of almost all the merchandise which goes to Calecut, most of it is to be found in that land, and because others go there first without going to Calecut. In this city of Cochim there are many ships, and he learned that two merchants alone had as many as 50 ships. In that kingdom there are many true Christians of the conversion of Saint Thomas, and their priests follow the manner of life of the apostles with much strictness, having nothing of their own except what is given them as alms. And they practise celibacy, and have churches in which they say mass, and they consecrate unleavened bread, and wine which they make from dried fruit with water, for they cannot make other. In their churches they have no images save the cross, and all the Christians wear the apostolic garments, and never cut their beards and hair. And there he found definite information concerning where the body of Saint Thomas lies, which is 150 leagues from there, on the sea coast, in a city which is called Maliapor [Mailapur], of a small population; and he brought me earth from his tomb.[1] And all the Christians and also the Moors and Gentiles, on account of the great miracles which are performed, go to his house on pilgrimage. He also brought us two Christians who came of their own accord and with the permission of their prelate, so that we might send them to Rome and to Jerusalem, to see the things of the Church there, and to be informed about them, for they consider that they are better ruled by being ordained by Saint Peter, who, they believe, was the chief of the apostles. And he also learned certain news of great Christian nations which are on the other side of that kingdom, who come on pilgrimage to the aforesaid house of Saint Thomas, and have very great kings who obey One only. They are white men of fair hair, and are considered strong. The land is called Malchima,[2] and from it come porcelain, and musk

[1] This earth was supposed to have great curative value.
[2] This is probably derived from the Hindustani *Maha-Chin*, Great China.

and amber, and aloe-wood, which they bring from the river Ganges, which is on this side of them. And there are such fine vases of porcelain there, that a single one of them is worth a hundred cruzados. And while he was in the kingdom of Cochim, when the treaty had been agreed to and the ships loaded, there came to him messages from the King of Cananor, and from the King of Colum [Quilon] who are near by, requesting him to come to them because they would make more profitable trade with him, but, because he had already made the treaty, he declined to go. At this time, as he was about to depart from Cochim, the same king sent word to him that a large fleet from Calecut was coming against him, and that as many as 15,000 men were in it. It did not seem well to my captain to fight with it, because he had his ships loaded, and had few men, and it did not seem to him that there was time or necessity for taking the risk, since he feared that they might kill or disable some of them, and on account of the length of the journey which he had to go, which was 4,000 leagues from here. But he set sail, with them following him, and as they did not dare to go far out to sea, they turned back, because they feared to go against him. From there he went his way, which was to the kingdom of Cananor, [ruled by] one of those kings who invited him. And as he was passing, as soon as those on land caught sight of him, they sent him another message, asking him to stop there, because the king wanted to send a messenger to me by him, whom he brought me. And in the single day that he was there, he ordered so much spicery to be brought to the ships that he might have entirely filled them, had they been empty; and they gave what they might carry free, as a present to win my friendship. And all his chief men came also to my captain, telling him on behalf of the king that they would see to it that he was treated there in a different manner than in Calecut, assuring him that if he wanted to make war on Calecut they would help him, and that he in person would go on land, and all his fleet on the sea. And after thanking him greatly in my name, he took leave of him, saying to him that in the other fleet which I was to send soon, I would send him my answer regarding everything. He went his way, and in the middle of that crossing he took a very large ship loaded with merchandise. It appeared to him that it was a ship of Mecca which was just coming from Calecut. And finding that the aforesaid ship belonged to the King of Cambaia [Cambay], he abandoned it, sending word by it to the said king that he had released it because he did not intend to make war with any one; he had made it only on those who had broken the word which they had given to him in my name. Continuing farther on his way, he lost one of the ships which was laden, for it ran aground during the night. Its people were saved, and he ordered the ship to be burned because it could not be dislodged safely. From this place he sent a ship to obtain news of the mine of Çofalla which I have mentioned before.[1] This has just arrived, and brought me definite information of it and also concerning the trade and the merchandise of the country and of the great quantity of gold which is there; and there he found news, that among the men who carry gold from there to the coasts, they saw many who have four eyes, namely, two in front and two behind. The men are small of body and strong, and it is said that they are cruel, and that they eat the men with whom they have war, and that the cows of the king wear collars of heavy gold around their necks. Near this mine there are two islands on which they gather much pearl and amber. My aforesaid captain departed from there, and reached Lisboa 16 months from the day he had left it, and, blessed be Our Lord, in all this voyage he lost only three men from sickness, and all the others are healthy and of good spirits.[2] And now a certain message comes to me saying that one of the ships that was going to Çoffala which he believed lost, is coming, and will be here shortly. They say that it entered the Red Sea, and that it is bringing from there some silver and also some information concerning matters there, although I am already informed in detail concerning the said Red Sea, having been informed thereof by my above-mentioned captain, who had information concerning it in many ways.[3] I leave the other details of this

[1] There is no intimation either in this letter of the king or in any account of Cabral's voyage that Pedro da Covilhan had visited Sofala, and no information is given which da Covilhan might have included in a letter to John II.

[2] This is a mistake, since many had died of scurvy.

[3] The Anonymous Narrative, which is given on pp. 56–94 of this volume, has a description of the Red Sea. It is possible that this reference is an indication that this narrative was the official report of Cabral, though not written by him.

matter to Pero Lopes, who was present at everything.[1] Very exalted and very excellent and very puissant Sovereigns, Father and Mother, may Our Lord have your life and royal estate in His holy care.

Written in Santarem the 29th of July.

EL REY.

[1] There were thus at least three Spaniards with the fleet: Master John, Sancho de Tovar, and Pedro Lopez de Padilla. Pedro Lopez may have been the bearer of this letter to the Spanish sovereigns.

THE ANONYMOUS NARRATIVE

ONE of the earliest and the most complete contemporary accounts of the voyage of Cabral was written by a member of the fleet. The author is unknown, but he was without doubt a Portuguese and a man of more than ordinary intelligence and education. From the careful and concise manner in which the account was written it appears to have been either an official record of the voyage or a narrative intended for publication. Some version of this account was known to the Portuguese historians who wrote at a later date, but no contemporary copy can now be found in Portugal. It seems to have reached Italy soon after the fleet returned. Because of the interest taken in Cabral's voyage, this narrative was well known in Venice, for at least four early manuscripts still exist in the Venetian dialect, and it was included in the first edition of *Paesi*.

Two theories may be suggested for its presence in Venice: one, that it was sent there originally in the Portuguese language in either manuscript or printed form and that it was translated into Italian at Venice; the other that it was the book to which Angelo Trevisan refers as the work of Il Cretico,[1] the secretary of the Venetian ambassador to Spain. In favour of the first theory it may be held that there are no indications of Italian influence in the account and it seems to have been written in the form of a diary, from the viewpoint of a Portuguese and not of an Italian. Had it been composed or modified by an Italian the portion relating to the discovery of Brazil, which was of little interest to the Venetians, would probably not have been included, and it would undoubtedly have contained more about the trade in spices, regarding which they were greatly concerned. One of the early manuscripts states that it was translated from Portuguese into Italian. This statement is also made in the *Paesi*, where it appears in the headings of two books. Fracanzano, to whom the editing of *Paesi* is ascribed, further states in his dedication to Giovanni Maria Angiolelli that it was translated from Portuguese. All of the existing manuscripts

[1] Further information concerning Il Cretico and Trevisan is given later, on pp. 114–17.

differ, and they may have been independent translations of a Portuguese manuscript or possibly of a printed text. In support of the theory that it was the work of Il Cretico and that it was the book which Trevisan told Malipiero, his former employer, that Il Cretico was engaged in writing, we have a contemporary copy among the letters of Malipiero. This manuscript is the one most nearly like the text in *Paesi*. In it the narrative begins with 'In the year 1500', as might be expected if it were to form part of Malipiero's annals. It is uncertain whether Il Cretico knew the Portuguese language, and it is quite probable that he did not. Furthermore, the style of the narrative is not that of the learned professor of Greek as shown in his letter to the Signoria, and it does not contain the Latin expressions which we would expect Il Cretico to use.[1]

It seems possible, with the large population of the Venetian Republic and the general interest of the people in this voyage, that the narrative may have been printed separately. There were no restrictions against publishing it in Venice as there may have been in Lisbon. If it had been sent to Venice by Trevisan we might expect it to be printed there, as had happened with the account of the Spanish voyages from the notes of Peter Martyr.[2] The manuscript copyists of this printed narrative then evidently

[1] In the text of *Paesi*, published six years after Cabral's return, there are further complications. The first three books of that volume are devoted to Portuguese voyages and include the narrative of Cadamosto, two letters of Girolamo Sernigi regarding da Gama's voyage, and the Anonymous Narrative. There then occurs a definite 'FINIS' before the accounts of the Spanish voyages. These three accounts are continuous, without titles. The Cadamosto voyage, with its accompanying account of that of de Sintra, ends with 'Finis' and then a note, but there is no break in the text. The beginning of the second book is made arbitrarily during the Cadamosto voyage with the title *Voyage from Lisbon to Calicut translated from Portuguese into Italian*, a title evidently intended for the Anonymous Narrative. The three accounts are written in the Venetian dialect and seem to be uniform. This suggests that they might have been translated together from Portuguese, as stated in the titles to the second and third books. The three narratives, however, evidently existed in Italy several years prior to the publication of *Paesi*, although the letters of Girolamo Sernigi were originally written in the Florentine dialect. The collection of Portuguese voyages given in *Paesi* was therefore either translated as a whole from a Portuguese source or more probably was made from a manuscript copy of the three narratives in Venetian. Because of the careless way in which it was printed it does not seem reasonable to suppose that Fracanzano had made the translation or that it had been done for him. If the three accounts were not translated directly from the Portuguese, the Anonymous Narrative as given in *Paesi* would seem to have been taken from a Venetian source.

[2] The letter of Il Cretico which follows the Anonymous Narrative in the Contarini A MS. had been published. Vagliente copied printed pamphlets in his manuscript collection of voyages, and the author of the so-called letter of King Manuel of 1505 had access to a copy of the Anonymous Narrative, probably at Rome.

changed and abbreviated it. The title seems to have been *The Voyage from Lisbon to Calicut.*[1]

Some clue as to the identity of the Portuguese author may be obtained from the narrative itself. He was on Cabral's ship or that of Simão de Miranda or Pedro de Ataíde after the storm, and he returned either with Cabral or Simão de Miranda. He seems to have been present when Cabral met the Zamorin and was on shore at the time of the massacre and was among those saved. Since Cabral was on board his ship during the uprising, he could not have been the author. Only Frei Henrique, Nuno Leitão da Cunha, and a sailor are mentioned, of the twenty who escaped. It may have been the work of some nobleman who went with the fleet, but it seems more probable, from the careful manner with which it was written, that it was composed by some one whose duty it was to make this record, possibly one of the writers. The only one holding this position whose name is known and who might have been the author is João de Sá, who had gone with Vasco da Gama as a writer and undoubtedly held a position of trust under Cabral. His duties would take him ashore at Calicut, and he returned with the fleet. Since Ravenstein considers that de Sá may have been the author of the so-called *Roteiro* of the voyage of Vasco da Gama, he may have had a similar duty to perform with Cabral's fleet.[2]

From what is known of the voyage of Cabral from other sources the Anonymous Narrative is substantially accurate. It was written by one who was on the voyage and who lived to return. It thus ranks second only to the letters of Pedro Vaz de Caminha and Master John as an authoritative source.

Four manuscripts of the Anonymous Narrative have been preserved. One of these is to be found with the letters of Trevisan in the Sneyd Collection now at Newcastle-on-Tyne. Two manuscripts bound together, known as Contarini A and B, and another in somewhat condensed form are in the Mar-

[1] *Navigatione de Lisbona a Callichut, de lengua Portogallese in taliana* as given in *Paesi*, or *Copia del viazo de lisbona a Cholocut de lengua portogalesse in lengua taliana*, as shown on the first page of the Contarini A MS.

[2] There is nothing in the text to indicate that this narrative was written by a pilot, a statement which was first made by Ramusio. That author was often inaccurate. In this case he seems to have still had in mind the account of the *Navigation from Lisbon to São Thomé* written by a Portuguese pilot, which he had previously inserted in his collection of voyages.

ciana Library. Of all these the Sneyd MS. seems to be the oldest. The Contarini B MS. seems to be contemporary and the Contarini A seems to be later. The fourth manuscript is included in a volume entitled *Viaggiatori Antichi* and was written after 1523. The first printed text which is known is that given in the first edition of *Paesi nouamente retrovati*. It is to be found in all editions of this collection, and was included by Simon Grynaeus in the editions of his *Novus Orbis* and in the German translation. It was published by Ramusio in the first volume of his *Navigationi et Viaggi*, and is contained in all subsequent editions and in the French translation of Temporal. It is also included in several minor collections of voyages during the sixteenth and seventeenth centuries.

The translation given is from the text of the first edition of the *Paesi* (II, III, ch. lxiii to ch. lxxxiii, incl.) published at Vicenza in 1507. Comparison has been made with others which followed.

WHEREIN KING MANUEL IN PERSON CONSIGNED THE ROYAL STANDARD TO THE CAPTAIN

In the year 1500 the Most Serene King of Portugal, called Don Manuel by name, sent his armada of ships, large and small, to the parts of India, in which armada there were twelve large and small ships. The captain-general[1] of this armada was Pedro Aliares Cabrile, a fidalgo. These ships departed, both well equipped and in good order, with everything which they might need for a year and a half. Of these twelve ships,[2] he ordered that ten should proceed to Calichut [Calicut] and the other two[3] to Arabia,[4] directing their course so that they might make a place called Zaffalle [Sofala] because they wished to establish trade with merchants in the said place, which place, Zaffalle, is found to be on the way to Calichut. In like manner

[1] *capo generale*. When Cabral is referred to later in the narrative it is either as *capitaneo* or *capitaneo magiore*. This seems to indicate that the beginning of this narrative was written by another person. It seems also to have been somewhat condensed from the original. Nothing is said concerning the voyage from the Cape Verde Islands to Brazil.

[2] The store-ship of Gaspar de Lemos is evidently not counted.

[3] Those of Bartolomeu and Diogo Dias.

[4] That is, the country under the control of the Arabs, in this case East Africa.

the other ten ships carried merchandise which they might need for the said voyage. And on the 8th of the month of March of the said year they were ready, and on that day, which was Sunday, they went a distance of two miles from this city to a place called Rastello, where there is a church called Sancta Maria de Baller [Belem].[1] To this place the Most Serene King went in person to consign to the captain the royal standard for the said armada.

Monday, which was the 9th day of March, the said armada departed on its voyage with good weather.

On the 14th day of the said month the said armada passed the Island of Chanaria [Grand Canary].

On the 22nd day it passed the Island of Capo Verde.[2]

On the 23rd day one ship became separated from the said armada, so that no news of it has been heard from that day to this, nor can anything be learned of it.

HOW THE SHIPS RAN BECAUSE OF A STORM

On the 24th of April,[3] which was Wednesday of the octave of Easter, the aforesaid armada came in sight of land, with which they had great pleasure; and they went to it to see what land it was.[4] They found it a land very abundant in trees, and there were people who were going there along the shore of the sea. And they cast anchor at the mouth of a small river. And after the said anchors were cast, the captain ordered a boat to be launched in the sea, in which he sent to see what people they

[1] Neither the justly celebrated Monastery of the Jeronimos at Belem nor the Tower of Belem existed at this time, although work had begun on the former. The Monastery occupies the site of the Restello, a chapel built by Prince Henry the Navigator, which no longer exists. It was here that Vasco da Gama spent the night before he departed on his voyage to India. Dom Manuel had vowed that if the voyage was a success he would erect there a church worthy of the results. This was begun a few weeks after the return of da Gama. The ceremonies prior to the departure of Cabral's fleet further identified this place with the hopes and ambitions of Dom Manuel for the control of the Eastern seas. The Tower of Belem, which was formerly on a rocky island in the Tagus a short distance below the Monastery, was built in 1520. The silt of the river has since extended the shore line to the Tower, and the former site of the Restello is also considerably farther from the river bank than at the time of the departure of Cabral.

[2] Probably São Nicolau.

[3] This was the 22nd of April; see letter of Caminha.

[4] 'On the 24th of April they saw land, at which they were very much pleased, because in the direction in which it lay there were none which had hitherto been discovered' (de Goes).

were. And they found that they were people of dark colour, between white and black, and well built, with long hair. And they go nude as they were born, without any shame whatever, and each one of them carried his bow with arrows, as men who were in defence of the said river. On the aforesaid armada there was no one who understood their language. And having seen this, those in the boat returned to the captain; and then night came on. During that night there was a great storm.[1]

On the morning of the following day we raised anchor, and in a great storm we skirted the coast towards the north (the wind was the sirocco[2]) to see whether we might find some port where the aforesaid armada might stay. Finally we found a port where we cast anchor. There we found some natives who were fishing in their little barks. One of our boats went to where these men were and took two of them and these they brought to the captain to learn what people they were, and, as has been said, they did not understand one another either in speech or by signs. And that night the çaptain kept them with him. On the following day he ordered them to be dressed in shirts and coats and red caps [*berettas*]. They were very content with this attire and marvelled at the things which were shown them. He afterwards ordered them to be put on shore.

A ROOT FROM WHICH THEY MAKE BREAD, AND THEIR OTHER CUSTOMS

Likewise on that same day, which was the octave of Easter, the 26th day of April,[3] the chief captain determined to hear mass, and he directed a tent to be set up in a place where he ordered an altar to be erected. And all those of the said armada went to hear mass and a sermon; whereupon many of those men joined them, dancing and singing, with their horns. And immediately after mass had been said they all left for their ships. The men of the land entered the sea as far as their armpits, singing and making merry and festivity. And then, after the captain had dined, the people of the said armada returned to land, taking solace and pleasure with those men of the land, and they began to trade with the men of the armada, and gave their bows and

[1] The narrative from here seems to follow the original Portuguese account and 'we' replaces 'they'. [2] i.e. south-east. [3] The date is here given correctly.

arrows for little bells and leaves of paper and pieces of cloth. Thus all that day our men took pleasure with them. And we found in that place a river of sweet water, and we returned late to the ships.

On the following day the chief captain decided to take in water and wood, and all those of the said armada went on shore. And the men of that place came to help them with the aforesaid wood and water, and some of our men went to the place where these men dwell, which was three miles away from the coast of the sea; and they bartered for parrots and a root called *igname*, which is their bread, which the Arabs eat.[1] Those of the armada gave them bells and pieces of paper in payment for the said things. In this place we remained five or six days. In appearance these people are dark, and they go nude without shame, and their hair is long, and they pluck their beards. And their eyelids and over their eyebrows are painted with figures of white and black and blue and red. They have the lip of the mouth, that is, the lower lip, pierced. In the opening they put a bone as large as a nail, and others wear there a long blue stone or a green one, and they hang from their lips. Women likewise go nude without shame and they are beautiful of body, with long hair. And their houses are of wood, covered with leaves and branches of trees, with many wooden columns. In the middle of the said houses and from the said columns to the wall they hang a net of cotton, which holds a man. And between the nets they make a fire. Thus in a single house there may be forty or fifty beds set up like looms.

PARROTS IN THE NEWLY DISCOVERED LAND

In this land we saw no iron[2] nor any other metal. They cut wood with stone. And they have many birds of many sorts, especially parrots, of many colours; among them are some as large as hens; and there are other very beautiful birds. Of the feathers of the said birds they make the hats and caps [*cappelli e*

[1] The Portuguese did not recognize that the cassava or manioc root was not the *igname* or yam. The latter was known to them and also to the Arabs on the ships. It is practically certain that the Tupinamba did not know the yam (Métraux, A., *La Civilisation matérielle des tribus Tupi-Guarani*, Paris, 1928, p. 66).

[2] Iron was not known to the Tupinamba Indians nor on either coast of South America prior to the coming of the whites.

berette] which they wear. The land abounds with many kinds of trees and much and excellent water and *ignames* and cotton.[1] In this place we did not see any animals. The land is large, and we do not know whether it is an island or mainland, but on account of its size we believe that it is *terra firma*. Its climate is very good. And these men have nets and are great fishermen and fish for various kinds of fish. Among these we saw a fish which they caught. It must have been as large as a barrel and longer and round, and it had a head like that of a pig and small eyes, and it had no teeth and had ears the length of an arm and the width of half an arm. Below its body it had two holes and the tail was an arm's length long and equally wide. It had no feet anywhere. It had hair like a pig and the hide was as thick as a finger, and its meat was white and fat like that of a pig.[2] During these days which we stayed there, the captain determined to inform our Most Serene King of the finding of this land, and to leave in it two men, exiles [*banditi*], condemned to death, who were in the said armada for this purpose. And the said captain promptly dispatched a small supply ship which they had with them, in addition to the twelve ships aforesaid. This small ship carried the letters to the king. In these were contained what we had seen and discovered. After the said small ship was dispatched, the captain went on shore and ordered a very large cross to be made of wood, and he ordered it to be set up on the shore, and also, as has been said, left two convicts in the said place. They began to weep and the men of the land comforted them and showed that they pitied them.

A STORM SO GREAT THAT FOUR SHIPS PERISHED

The following day, which was the 2nd of May of the said year, the armada made sail on its way to go round the Cape of Good Hope. This voyage would be across the gulf of the sea,

[1] Cotton was carefully cultivated. According to Claude d'Abbeville the shrub which bore cotton was cut close to the ground every five or six years to increase production.

[2] This was undoubtedly a manatee (*Trichechus inunguis*), a herbivorous mammal, which inhabits the shallow waters of rivers and estuaries. It is from eight to ten feet long with a wide shovel-shaped tail. The fore limbs are flippers or paddles and there are no hind limbs. The body is round and smooth. The eyes and ears are small. These Sirenia are now found particularly in the regions of the Amazon and Orinoco. A similar species is found in the West Indies and the neighbouring mainland.

more than 1,200 leagues, that is, four miles to a league. On the 12th day of the said month, while on our course, there appeared a comet with a very long tail in the direction of Arabia. It was in view continuously for eight or ten nights.

On Sunday, which was the 24th day of the said month of May,[1] as all the armada was sailing together with a favourable wind, with the sails half set and without bonnets because of a rain which we had the day before, while we were thus sailing, there came on us a head wind so strong and so sudden that we knew nothing of it until the sails were across the masts. And at that moment four ships were lost with all on board, without our being able to give them aid in any way.[2] The other seven ships which escaped were also almost lost. And thus we took the wind astern with the masts and sails broken. And we were at the mercy of God; and thus we went all that day. The sea was so swollen that it seemed that we were mounting up to the heavens. The wind changed suddenly, although the storm was still so great that we had no desire to set sails to the wind. And going thus with this storm, without sails, we lost sight of one another, so that the ship of the captain with two others took a different route.[3] And another ship called *Il Re* with two others took another route,[4] and the other one, alone, took still another.[5] And thus we went twenty days through this storm without setting a sail to the wind.

CONCERNING ZAFFALLE, A GOLD-MINE

On the 16th day of June[6] we came in sight of the land of Arabia and cast anchor close to the shore. There we had much sickness and no one went on shore. This land is thickly populated, and in it we saw many people; and then we raised anchor and went along the shore with good weather, and we saw great rivers and many animals, so that every place was inhabited.

Somewhat before[7] Zaffalle, which is a gold-mine, we found

[1] Castanheda and de Barros also give this date, while de Goes says the 25th.

[2] Those of Bartolomeu Dias, Luis Pires, Aires Gomes da Silva, and Simão de Pina.

[3] Cabral's flagship, and those of Simão de Miranda and Pedro de Ataíde.

[4] The ship of Sancho de Tovar with those of Nicoláu Coelho and Nuno Leitão da Cunha.

[5] That of Diogo Dias.

[6] This is a mistake for the 16th of July, which is the date given by de Barros.

[7] 'After Sofala' is evidently meant.

people near two islands who were in two Moorish ships which were coming from this gold-mine, and they were going to Melinde. And when those of the said two ships caught sight of our ships, they began to flee. They headed for the shore and all cast themselves into the sea in order to reach land, and they threw all which they had into the sea so that our people might not take it away from them. Our captain ordered him[1] to come before him, after the aforesaid two ships had already been captured by our men, and he asked first whence they came. He replied that he was a Moor, a cousin of the King of Melinde, and that the ships were his, and that he was coming from Zaffalle with gold, and that he was bringing his wife with him. She and also one of his sons, while trying to flee to land, were drowned. When the captain of our armada learned that he was the cousin of the King of Melinde, which king he considered a very good friend of ours, he was very sorry and did him much honour. He ordered that his ships with all their goods, which he had taken, should be returned. The Moorish captain asked our chief captain whether he had with him any enchanter who might recover the gold which they had cast into the sea. Our captain replied that we were Christians and that among us such things were not the custom. Then our captain inquired concerning Zaffalle, which was not yet discovered except by reputation.[2] This Moor gave him the information that Zaffalle was a mine of much gold and that a Moorish king possessed it,

[1] i.e. the captain of the Moorish ship. De Barros and de Goes say he was named Sheik Fateima. De Barros also states that he was an uncle of the King of Malindi.

[2] Vasco da Gama seems to have been informed regarding the coast of East Africa before he arrived there. In addition to the references to it by classical writers, it was mentioned by Mas'ūdī (A.D. 943), by Edrisi (A.D. 1154) and by other Arabian geographers. Ibn Batuta (1320–40) visited Mogadishu, Mombasa, and Kilwa. Although he speaks of Sofala, he did not go there. Father Álvares states that Pedro da Covilhan informed him that he had been to the coast of Sofala. He mentions none of the cities visited, however, and the statement which he makes is too indefinite to indicate that, when he was there in 1489–90, he went farther south than Kilwa, the chief city of that coast. (*Verdadera Informacam das Terras de Preste Joam das Indias*, ed. Lisbon, 1889). This question was discussed by Conde de Ficalho (*Viagens de Pedro da Covilhan*, Lisbon, 1898), who was of the opinion that da Covilhan visited Sofala. The coast of Sofala at that time, however, meant the coast ruled by the King of Kilwa (see Bittner and Tomaschek, op. cit.). The King of Portugal undoubtedly obtained knowledge regarding the East African coast through Venetians and from Arabs in Morocco who had made the pilgrimage to Mecca. Da Gama must have secured sufficient information regarding Sofala from the Arab pilots to warrant Dom Manuel sending two of the vessels of Cabral's fleet to that port. All narratives state that Sancho de Tovar discovered it when he stopped there on this voyage.

that this king lived on an island which is called Chiloa [Kilwa],[1] and that it was on the route we were to take, and that Zaffalle was behind us. The captain took leave of him and we went on our way.

On the 20th day of the month of June[2] we reached a small island which belongs to the same King of Zaffalle, Mozonbige [Mozambique]. It has a small population and in it there are rich merchants. From this island we took supplies and a pilot who would conduct us to Chiloa. This island has a very good port and is near the mainland. From here we departed for Chiloa, along the coast, where we found many inhabited islands which belong to this same king.

We reached Chiloa on the 26th day of the said month, and in that place six sails joined;[3] the other one was never found.[4] This island is small, near the mainland, and is a beautiful country. The houses are high like those of Spain. In this land there are rich merchants, and there is much gold and silver and amber and musk and pearls. Those of the land wear clothes of fine cotton and of silk and many fine things, and they are black men.[5]

HOW THE CAPTAIN, HAVING RECEIVED THE SAFE-CONDUCT, TALKED WITH THE KING

As soon as we arrived there the captain sent to ask a safe-conduct from the king, and the king ordered that it be given to him immediately. As soon as the captain received the safe-

[1] For the history of Kilwa and other ports on the coast of East Africa prior to the arrival of the Portuguese, see G. M. Theal, *The Portuguese in South Africa* (London, 1896); M. Guillain, *Documents sur l'histoire, la géographie et le commerce de l'Afrique orientale* (Paris, 1856).

[2] This is again an error and should be the 20th of July, the date given by de Barros and de Goes.

[3] The coincidence of the arrival of these vessels after having been separated for two months is remarkable. No account tells of the voyage of the ships of Nicoláu Coelho, Nuno Leitão da Cunha, and Sancho de Tovar from the time they became separated from the rest of the fleet until they rejoined the flag-ship. This would indicate that the narratives of the voyage were written by those on the other ships. Corrêa states that they joined at Mozambique. This seems more probable because it was the place designated in the instructions given for future voyages, for ships to reassemble should they became separated.

[4] This seems to indicate that the narrative was written as a diary before the fleet reached Cape Verde on the return voyage, since the narrative states later that the ship of Diogo Dias was found there.

[5] The Arabs were classified by the Portuguese as either white or black, the white being those from Arabia.

conduct, he sent Alfonso Furtado on shore with seven or eight well-dressed men as an embassy. He instructed them to say that they were ships of the King of Portugal, and that they came there from him to make a treaty with him and that they had much merchandise of kinds which he would like. And, moreover, he ordered them to say that it would give him pleasure to meet him. The said king replied to him that he was very content and that the following day he would meet him if he would be willing to go on shore. Alfonso Furtado replied that the captain had orders from his king not to go on shore, and that if he wished they might talk in their boats. And this they agreed to do the following day. And the next day the captain made ready with all his people, and the ships and the boats with all their banners raised and his heralds and the artillery in order. The king of the said land also ordered his *almache*,[1] that is, boats, to be put in order, with much festivity and noise, according to their custom. The captain proceeded with his trumpeters and pipers. And they came within sight of each other. And as they were approaching each other, the bombards[2] were ready with their matches and were fired. The noise was so great from this discharge that the said king with all his people was stupefied and frightened.[3] And at once they held a consultation, and having talked they hurriedly took leave of each other. The captain returned to his ship, and on the following day again sent Alfonso Furtado ashore to begin to negotiate. He found the king very differently disposed toward the captain than he had been at first, excusing himself by saying that they had no need of our merchandise and that it seemed to him, the said king, that we were corsairs. And so Alfonso Furtado returned to the captain with this message. And thus we remained for two or three days, for we could accomplish nothing. And while we were there they did nothing but send men from the mainland to the island, for they

[1] Small native craft, the *almadia* of the Portuguese.

[2] Bombards were breech-loading cannon (see Whiteway). For *bombardeiros* see Pieris, P. E., and Fitzler, M. A. H., *Ceylon and Portugal* (Leipzig, 1927), part 1, pp. 295–301.

[3] Artillery was not used on Arabian or Hindu ships in the Indian Ocean at this time, and there were very few guns on land. The artillery of the Portuguese gave them a decided advantage in the early encounters with these ships, not only because greater damage could be done, but because boarding by superior numbers could be prevented.

feared that we might take the aforesaid island by force.[1] And when the captain saw this, he determined to leave, and ordered the sails to be set for the voyage to Melinde. And along the coast we found many islands inhabited by Moors. There is another city there, which is called Mombaza [Mombasa]. The king is a Moor.

All this coast of Arabia is inhabited by Moors. Both on the island and on the mainland there are said to be Christians who wage many wars. We did not see any of them.

HOW THE GIFT AND THE LETTER FROM THE KING OF PORTUGAL WERE PRESENTED TO THE KING OF MELINDE

We arrived at Melinde on the 2nd day of the month of August of the said year. In that place three ships of Gombaia [Cambay] were lying at anchor, and each one of these ships must have had a capacity of 200 *botte*.[2] Their hulls are well built of good wood, tied together with cord (for they have no nails), and they are covered with a mixture in which there is much incense. They have no castles except in the stern. These ships come to trade from parts of India. When we arrived there, the king sent those to visit us with many sheep, hens and geese, and lemons and oranges, the best that there are in the world. In our ships there were some men sick with the scurvy [*amalati de la boccha*], whom the oranges made well. As soon as we had cast anchor near the land, the captain ordered all the bombards to be fired and the ships to be decked with banners,

[1] De Goes says that Cabral learned of this from Molei Homan, brother of the King of Malindi, who was then at Kilwa. The following account of Cabral's visit is given in a Persian manuscript: 'In the year 906 came Qabītān [Cabral] with several ships to Kilwa. He demanded wood and water and that the Sultan or his son should be sent to confer with him. However, the Amīr and the people would not venture to let the Sultan go in person, so they disguised one Lugmān, son of Al-Malik al-Adil, in the fashion of royalty, and sent him instead. Then they carried the water down to the shore in vessels, and signalled to those on board to come and fetch it. But at this moment one of the Amīr's servants, named Hājj Ibrāhīm, went down to the beach, and ordered all the water to be taken away, so that when the Christians arrived they found none, and returned in anger to their ships. They then went to Malindi, where they were again cordially received and supplied with whatever they demanded. But before their final departure they chose seven men that were Christian perverts. Two of these they settled at Malindi: four they sent to Guzerat, to the Sultan Mahmūd, and the seventh to Kilwa.' (A. S. Strong, 'The History of Kilwa', *Journal of Royal Asiatic Society*, Apr. 1895.)

[2] A *botte* was about one-third of a Portuguese ton. For more exact information see Ravenstein, *Vasco da Gama*, p. 163.

and he sent on shore two factors of the king, one of whom could speak Moorish, that is, Arabic, to learn how the king was and to inform why we came, and that on another day he [the captain] would send his embassy with the letter which the King of Portugal sent him. The king had great pleasure in our coming; and at the request of the king the factor who knew how to speak Arabic remained on shore. The next day the king sent two Moors of high rank who spoke Arabic to the ships to visit the captain. He instructed them to say that he had great pleasure at his coming, and he begged him to request anything which he might need from this land just as he would do in Portugal, for he and all of his kingdom were at the command of the King of Portugal. The captain at once ordered that the letter with the present which the King of Portugal sent him should be sent on shore. The present was this: a rich saddle, a pair of enamelled bridles for a horse, a pair of stirrups and their spurs, all of silver, enamelled and gilded, a breast strap and cords of the proper kind for the said saddle, and furnishings of very rich crimson, and a halter worked in gold thread for the aforesaid horse, and two cushions of brocade and two other cushions of crimson velvet, and a fine carpet, and a piece of tapestry, and two pieces of scarlet cloth (this present was worth more than a thousand ducats in Portugal), and also a length of crimson satin and a piece of crimson taffeta. They agreed in council that Areschorea [Ayres Correia], who went as chief factor, should take this present. This Areschorea went on shore with the letter[1] and the said present, and there went with him many principal men and trumpets.[2] And similarly the said king sent all his important men to receive the said factor. And the house of the said king was on the shore of the port. Before they arrived at the house of the king many women came to meet

[1] No copy of this letter is known to exist. Its contents may be judged from that sent to the King of Calicut.

[2] Vasco da Gama had left a pillar or *padrão* at Malindi. When Cabral arrived there João de Sá was sent on shore with a message. There went with him a man who had accompanied da Gama. On inquiring for the *padrão* 'the king replied that he had guarded it very well in a house. And taking João de Sá by the hand he led him to the house where it was, with the arms freshly painted with ochre as if it had just been made.' He explained that it was so protected until the coming of the Portuguese because of the enmity of the King of Mombasa, 'who was at war with him with fire and blood, in which he had lost many people and much property, because the King of Mombasa was the most powerful of any' (de Barros).

them with vases filled with fire, in which were placed so many perfumes that the odours pervaded the land; and thus they entered the house of the said king, who was seated on a throne, and many of the principal Moors with him. The king was greatly pleased, and they gave him the present and the letter, which in one part was written in Arabic, and in another in Portuguese. As soon as the king had read the said letter he talked with the said Moors, and they had great pleasure among themselves. All gathered in the middle of the room uttered a cry, rendering thanks to God that they had for a friend so great a king and lord as the King of Portugal. Immediately he ordered arms and lengths of silk cloth to be brought, and he ordered them to be given to those who had brought the present. And he told Areschorea that he wished him to remain on land until the ships left, because he had much pleasure in talking with him. Areschorea replied that he could not do so without permission from the chief captain. The king sent his brother-in-law bearing his ring to the captain, requesting that he should allow Areschorea to remain on shore, and [telling him] that he might send on shore for all the things which he needed, and that he might take in water. The captain was satisfied with this. At once the king ordered that Areschorea be given a very honourable lodging, and that he be supplied with everything which he needed, that is, sheep and chickens and rice and milk and butter and dates and honey and fruit of every kind, save bread, which they do not eat.[1] And thus the said Areschorea remained three days on land, the king talking continually with him of the affairs of the king, our lord, and of the affairs of Portugal, telling him that he would be very glad to see the captain again. Areschorea told him that the captain had no authority to disembark on land, but that they could see him in a boat, as the King of Chilloa had done. The said king refused this, but Areschorea persuaded him to do so, and immediately he sent word to the captain, who made ready with his boats, leaving the ship in good care. The boat in which he went had its canopy spread, and its people were armed under their garments, which were of very fine scarlet. And the king ordered two

[1] According to Corrêa the King of Malindi had secured wheat from Cambay in anticipation of Cabral's arrival.

boats of the land similarly prepared with their canopies, and he also ordered a horse harnessed in the manner of Portugal; and his men on land did not know how to do this, so our men had to arrange it. The king descended some steps, and at the foot of the steps all the richest and most honourable people were awaiting him. These had a sheep, and when the king mounted the horse they slaughtered the said sheep, and the king rode over it on horseback. And all the people shouted very loudly with very high voices. This they did for ceremony and enchantment, and the custom is thus in Zambochob [Zanzibar].[1] Then he had a talk with the captain, who finally told him that he wished to leave but that he needed a pilot who would conduct him to Calichut. The king told him that he would order one to be given to him, and thus they separated one from the other. When the said king went on shore he at once sent Areschorea to the ships with much meat and fruits for the captain, and he also sent him a Guzerati pilot from the ships of Chombaia which were in the port. The captain also left two Portuguese convicts, one of them to remain in Melinde, and the other to go with the ships to Chombaia.[2] The following day, which was the 7th day of August, they departed and began to cross the gulf to Calichut.

CONCERNING THE RED AND PERSIAN SEAS AND THE ISLAND OF AGRADIDA[3]

In this crossing, which took us along all the coast of Melinde, we left a very rich and beautiful Moorish city which is called Magadasio [Mogadishu]. And beyond this there is a large island with another very beautiful walled city. The island has

[1] The name Zanzibar, literally 'the region of the blacks', was applied by the Arabs to that part of the East African coast which they controlled.

[2] De Barros and de Goes say that these two convicts, João Machado and Luiz de Moura, were to go by land to the court of Prester John. Corrêa states that João Machado had been left at Mozambique by da Gama and was a convict who had killed a man in the Rocio at Lisbon. While at Mozambique he was held in great favour by the sheikh of that city and gave him much information about Portugal. He later went to Malindi and from there, dressed as a Moor, to Cambay. Later he went to Goa, where he was of assistance to the Portuguese.

[3] This information may have been obtained from the native pilots or Arabian charts. The first portion of this chapter is also included in the Venetian manuscripts Contarini A and B, of the Marciana Library.

a bridge[1] in the land which is called Zognotorre. And farther along the coast is the mouth of the strait of Mecca, which must be a league and a half wide, that is, the said strait.[2] And there within is the Red Sea, and thus the House of Mecca and Saint Catherine of Mount Sinai. And from there are carried spices and precious stones to Caiero and to Alexandria across a desert by means of dromedaries, which are a special kind of camel. And concerning this sea there are many great things to relate. And passing the mouth of the strait on the other side, is the sea of Persia, in which are great provinces and many kingdoms which belong to the Grand Sultan of Babilonia.[3] In the middle of this Persian Sea there is a small island which is called Gulfal [Julfār][4] where there are many pearls. And in the mouth of this Persian Sea is a large island which is called Agremus [Ormuz]. This belongs to the Moors, also the king who is the lord of Gulfal. And in this Agremus there are many horses which they take to all parts of India to sell and they bring a great price. And in all these lands there is great traffic of ships. And passing this Sea of Persia there is a province which is called Combaia, whose king is great and powerful. And this land is the most productive and rich in the world. In it there is much wheat and other grain and rice and wax and sugar, and here is produced all the incense of the world,[5] and many cloths of silk and of cotton. And there are many horses and elephants. The king was an idolater, and recently a Moor was crowned because of the influential Moors who are in his kingdom. And there are still many idolaters among them. These people are great merchants, who on the one hand trade with Arabia, and on the other with India, which begins where they are. And thus they go along this coast as far as the kingdom of Calichut. On this coast are great provinces and

[1] This is an error; a port is evidently meant. The island referred to may have been Socotra.

[2] The strait of Bab-el-Mandeb is twenty miles wide.

[3] Mesopotamia, then under the control of the Turks, ruled by Bayazid II. At this period Egypt was also called Babylonia.

[4] The author confuses the name of this island, whose waters were celebrated for their pearl fisheries, with Julfār, a town on the mainland.

[5] This is not strictly true. While much incense was produced here, large quantities were imported, particularly frankincense from Somaliland and Arabia. What is referred to is probably the combinations of incense materials to form powders, incense sticks, and pastels, of which enormous quantities were used in India.

kingdoms of Moors and of idolaters. And all that which is in this chapter was not seen by us.

We came in sight of India on the 22nd day of August. This was a land in the kingdom of Goga. And as soon as we recognized it we went along it until we arrived at a small island which is called Angradida [Anjediva] which belongs to a Moor. In the middle of it is a large lake of sweet water. It is uninhabited and a desert. From there to the mainland is a distance of two miles. This was once inhabited by Gentiles. And because it is on the route of the Moors of Mecca[1] to Calichut they stop there because they require water and wood. And as soon as we arrived there we cast anchor in the sea; and we went on shore and spent nearly fifteen days taking on water and wood, and watched to see whether the Meccan ships would come; we wished to capture them, if we could do so. And thus the people of the land came to speak with us, and told us of many things. Our captain ordered us to show them great honour. And on this island there is a small chapel [*armada*][2] in which, during these days when we were there, many masses were said by the clergy, whom he had to remain with the factor in Calichut. And thus we all confessed and partook of communion. And we took on the said water and wood. Since the ships of the said Moors of Mecca did not come, we departed for Calichut, which is seventy leagues distant from this island.

HOW THE CAPTAIN WENT TO THE KING OF CALICHUT

We reached Calichut the 13th day of September of the said year. And at one league from the city a fleet of boats came out to receive us. In it came the Chunal[3] of the said city and a very

[1] The Portuguese found three classes of Mohammedans when they reached India: the seafaring Arabs and Egyptians or 'Moors of Mecca' who engaged in the trade relations of the Indian Ocean, and particularly with the west coast of India; the *moplas* or *mappilas*, the native people of Malabar whose ancestors had originally belonged chiefly to the lower castes but who had been converted to the Moslem faith; and those of that faith who had come overland from the north in the last quarter of the thirteenth century. It must not be forgotten that in the year 1500 the great Sultanate of Delhi was ruled by Sikandar Lodi and that nearly all of India north of the Kistna was under Mohammedan rule. The Pepper Coast of Malabar formed but an insignificant part of the Indian peninsula and was subject to the Hindu kingdom of Vijayanagar. With the great Mohammedan states of India the Portuguese had, at first, little contact. Their relations were with the Arab merchants and the *mappilas*.

[2] A temple is evidently meant.

[3] The *Catual*, or governor, of the port.

wealthy merchant of Guzerate and the chief residents of this city of Calichut. They came on board the flagship, saying that the king was greatly pleased at our coming. And thus we cast our anchors into the sea before the city and loudly began to fire off our artillery, at which the Indians marvelled greatly, saying that no one had power against us except God. And thus we remained that night. The morning of the following day the captain determined to send the Indians ashore whom we carried from Portugal in our ships. These were five; that is, one Moor who had become a Christian among us and four Gentile fishermen,[1] all of whom spoke very good Portuguese. The aforesaid captain sent these on shore very well dressed, that they might speak with the king and that they might tell him why we came, so that he might order a safe-conduct given us so that we might go on land. This they did. The Moor spoke with the king because the others, who are fishermen, did not dare to approach the king, nor could they look upon him, because the king considers this the custom for his rank and magnanimity, as will be explained later on. The king ordered that the said safe-conduct be given and that any of us who wished might go on land. And seeing this, the captain at once sent Alfonso Furtado with an interpreter who knew how to speak Arabic. He was to tell the king that these ships belonged to the King of Portugal, who had sent them to this city to make a treaty of commerce and of good peace with them; and for this it was necessary for the captain to go on shore; that he carried instructions from our King of Portugal that no one should go on shore without having others as a hostage for his person; and that His Highness, the said King of Calichut, should send to the said ships those men of the city whom the said Alfonso Furtado had in mind.[2] The said king, having heard the said embassy, refused firmly, saying that those men whom they asked of him were very old and venerable men who could not go on the sea and that he would give him others. Alfonso Furtado told him that he could not take any except

[1] This was the Moor, Baltasar. These five had been taken to Portugal by Vasco da Gama.

[2] According to de Barros they had been selected by Monçaide, the 'Moor of Tunis', whom Vasco da Gama had brought back to Portugal (see Ravenstein, *Vasco da Gama*, p. 180).

those, because they were given in the instructions of the captain from his King of Portugal. The king marvelled greatly at this; and they continued in this difference for two or three days. Finally the king agreed to send them, and it was told to the captain at once. And the captain made ready to go on shore and to remain two or three days, and he took with him twenty or thirty of the most honourable men and those in good standing, with his officials, as was fitting for the service of a prince. And he carried all the silver which was in all of the ships. He left as chief captain in his place Sancto de Trovar, to whom he gave instructions to do honour to those men of the land who had been given as hostages for the captain. The following day the king came to a house which he had near the sea shore to receive the captain, and from there he sent the aforesaid men of the land to the ships. They were five men, very honourable, and they carried with them a hundred men with swords and bucklers. With those men were fifteen or twenty drummers. And the captain departed from the ship with his boats; he had already sent on shore all the things which he needed. And as soon as the captain had embarked, the aforesaid five men set forth from the city. These did not wish to enter the ships until the captain came on shore. And over this they were in disagreement for a long time. Thereupon Areschorea entered one of their *sambucos*, that is, a boat, and persuaded them to enter the ship, the captain already being on his way to the land. And as the captain landed, many noblemen came to receive him.[1] They carried him in their arms and all those who came with him, so that they did not set foot on the ground until in this manner they arrived at the place where the king was.

THE APPAREL OF THE KING OF CALICHUT IN HIS RESIDENCE

The king was in a high house, placed within a canopy with twenty cushions of silk tapestry. And the covering of the canopy was of cloth of silk which looked like purple. And he

[1] Those who went ashore were richly dressed with silks and jewels. Cabral himself wore an *opa*, or long flowing robe of brocade which was the fashion at that day. The Zamorin wore only a *purava*, and his body was covered with jewels (de Barros).

was nude above and below the waist. And he had around him a cloth of very fine white cotton, which was wound many times around him and worked in gold. He had on his head a cap of brocade made like a long and very high helmet, and he had his ears pierced. In them he had large pieces of gold with rubies of great price and likewise diamonds, and two pearls, very large, one round and the other pear-shaped, larger than a large filbert. And he had on his arms bracelets of gold from the elbow down, full of rich stones, with jewels and pearls of great value. And on his legs he had great riches, and on one toe of his feet he had a ring in which was a carbuncle ruby of great brilliance and value. Likewise on the fingers of his hands he had many rings full of jewels with rubies, emeralds, and diamonds. Among them was one the size of a large bean. And he had two belts of gold full of rubies belted over the cloth. And the riches which he had on him were priceless. And he had near him a large silver chair, the arms and back of which were of gold and full of stones, that is, of jewels. He had in his house a litter with which he had come from the larger house.[1] In this litter he enjoyed remaining continually, and it was carried by two men. It was rich beyond description. And he had also as many as fifteen or twenty trumpets of silver and three of gold. One of these was of such size and weight that two men had enough to do to carry it. The mouths of these three trumpets were full of rubies. And nearer to him he had four silver vases and many of gilded bronze, large candlesticks of brass, and others full of oil and small wicks. These were burning in the house, which was not necessary; he had them there for grandeur. And his father was there, standing five or six steps away, and also two of his brothers, all like himself with great riches upon them. And there were also many other honourable gentlemen who stood at a greater distance and also had great wealth upon them, in the same manner as the king. And when the captain entered he wished to go to the king to kiss his hand, but they made a sign to him that he desist, for it was not the custom among them that any one should approach the king; and thus he remained where he was. The king made him sit

[1] The French translation of 1508 reads, 'In his house he had a bed which was made like those which are below the large beds of this country.'

down, to do him honour. And he began to give his embassy. He read the letter of the King of Portugal which was written in the Arabic language,[1] and immediately he sent to his house for the present of the things which we shall mention below.

THE PRESENT WHICH WAS GIVEN TO THE KING, WITH THE DISORDER WHICH FOLLOWED

To begin with, a basin of silver for washing the hands, made with figures in relief, all gilded and very large; a dish of gilded silver with its lid similarly worked, with figures in relief; two silver maces with silver chains for the mace bearers, and four large cushions, that is, two of brocade, and two of crimson, and a large carpet and two fine tapestries, very rich, one with figures and the other with foliage, and also a bronze vessel for washing the hands of the same work as the basin. And when the king had received this present and the letter and the embassy, he showed great pleasure. And he told the captain that he should send for the men whom he had put in his hands as hostages, for they were gentlemen and could not eat, drink, or sleep on the sea, and that if for any reason he wished to return to the ships, that the next day he would return them to him, and that he could come on shore to do all that he might find necessary. The captain withdrew to his ship and left Alfonso Furtado with seven or eight men with him to wait at his house. When the captain left the shore a *zambuco* with men of Calichut went ahead of him to the ship to inform those who were hostages that the captain was returning thither. And straightway they threw themselves into the sea. Areschorea, the chief factor, quickly entered a boat and took two of the honourable men and two or three servants; and the others escaped by swimming to shore. And at this moment the captain reached the ship and ordered the two worthies put below deck. And then he sent word to the king that upon his arrival he had found this annoyance, which one of his clerks had brought about; that he had thereupon ordered the two worthies to be retained because many of his own men were on shore as well as much property, and that His Serenity should send these to him; and that he would send his men in return,

[1] A translation of this letter is given on pp. 187–90.

whom he was treating very well. With this embassy there went to the king two of those men who had been taken with the ambassadors. And all that night the captain awaited the reply. And the next day the king came to the seashore with more than ten or twelve thousand men, and our people who were on land were seized for the purpose of sending them in his *almache* to make an exchange for those whom the captain had held; and while matters were thus, twenty or thirty *almache* came, and our boats set out with the aforesaid men who were hostages. And the *almache* did not have the courage to come alongside our boats, nor ours to their *almache*. And thus that entire day was spent without doing anything. And when they returned to land with our men they began to show them great discourtesy, frightening them by saying that they wished to kill them. That night our men were in great tribulation. The following day the king again sent word to the captain that he was sending him his men and his goods with the *almache* without carrying any arms and that he should thus send his boats. He immediately ordered it, and with them Sancto de Tovar, his captain, who reached the place where the *almache* were, and they began to receive all the silver and all the other things which they had on land; so that nothing remained but one *almofresse*, that is, a sack containing a bed and its furnishings. And while nearly all the men were thus, one of those gentlemen, who was in our boats which Sancto de Tovar had, took it in his arm and threw it into the sea; and when our men who were in the *almache* saw this they became so indignant and angry that they threw all the men of the *almache* into the sea, and there only remained in the *almache* and in our boats one old man, who was one of the principal men and a hostage of ours, and two boys of our number remained in the *almache*, for they could not escape. And the next day the captain, taking pity on the old man who was a hostage and who had had no food for three days, sent him ashore and gave him all the arms which had remained in the ships belonging to those who had thrown themselves into the sea, and he sent to ask the king to return these two youths. The king sent them. After two or three days passed in this manner and no one went to land or from land to us, the captain and the others conferred. The chief factor said that if the King of

Calichut would send two men for security he himself would go ashore. The captain and the others were satisfied with what the factor had said, but it was not known whether there was any one who dared to go on shore; and immediately a cavalier named Francescho Chorea said that he would go on land to talk with the king, and this he did. He told him how Areschorea was preparing to come on shore to make a treaty with his serenity and that he should send them two merchants as hostages, one of them a very rich merchant from Guzerat. The aforesaid Moor, called a Guzerate, replied to the king that he would send him two of his nephews, whereat the king was very content. The following day Francescho Chorea sent the reply to the captain, and Areschorea quickly made himself ready; and the king sent the hostages to the ship, and Areschorea went ashore; and in his company eight or ten men. And late that day Areschorea returned to the ship to sleep. And the following day he returned to shore to carry out all that had been agreed on. The hostages, however, remained on the ship. The king ordered him to be given the best house, which belonged to a Guzerate merchant, and gave this merchant the task of teaching the factor the customs and manners of the country. And thus Areschorea began to negotiate and carry on trade. The language which our men spoke was Arabic, so that no one could converse with the king except through Moors as intermediaries. These are bad people and were much opposed to us, so that they were at all times deceitful and prevented us from sending anyone to the ships. And when the captain saw that every day we were sending men to shore and that no one was returning with reply, he determined to leave and ordered sails set. We were thus captive on shore in a house well guarded by many people. We saw that the ships were leaving. The Guzerate, for consideration of his nephews, who were on the ship, told Areschorea that he should send a youth in an *almache* to the ships. This youth was conducted to the captain, and the captain, heeding the protest of Areschorea, returned to port, and thus Areschorea began to deal with the aforesaid king; and he drew up the treaty, obtaining little by little what he wished. And since this Guzerate urged this on account of his men who were given as hostages on the ships, the king charged a Turk, an important merchant, to attend to our affairs, and quickly he had us leave that house for another, nearer the house of the said Moor, and soon we began to see some of our merchandise, of which we bought part.[1]

And we remained thus for two months and a half until the aforesaid treaty was finally completed and agreed to. This was accomplished with much effort on the part of Areschorea and those who were with him. When the treaty was completed, which was done by much bargaining, the aforesaid king gave him a house near the sea which had a garden. In the said house Areschorea set up a banner with the arms of the king.[2] And as for the treaty, the said king gave him two letters signed in his hand, one of which was of copper with his signature engraved in brass.[3] This was to remain in the house of the factor, and the other one of silver with its signature engraved in gold, which we were to carry with us to our King of Portugal. When these letters were finished, Areschorea went immediately to the ship and delivered this letter of silver to the captain, and took ashore the men who were on board as hostages. And from that day on they began to show confidence in us so that it seemed as though we were in our own land. And one day, while things were thus, a ship came there which was going from one kingdom to another. That ship was carrying five elephants; among them was a very large one of great price because it was trained for war.[4] The ship which carried it was very large and had many well-armed people. And when the king learned of the coming of the

[1] 'And because these houses belonged to a Guzerati Moor who immediately began to show little truth to us, Aires Correa asked others of the king, who then ordered us given better ones and nearer the shore. These belonged to a Moor, named Cojebequij, who was one of the richest men of that city, and was furthermore like our people, and a very good friend and servant of the Portuguese. He later destroyed the King of Calechut and took his property, which was worth more than 800,000 cruzados. When a boy I later saw this Cojebequij. He came to this kingdom, where he came to ask satisfaction for his losses from the King, Dom Manuel, and he asked favours of him, which he gave him, and he gave him honourable offices in India, with which he returned to his land.' (De Goes.)

[2] This flag of Portugal was the first raised in India on land belonging to the Portuguese.

[3] The Zamorin's signature consists of the Malayālam letter Zal: a facsimile of this is given in Juromenha's edition of Camoen's works. On the use of silver and gold plates for writing documents, see A. C. Burnell, *Elements of South Indian Palaeography*, 2nd ed., 1870, pp. 90, 93.

[4] Regarding the elephants of South India see Sir James Tennant, *Ceylon*, vol. ii, pp. 271–404.

aforesaid ship, he sent to tell the captain that he begged him to capture that ship which was carrying the elephant; he said he had offered much money for it, but they did not want to give it up.[1] The captain sent word that he would do so, but that he would have to kill if they did not wish to surrender. The king was content with this and sent a Moor with them to see how he took the ship and to tell them what was intended. At once the captain sent a caravel with a large bombard and well armed, with sixty or seventy men.[2] They pursued the ship for two nights without being able to capture it. The next day they caught up with it and asked them if they wished to surrender. The Moors began to laugh because they were numerous, and their ship was very large, and they began to shoot arrows. And when the captain of the caravel saw this, he ordered the artillery fired so that they struck the said ship, and it surrendered at once. Thus they took it to Calichut with all its people. The king came forth to the shore to see it. And the captain of the caravel went at once to deliver the ship's captain and likewise the ship to the king. The king marvelled greatly that so small a caravel and with so few people could take so large a ship in which were three hundred men at arms. The king received the ship and the elephants with great pleasure and solace, and the caravel returned to the ships.

CUSTOMS AND MANNERS OF CALICHUT

The city is large and has no wall around it, and in certain places of the land there are many empty spaces and the houses are distant one from the other. They are of stone and lime and carved within. On top they are covered with palms, and the doors are large and well worked, and around the houses there is a wall within which they have many trees and lakes of water in which they bathe and wells of water from which they drink.

[1] 'And he learned that a ship had left Cochij, a city twenty leagues distant, which had come from Ceilão. This carried seven elephants, which were carried as merchandise to the King of Cambaya. They belonged to two merchants of Cochij named Mammale Mercar and Cherina Mercar' (de Barros). De Barros continues, saying that the Zamorin informed Cabral that the ship belonged to the Moors, that it came from Ceylon with two ship-loads of spices, and that ginger was to be loaded at Cananore. Cabral was to have all of these spices if he captured the war elephant for the Zamorin. When the ship was captured, however, no spices were found. All that Cabral received for his trouble was one of the elephants which had been killed, and this was eaten by the crew.

[2] This was the caravel of Pedro de Ataíde.

And throughout the city there are other large lakes of water to which the people go frequently to bathe, and this because every day they bathe their entire bodies two, three, or four times. The king is an idolater, although others have believed that they are Christians.[1] These have not learned so much about their customs as we who have had considerable trade relations in Calichut. This king they call Gnaffer. Almost all his nobles and the people who serve him are men dark as Moors. And they are well-built men, and go nude above and below the waist. They wear fine white clothes of cotton and of other colours girded around them. They go barefoot, without caps, save the great lords, who wear caps of velvet and brocade, some of which are very high. Their ears are pierced, with many jewels in the openings. They wear gold bracelets on their arms. These nobles carry sword and buckler in their hands, and the swords are bare and wider at the point than elsewhere. Their bucklers are round like the *rotelle* of Italy. These are black and red. Thus they are the greatest jugglers with sword and buckler in the world, and have no other occupation. There are at the court numberless people who do these things. They marry one wife or five or six women, and those who are their best friends gratify them by sleeping with their wives, so that among them there is neither chastity nor shame. And when the girls are eight years old they begin to secure gain by this means. These women go nude almost like the men and wear great riches. They have their hair marvellously arranged and are very beautiful, and they entreat the men to deprive them of their virginity, for as long as they are virgins they cannot procure a husband. These people eat twice a day. They do not eat bread, nor do they drink wine or eat meat or fish, but only rice, butter, milk, sugar, or fruits. Before they eat they wash, and if, after they have washed, any one who has not washed touches them they do not eat until they have again washed, so that in this they make great ceremony. All day long both men and women go about eating a leaf which is called *betella*, which makes the mouth red and the teeth black, and those who do not do this are men of low degree. When some one dies, because they must wear black, they polish their teeth and do

[1] Those of da Gama's fleet.

not eat it for several months. The king has two wives, and each one of them is attended by ten priests and each one of them sleeps with her carnally to honour the king, and for this reason the sons do not inherit the kingdom, but only the nephews, sons of the sister of the king. And, moreover, there dwell in the house a thousand or fifteen hundred women, to give greater magnificence to the state. These have no other duty save to clean and sprinkle the house before the said king wherever he wishes to go, and they sprinkle with water mixed with cow's dung. The houses of the said king are very large, and in these houses there are many fountains of water in which the king bathes. And when the king goes forth he goes in a very rich litter [*choridore*].[1] Two men carry this, and thus they go with many players of instruments and many gentlemen with swords and bucklers, and many archers and guards before him, and porters and a canopy above him. Thus they do him more honour than any other king in the world, because no one dares to approach within three or four paces of him. And when they give him anything they give it to him on a branch, for they must not touch him. And thus when they speak to him they speak with the head lowered and the hand before the mouth, and no gentleman appears before him without sword and shield. And when they do reverence they place the hand above the head as one who gives thanks to Our Lord, and no official or

[1] Castanheda gives the following description of an *andor* when telling of the meeting of Vasco da Gama with the Kotwal of Calicut.

'And after he was received he was taken in an *andor*, which the King of Calicut sent him, in which to come, because in that land it is not the custom to go on horseback. And they go in these *andores*, which are like travelling beds [*leytos dandas*], except that they are uncovered and almost flat. When these are to be used they are carried on the shoulders of four men, as for state, and this is because they have no animals in the land, because in other parts where there are animals they are not carried by men. And they also post with them if the kings or lords go on a long journey and if they wish to go in a very short time. They can go seated or reclining according to their wish, and they are covered with umbrellas which are also carried by men who are called *boys*, and are thus protected from the sun and rain. There are also other *andores* which have an arched cane above, which two men can carry because they are very light.' (Castanheda, bk. i, ch. xvi.)

The latter type are described by Corrêa. 'These [*andores*] consist of great canes which are bent overhead and arched, and from these are hung certain cloths a half-fathom wide and a fathom and a half long. And at the ends are pieces of wood to bear the cloth which hangs from the cane; and laid over the cloth there is a great mattress of the same size, and this is all made of silk stuff wrought with gold thread, and with many decorations and fringes and tassels; whilst the ends of the cane are mounted with silver, all very gorgeous and rich, like the lords who so travel.' (*Lendas da India*, i, p. 102.)

man of low quality may see the king or speak with him, and especially fishermen. If a gentleman goes along a street and two fishermen should come towards him along the said way, the said fishermen either flee or receive many blows. When the king dies, these gentlemen and his wives burn the king with sandalwood to honour him (the people of low rank bury), and they sprinkle their heads and shoulders with ashes. They wear their beards full. They are great story tellers and writers. They write on a palm leaf with an iron pen without ink.[1] And regarding the other class of men: there are great merchants who are called Guzerates who are from a province which is called Combaia.[2] These and the natives are idolaters and adore the sun and the moon and cows, and should any one kill a cow, he is killed for it. These Guzerate merchants eat nothing which receives death, nor do they eat bread or drink wine, and if some youth should eat meat in error they send him out to seek the will of God on this earth, even though he be of the highest descent and a son of a great lord or merchant. These believe in enchantments and diviners. They are whiter men than the natives of Calichut. They wear their hair very long and also their beards. They go clothed in cloth of fine cotton; they wear veils and their hair wrapped about as the women do, and they wear sandals. They woo and marry one woman as we do. They are very jealous and hold to their wives, who are very beautiful and chaste. They are merchants of cloth and of adornments and of jewels.

CONCERNING THE MERCHANTS AND THE VOYAGE OF SPICES TO CAIRO AND ALEXANDRIA

There are other merchants who are called Zetieties[3] and they are from another province. They are idolaters, and great merchants of jewels and of pearls and of gold and silver. They

[1] For the method of writing on the leaves of the talpot palm and the formation of their book, see Tennant (op. cit., pp. 512–13).

[2] The Guzerat merchants, having their head-quarters in Cambay, had many branches and factories, and their shipping and trade relations extended throughout the Indian Ocean from East Africa to Indo-China. The trade with Malacca was extensive, and many Guzerat merchants resided there. It has been estimated that between three thousand and four thousand voyaged to Malacca for trade each year, particularly after the Chinese junks came less frequently to Indian ports.

[3] These were the Chettys, a Tamil commercial caste in south India. Since they came from the Coromandel coast they were considered foreigners.

are blacker men. They go nude and wear small head-dresses, and under the head-dress they wear hair like the tail of an ox or a horse. These people are the greatest enchanters that there are in the world, for every day they talk with the devil invisibly. The wives of these men are very corrupt in wantonness, like the natives of the land. In this city there are Moors from Mecca and from Turkey and Babylonia[1] and Persia and from many other provinces. They are great merchants and rich men, and they have all the merchandise which comes to this city of Calichut, that is, jewels of many sorts and very rich things: musk, amber, benzoin, incense, aloe-wood, rhubarb, porcelain, cloves, cinnamon, brazil-wood, sandal-wood, lac, nutmegs, mace. All of these come from a distance, save ginger, pepper, tamarind, myrobalan, and cassia-fistula and also wild cinnamon, which all grow in the land of Calichut. These Moors are so powerful and rich that they command all the land of Calichut, and in the mountains of this kingdom there is a very great and powerful king who is called Naremega [Narasimha], and they are idolaters. The king has two or three hundred wives. The day he dies they burn him and all of his wives with him. And this custom prevails for nearly all the others who are married when they die. A ditch is made in which they burn him, and then his wife, dressed as richly as possible, attended by all her relatives, with many instruments and festivity, is led to the trench, and she goes dancing backwards. The trench has a fire burning in it and into this she lets herself fall. Her relatives are provided and ready with pots of oil and butter, and as soon as she has fallen into it they throw the said pots over her so that she may burn more quickly.

In this kingdom there are many horses and elephants because they wage war, and they have them so taught and trained that the only thing which they lack is speech, and they understand everything like human beings. And this we ourselves have seen in Calichut. The elephants which the king has, on which he rides, are the strongest and most ferocious animals in the world, for two of them draw a ship to land. The ships of this land navigate only from October or November until the end of March. Their summer is in these months, and the other months

[1] i.e. Egypt.

are winter, and in them they do not navigate their ships and they keep them on land. In the month of November the ships of Mecca leave Calichut with the spices and carry them to Vida [Jidda],[1] which is the port of Mecca. And from there they carry them to Cairo overland and to Alexandria.

THE GREAT SLAUGHTER OF THE MOORS AND CHRISTIANS IN CALICHUT

After we had been in the land about three months and the treaty had been signed and two of our ships loaded with spices, the captain one day sent on shore to tell the king that he had been in his land for three months and had loaded only two ships, and that the Moors were concealing the merchandise from them and the ships of Mecca were secretly loading and were thus departing, and that the said captain would be greatly obliged to him if he would have this attended to with dispatch, because the time of his departure was already approaching. The king replied to him that he would be given all the merchandise he wished, and that no Moorish ship would be allowed to load until our ships were loaded, and if any Moorish ship should leave that the captain might take it to see whether the ship had any merchandise, and that he would have it given to them at the price which the said Moors had paid for it.

On the 16th day of December of the said year, as Areschorea was settling accounts with two factors[2] and writers[3] of two of our ships which were already loaded for departure, a Moorish ship left with much merchandise. The captain took it, and the captain of that Moorish ship,[4] and the most honourable of his men among them disembarked and made great lamentation

[1] Jidda held an important position as a trade centre because as the port of Mecca, 46 miles inland, it connected with the caravan routes to the north and east. It had gradually taken away much of the Indian trade from Aden, because the ships could reach the caravan routes at Jidda and thus avoid transhipment. In 1426 more than forty ships from India and Persia were to be found at one time in the port of Jidda and in 1431 and 1432 junks were in the harbour which had come directly from China. (Heyd, *Histoire du Commerce du Levant au moyen âge*, Leipzig, 1885, vol. ii, p. 445.)

[2] Afonso Furtado and Duarte Gil Barbosa are the only other two factors whose names are given, but the latter may not at this time have been appointed a factor.

[3] One of these was probably Pedro Vaz de Caminha and the other may have been João de Sá. The former had been the writer on the flagship and the latter may have been on the ship of Simão de Miranda.

[4] De Goes states that this ship belonged to a rich Moor of Calicut named Cogecem Micide.

and uproar, so that all the Moors assembled and went to talk with the king, telling how we had on land more riches than we had carried to his kingdom, and that we were the worst robbers and thieves in the world, that as we had taken their ship in his port so would we do from that day onward, and that they were obliged to kill all and that His Highness should rob the house of the factor. The king, as a seditious man, agreed that this should be done. And we, not knowing anything of this, allowed some of our men to go on shore to do their trading throughout the city. We saw all the people come against our men, slaughtering them and wounding them; and the rest of us went to give them aid; so that on that shore we slew seven or eight of them, and they two or three of us. And we were about seventy men with swords and helmets, and they were innumerable, with lances and swords and shields and bows and arrows. And they so pressed us that it was necessary to retreat to the house; and during the retreat they wounded five or six men. And thus we closed the door with much effort, and they fought against the house even though it was surrounded by a wall as high as a man on horseback. We had seven or eight cross-bows with which we killed a mountain of people. More than three thousand of their warriors assembled. And we raised a banner so that those on the ships might send us aid. The boats drew near the shore, and from there they fired their bombards and did no damage. Then the Moors began to break down the wall of the house so that in the space of an hour they razed it entirely. They sounded trumpets and drums with great shouts and pleasure, so that it seemed as though the king were with them because we saw one of his attendants. And Areschorea saw that we had no remedy whatever, and because we had been fighting for two hours so fiercely that our men could hold out no longer, he determined that we should sally forth to the shore, breaking through them to see whether the boats might not save us. We did this. And thus the greater part of our men arrived near enough to enter the water, and the boats did not dare to approach to receive us.[1] And thus, because of little assistance,

[1] According to de Barros the Moors had made mounds of sand and pits on the shore the previous night, so that the boats from the ships would be delayed in saving the Portuguese who might escape.

Areschorea was slain and with him fifty and more men.[1] And we escaped by swimming, to the number of twenty persons, all severely wounded. Among these a son of the aforesaid Areschorea escaped; he must have been about eleven years old.[2] Thus we entered the boats, almost drowned. The captain of the said boats was Sancho de Tovar, because the chief captain was sick. And thus they took us to the ship. And when the chief captain saw this dissension and bad treatment, he ordered ten Moorish ships which were in the port to be taken, and all the people whom we found in the said ships to be killed. And thus we slew to the number of five hundred or six hundred men, and captured twenty or thirty who were hiding in the holds of the ships and also merchandise; and thus we robbed the ships and took what they had within them. One had in it three elephants which we killed and ate; and we burned all nine of the unloaded ships; and the following day our ships drew nearer to land and bombarded the city, so that we slew an endless number of people and did them much damage, and they fired from on shore with very weak bombards. And while things were thus, two ships passed at sea and went to Pandarada [Pandarani], which is five leagues from here. And the ships went towards land where there were seven other large ships, in shallow water, and loaded with many people. We could not capture them because they were in very shallow water, and the captain quickly decided that we should go to Chochino [Cochin], where we might load the ships.

HOW THE SHIPS WERE LOADED AT CUCCHINO

And we departed for Cucchino, which is thirty leagues from Calichut, and is a kingdom of itself. They are idolaters of the same language as Calichut. And thus going on our way we found two ships of Calichut loaded with rice, and we went straight to them, and the people fled to shore in their boats and we took the ships. The captain, seeing that they did not carry

[1] Paulo da Trindade, in his history of the Franciscan Order in the East (*Conquista spiritual do Oriente*, MSS. Vat. lat. 7746, 1638, ch. 64), states that three Franciscans were killed at this time, 'the first Christian martyrs in India'. He was not able, however, to ascertain their names.

[2] De Barros says that Antonio Correia, the young son of Ayres Correia, was saved by Nuno Leitão da Cunha, the captain of the *Anunciada*.

merchandise, ordered them to be burned. And we reached Cucchino the 24th day of December, and cast anchor in the mouth of a river. The captain sent on shore a poor man of the Guzerate nation who voluntarily left Calichut to come to Portugal. And he was to tell the king[1] what had happened to the rest of us in Calichut and that the captain had sent him to say that he wished to load his ships in his kingdom, and for payment he carried money and merchandise. The king replied that he was grieved that so much injury had been done him, and that he had great pleasure in our coming to his land, for he knew what good people we were, and all that we wished for would be done. The Guzerate who went ashore told the said king that there was need for some security, which was obtained by exchanging man for man, and that he might send him as hostage any one of his men, and that immediately the men of our ships would go ashore. The king at once sent two of his principal men with other merchants, and samples of merchandise and hostages, who should go to the ships and should tell the captain that he would do all that he wished. The captain immediately sent the factor[2] with four or five men ashore with orders to buy merchandise, keeping with him, however, the men who were hostages, treating them very honourably. Every day they were exchanged because the gentlemen of those parts do not eat on the sea; if by chance they did eat, they could not see their king again. And thus we were twelve or fifteen days loading the ships a distance from Cucchin, at a place called Carangallo [Cranganore]. In this place there are Christians, Jews, Moors, and infidels [*Zafaras*]. Here we found a Jewess of Seville who came by way of Cairo and Mecca, and from there two other Christians came with us; they said that they wished to go to Rome and to Jerusalem. The captain had great pleasure with these two men. When the ships were nearly loaded, there came an armada from Calichut in which there

[1] For the full name and titles of the King of Cochin see Doc. viii in *Esmeraldo de situ orbis* edited by Raphael Basto.

The woodcut by Hans Burgkmair, herewith reproduced, is supposed to be a likeness of the King of Cochin in 1505. It appears in a pamphlet entitled *Die Reyse vā Lissebone*, Antwerp, 1508, the authorship of which is attributed to Amerigo Vespucci or to Balthazar Sprenger, and also in broadside. See C. H. Coote, *The Voyage from Lisbon to India, 1505–6*, London, 1894; H. Harrisse, *Americus Vespuccius*, London, 1895; F. Schulze, *Balthasar Springes Indienfahrt*, Strassburg, 1902.

[2] Gonçalo Gil Barbosa.

THE KING OF COCHIN IN 1505
(*From "Die Reyse vá Lissebone," Antwerp, 1508*)

were from eighty to eighty-five sails, among which were twenty-five very large ones.[1] When the king had news of the arrival of this armada he sent word to the captain that if he wished to combat with them he would send him ships and men. The captain replied that it was not necessary. The said armada, because it was already night, proceeded a league and a half beyond us. At nightfall the captain ordered full sail set, taking with him the men whom he had as hostages in exchange for those who remained on land, who were seven men.[2] It appeared to the captain that he could defeat it without other help. And that night a wind did not arise; so that he could go against the armada of Calichut. The following day, which was the 10th of January 1501, we went near them and they came to us, so that we drew very near, one to the other. The captain determined to fight with them, since they were so close that we were within a bombard shot from them. Sancho de Tovar, a captain, with his ship and one small ship remained behind in such a manner that the captain saw that order could not be established among them, and decided to take his course to Portugal, since he had the wind astern. Nevertheless, the fleet from Calichut followed us all that day until one o'clock at night. And thus that night we lost them from sight. And thus the captain decided to continue to Portugal, leaving his men there with the factor on land, and taking the two men of Chochino with us. He began to cajole them, begging them to consent to eat, for now they had not eaten for three days and then they ate with great grief and sorrow, and we continued on our way.[3]

[1] Dom Manuel in his letter to the Spanish sovereigns and de Goes both give 15,000 men. De Barros says 70 ships, of which 25 were large; de Goes, 20 large ships and other small ones; Osorio, 20 large ships.

[2] Cabral left, at Cochin, Gonçalo Gil Barbosa as factor; Lourenço Moreno and Sebastião Alvares as writers; Gonçalo Madeiro of Tangiers as interpreter; and three others, probably with the addition of some convicts and servants. Castanheda omits Sebastião Alvares and says there were four convicts to serve the other three.

[3] Three letters were written to Dom Manuel by the King of Cochin, dated the 20th and 23rd of November 1513 and the 11th of December 1513 (*Cartas de Albuquerque*, vol. iii, pp. 73–4). These letters are similar, but not exactly the same, and may have been translations of the same original.

In this letter the King of Cochin complains to Dom Manuel of the acts of the Portuguese captains and of the lack of consideration which had been shown him in the loading of spices and through their relations with the Zamorin. He gives a long recital of what he has done for Portugal and the promises which had been given him. 'Senhor, I have no other friend in all the world but Your Highness, nor any in whom I may so much confide. The King of Calecut and all my relatives came against me to take the

THE KINGDOM OF CHANONON, FRIEND OF OUR SHIPS

On the 15th of January we reached a kingdom on this side of Calichut, which is called Chanonon [Cananore]. It belongs to the Caferis,[1] whose language is like that of Calichut. As we were passing by the aforesaid kingdom the king sent word to tell the captain that he was greatly displeased that he had not come to his kingdom, and he begged him to cast anchor, and said that if our ships were not loaded, he would load them. When the captain learned this, he anchored and sent a Guzerate on shore to tell the king that the ships were already loaded and that they needed only a hundred *barchara* of cinnamon, which is four hundred *chantaras*. And immediately the king sent the said cinnamon to the ships with great diligence, trusting greatly in us, and the captain sent to pay for it in so many cruzados. And then much cinnamon came to the ship and there was no place in which to put it. The king sent word to the captain that, if it were for lack of money, we should not fail to load on as much as we wished on this account, that

Portuguese who were with me, and nevertheless I did not give them up, and I guarded them the best I could; and should all the world come against me I would have need of no one but Your Highness. The first time that Pedralvares Cabral came with six ships, when he came to the port of Calecut he went on shore and confided in the King of Calecut, and they killed all the Portuguese and took what merchandise of Your Highness there was on land. After all this happened and they came to this my port, I gave them all the aid they asked for, as well in the loading of ships as in all other things. When their ships were loaded an armada from Calecut came to fight with them, and two of my writers named Ytalaca and Parangova were in the ships as hostages. And they made sail and carried them to Portugal. And thus the Portuguese remained on shore with me. The King of Calecut and all the Moors of Crangalor beyond came against me, saying that I should turn over the Portuguese whom I had in my power or they would destroy all my land, and my relatives and my friends told me that these men were strangers and were from 4,000 leagues from my land, and that they did not know them, and that I should not lose my land because of them, and that I should surrender them, and that if I did not do so that they would not aid me and would join the King of Calecut, as in fact they did, and they came against me and killed two of my uncles and a nephew, princes, very honourable people, and they destroyed my land and port. And I guarded the Portuguese who were with me the best I could and I always took them with me whenever they wished to go. Within a year the King of Calecut returned again upon me to take my land, and I with my friends and my people and with the aid of yours defeated him, and he returned to his land much dishonoured and annoyed, without hope of again coming against me. Then he joined with Narsynagus and fought with my people, principally with one named Carutyquy, a nayre, who has 20,000 nayres; and with my aid he defeated him. And until now he has always had war with him and many of his people have been killed', &c.

[1] This word is properly the Arabic Kāfir, 'an infidel, an unbeliever in Islam'. As the Arabs applied this name to the pagan negroes, the Portuguese and, later, others used it more specifically to designate the black tribes of South Africa. (See Yule and Burnell, *Hobson-Jobson.*)

we could pay him on the return voyage, for he had well learned how the King of Calichut had robbed us and what good and truthful people we were. The captain thanked him very much, and showed the messenger, that is, the ambassador, the three or four thousand cruzados which remained, and then the king sent to inquire whether he wished anything more. The captain told him no, except that His Highness might send a man to visit Portugal. The king immediately sent a gentleman who was to come to Portugal with us. And the men of Chuchino, who had remained on the ship, wrote to their king that they were going to Portugal; and the captain also wrote similarly to the factor who remained there. In this place we did not remain longer than a day; and then we left to cross the gulf of Melindc. On the last day of January, when we were in the middle of the gulf, we found a ship from Combaia which was coming from Melinde; and without inquiry it appeared that it was a ship from Mecca, and we took it. It came very richly laden and it had more than two hundred men and women on board. And when the captain learned that they were from Combaia he allowed them to continue their voyage, except for a pilot whom he took from them; and thus they left, and we went on our way.

A SHIPWRECK IN THE GULF OF MELINDI

On the 12th of February, as night came on, when all the pilots as well as all the others who had charts believed themselves near land, Sancto di Tovar, who was captain of a large ship, said that he wished to go ahead with his ship. And he ordered all the sails to be set and thus he placed himself before the others. And when it was the hour of midnight he ran ashore and the ship began to burn. And when the captain saw this, he sent aid to him, but the wind increased so much during the night that they could not get it off, as everything was unfavourable. The captain immediately sent the boats to the ship to see whether the people might come from it. The ship was already open and so situated that it could not be dislodged. The wind increased so much that the other ships were in great danger, so that it was necessary to operate them by hand. Nothing was saved from it except the people in their shirts.

The ship was of two hundred tons [*tonelli*] and laden with spices.[1] And from there we departed with the ships and passed by Melinde, where we could not enter. And thus we came to Monsabiche [Mozambique], where we took water and wood. Here we put the ships on dry land. And from there the chief captain sent Sancto di Tovar in a small caravel [*charavellina*] with a pilot to conduct them to the island of Zaffalle so that they might know about it, and we remained there to repair the ships. And from there four of us departed and went to a point where there was good fishing for *parni*. And when we left there a storm struck us which made us turn back, and one ship became separated so that we remained three ships.[2]

THE SHIPS WHICH RETURNED TO LISBON

We arrived at the Cape of Good Hope on Palm Sunday [*Pascha fiorita*],[3] and from there we had good weather, with which we made the crossing and came to the first land near Cabo Verde at Bestenicha [Beseguiche], and there we found ourselves with three small ships[4] which our King of Portugal sent to discover the new land[5] and one ship which we lost from sight when we went there.[6] That went to the mouth of the strait of Mecca and stopped at a city where they took the boat with all the people who were in it. And thus the ship came

[1] After saving those on board the ship was burned to prevent its cargo from coming into the possession of the Moors. Those of Mombasa, however, obtained some of the cannon by means of divers and took them to their city, where they were later used against the Portuguese. (De Barros.)

[2] The flagship and those of Simão de Miranda and Nuno Leitão da Cunha. According to other writers the *Anunciada*, then under the command of Nicoláu Coelho, had proceeded to Lisbon, where we know it arrived on the 23rd of June, a fact which must have been known to the author of the Anonymous Narrative. This statement shows that this author was not on the *Anunciada*, as is sometimes claimed.

[3] This was the 4th of April, since Easter in 1501 fell on the 11th of April. The determination of this date has caused some discussion, because of the effort which has been made to reconcile the departure of Cabral's fleet from the Cape of Good Hope and its encounter with Vespucci at Beseguiche. Castanheda states that they doubled the Cape of Good Hope on the 22nd of May, and de Goes, who gives the same date, says it was the day of *Spiritu Sancto* or Whit-Sunday. This in 1501 would have been the 30th of May. The letter of 1505 states that the Cape was rounded on the *Pasqua de Mayo*.

[4] Further reference to this encounter is given in the letter of Vespucci to be found in this volume.

[5] *Giongemo al capo de bona Speranza il di de Pascha fiorita: & d̄ li ne dete bō tp̄o cū loq̄le a trauersamo & uenimo a la pria terra gionte cū lo capo Verde inbestenicha: & de li ci trouauamo cū. iii. nauili: e q̄l nr̄o re di portogallo mādaua a discoprire la terra noua. . . .*

[6] That of Diogo Dias.

with only six men, most of them ill, and they had nothing to drink but water which they collected in the ship when it rained. And thus we came and arrived in this city of Lisbon at the end of July. One day later there came the ship which we lost from sight when we turned,[1] and Sancto di Tovar with the caravel which went to Zaffalle,[2] who said that Zaffalle is a small island at the mouth of a river, inhabited by Moors, and gold comes from the mountain. It comes from another people who are not Moors. And they exchange in the said island gold for other merchandise. And when Sancto di Tovar arrived at this place he found there many Moorish ships, and he took a Moor as his security for a Christian of Arabia whom he sent on shore. And there he stayed two or three days. And the Christian did not come, nor did they recover him. And thus he came away with the Moor to Portugal, leaving the Christian there. Thus from the armada which went to Calichut six ships returned; and all the others were lost.

THE WEIGHTS AND MONEY WHICH THEY USE[3]

This is the price which spices and drugs are worth in Calichut and also the method of weighing and the money.[4]

A *baar*[5] of nutmeg, weighing four *cantaras*, is worth 450 *favos*. One ducat is worth 20 *favos*.

A *baar* of cinnamon is worth 390 *favos*.

A *faracola* of dry ginger is worth 6 *favos*; 20 *faracolas* make a *bacar*.

Ginger preserved in sugar is worth 28 *favos* a *faracola*.

[1] The caravel of Pedro de Ataíde.

[2] For Sofala see notes in *The Book of Duarte Barbosa* (Hakluyt Society, London, 1918, Ser. II, vol. xliv, pp. 6 et seq.) and G. C. F. Mangham, *Portuguese East Africa* (London, 1906).

[3] This supplement to the narrative of the voyage also occurs in all of the manuscripts. It shows an exactness in weights and values which indicates that it was made by one of the commercial men in the fleet, probably by either a factor or a writer, but not necessarily by the author of the Anonymous Narrative.

[4] For information regarding these spices and drugs and their uses at this period see Garcia da Orta, *Coloquios dos Simples e Drogas da India* (English tr. by Sir Clements Markham (London, 1913), or preferably the Portuguese text with comprehensive notes in the edition of Conde de Ficalho, Lisbon, 1891–5), Yule and Burnell, *Hobson-Jobson*, Schoff, *Periplus of the Erythraean Sea*, Yule's edition of *Marco Polo*, Heyd, op. cit. ii, pp. 555 et seq., G. Watt, *The Commercial Products of India* (London, 1908), and Dames's edition of *Barbosa*, vol. ii, p. 227.

[5] *Baar, bacar,* and *barchara* are forms of the Indian *bahar*.

A *bacar* of tamarind	is worth	30 *favos.*
,, zerumbet	,,	40 ,,
,, zedoary[1]	,,	30 ,,
,, lac	,,	260 ,,
,, mace	,,	430 ,,
,, pepper	,,	360 ,,
,, long pepper	,,	400 ,,
,, preserved *sebuli* myrobalans	,,	560 ,,
,, red sandalwood	,,	80 ,,
,, brazil-wood (*verzin*)	,,	160 ,,
A *faracola* of camphor	,,	160 ,,
,, incense	,,	5 ,,
,, benzoin	,,	6 ,,
,, cassia-fistula	,,	2 ,,
A *baar* of cloves	,,	600 ,,
,, white sandalwood	,,	700 ,,
A *faracola* of aloe-wood	,,	400 ,,
,, rhubarb	,,	400 ,,
,, opium	,,	400 ,,
,, spikenard	,,	800 ,,
A *peso* of musk	,,	400 ,,
A *mitricale*[2] of amber	,,	2 ,,

(An ounce is six and one-fourth *mitricali.*)

A *baar* weighs about twenty *faracolas*, and a *faracola* twenty-four and three-fourths *aratole* of Portugal, which *aratole* are of from thirty-two to thirty-three *libre* in Venice, according to custom.

The ducat is worth twenty *favos.*

These are the prices of merchandise which are carried from here to Calichut, namely:

A *faracola* of copper	is worth	45 *favos.*
,, lead	,,	18 ,,
,, silver	,,	54 ,,
,, alum	,,	20 ,,
,, white coral	,,	1,000 ,,
,, branched coral	,,	700 ,,
,, bastard coral	,,	300 ,,

[1] Zerumbet and zedoary are different forms for the name of a drug (also known as china root): see Dames's *Barbosa*, vol. ii, p. 92.

[2] *Mitricale* is the Arabic *mithkāl.*

An *almeno* is another weight, which, in Portugal, is two *arates* and a half, and would be about three and one-eighth *libre*, a little more or less, according to Venetian usage. With this weight they weigh saffron, which is worth eighty *favos.*

MENTION OF THE PLACES WHENCE SPICES COME

Hereafter mention will be made of the places from which the spices and drugs come to Calichut.

Pepper comes from a land which is called Chorunchel [probably Cranganore]. This is 50 leagues beyond Calichut on the sea-coast.

Cinnamon comes from Zallon [Ceylon]; and cinnamon is found only in this place, 260 leagues beyond Calichut.

Cloves come from Meluza [Molucca], 740 leagues beyond Calichut.

Ginger is grown in Calichut, and some comes from Cananor to Calichut; it is 12 leagues according to this part of Portugal.

Nutmeg and mace come from Melucha [Molucca], 740 leagues farther beyond Calichut.

Musk comes from a land called Pego [Pegu], 500 leagues beyond Calichut.

Large pearls come from Armuzo [Ormuz], 700 leagues this side of Calichut.

Spikenard and myrobalans come from Combaia, 600 leagues this side of Calichut.

Cassia-fistula grows in Calichut.

Incense is obtained more than 800 leagues this side of Calichut.

Myrrh grows in Farticho [Fartak], and more than 700 leagues this side of Calichut.

Aloe-wood and rhubarb and camphor and galingal come from Chini [China] beyond Calichut 2,000 leagues.

Zerumbet grows in Calichut.

Very large cardamons come from Cananore, more than 12 leagues this side of Calichut.

Long pepper grows in Samoter [Sumatra].

Benzoin comes from Zana [Siam], 700 leagues beyond Calichut.

Tamarinds in Calichut.

Zedoary in Calichut.

Lac comes from a land called Samatore, beyond Calichut, 400 leagues.

Brazil-wood [*brazili*] comes from Tanazaar [Tenasserim], 500 leagues beyond Calichut.

Opium comes from Ade [Aden], this side of Calichut more than 700 leagues.

These are the weights and money which are used in Calichut, with the locations of spices.

FINIS

THE ACCOUNT OF PRIEST JOSEPH

WHILE the fleet was being loaded with spices at Cochin two Christian priests from the neighbouring settlement of Cranganore sent word to Cabral asking permission to be taken to Portugal so that they might go from there to Rome and Jerusalem.[1] This request was readily granted. Vasco da Gama, having mistaken some of the ceremonies of the people of Calicut for those of the Catholic Church, had reported that the people were Christians. Cabral had found none there, and both he and the religious men who accompanied the fleet were greatly gratified to find a Christian settlement at Cranganore. These Syro-Malabar Christians were the first whom the Portuguese found in India. Cabral was, therefore, very willing to let these priests return with him to Portugal; he was able to learn from them the differences between their belief and his own, and also to ascertain that the Syriac Church of Malabar claimed a common origin with that of Rome.

Priest Mathias died either on the voyage or soon after his arrival in Portugal, but his brother, Priest Joseph, reached Lisbon in safety and was well received by the king. After remaining in Portugal for six months he was sent with a companion to Rome, where he had an audience with the Pope. From Rome he went to Venice, whence he returned to India, either by way of Jerusalem or by the sea route from Lisbon, carrying greetings from the Pope.

Priest Joseph was a man prominent in the religious life of Cranganore. For many generations the Syro-Malabar Christians there had been without a bishop. It was Joseph whom they sent with two others in 1490 as their representatives to Mar Simeon, the Catholicos in Mesopotamia, to secure bishops for India.[2] He was ordained priest by

[1] De Barros says, 'so that they might pass to Rome and from there to Jerusalem and Armenia to see their Patriarch' (*Asia*, Dec. I, bk. IV, ch. viii.)

[2] The account of this journey and of the sending of bishops to India is given in a letter written in 1504 addressed by four bishops from India to their patriarch, Mar Elias. In it they tell of Cabral's voyage as follows:

'By this way thus explored, the said king (whom may God preserve in safety!) sent

the Catholicos, and then returned to Malabar. It seems probable that Priest Joseph and his brother were similarly selected to proceed to Rome and Jerusalem in the Portuguese vessels as representatives of their co-religionists, who looked to the Pope as well as to their Catholicos for inspiration. They were probably also encouraged to take this journey by the religious men of the fleet. We have no further notice of Priest Joseph, but he may have been the Syro-Malabarian parish priest of Cranganore 'who came from Portugal' in 1518.

During the long voyage to Portugal and during his stay there much information was obtained from him, and it is also possible that at his audience with Pope Alexander VI at Rome a written or printed statement was presented. At any rate, the detailed account of South-west India which was obtained from him and is here published was probably printed either in Rome or in Venice prior to 1505, since extracts were incorporated in the so-called letter of Dom Manuel to the King of Castile, which was printed at Rome in that year. With the descriptions by Varthema and in the Anonymous Narrative it contained almost all the information about India available in print during the following forty years. Joseph is, in the main, accurate. His

six other huge ships, with which they crossed the sea in half a year and came to the town of Calicut. They are people very well versed in nautical science.

'In Calicut there live many Ismaelites, who, moved by their inveterate hatred of the Christians, began to calumniate them to the pagan king saying: "These people come from the West and they are very well pleased with the city and the country. Therefore they will now return to their king as soon as possible and will come again, bringing with their ships huge armies against you, and they will press on you and take your country from you."

'The pagan king believed the words of the Ismaelites and followed their advice and went out like a madman and they killed all the said Franks whom they found in the town, seventy men and five worthy priests who accompanied them, for they are not wont to travel or to go to any place without priests.

'The others who were in the ships weighed anchor and sailed away with great sadness and bitter tears, and came to our neighbouring Christians in the town of Cochi. This town also has a pagan king, who, when he saw them in deep distress and grief, received them hospitably and consoled them and swore never to abandon them until death.'

This letter was found by Joseph Simon Assemani, the eldest of the four celebrated Maronite Orientalists of that name, during his searches in Egypt and in the Levant for manuscripts relative to the Oriental Church. He brought it to Rome, and deposited it in the Vatican Library, of which he was librarian. It was translated into Latin, edited by him, and published in 1725 in his *Bibliotheca Orientalis*, vol. iii, pt. 1, pp. 589–99. It was republished by the Rev. Georg Schurhammer, S.J., in *Gregorianum*, vol. xiv, pp. 62–86.

statements are corroborated by the Portuguese historians of the sixteenth century and by more recent investigations concerning the Syrian Church in Malabar. There are no known manuscripts of the relation. The earliest existing account was printed in *Paesi*. The introduction to the account of Priest Joseph is apparently the only portion of *Paesi* which was written by Fracanzano himself. Where he obtained his information is not known, but he states that he had never seen Priest Joseph. It was included in all subsequent editions of that book and in the translations into Latin, French, and German. It was also given in different editions of *Novus Orbis* by Grynaeus[1] and in the German translation, as well as in smaller collections. It was not printed by Ramusio in his *Navigationi e Viaggi*.

The translation has been made from the 1507 edition of *Paesi*, where it occurs at the end of the sixth and last book, which is devoted to documents relating to the Anonymous Narrative of Cabral's voyage (ch. cxxix to ch. cxlii incl.).

HOW JOSEPH THE INDIAN CAME TO PORTUGAL ON BOARD OUR CARAVELS, AND THE KING CAUSED HIM TO BE ACCOMPANIED TO ROME AND TO VENICE

The King of Portugal, having learned at other times, through his ships and other Portuguese, how to go from the northern parts to the parts of India, and taking the counsel of some of his people who had come from those parts in the past, the aforesaid King Hemanuel decided in the year 1500 to send twelve ships and caravels. The captain of these was Pedro Aliares. He, having received the standard of his captaincy on the 8th day of March of the said year, departed from Portugal. And sailing through very great storms and perils until the 13th[2] day of the month of September of the aforesaid year, he reached Calichut

[1] De Barros refers to the Latin translation in Grynaeus, where it tells of the account of Priest Joseph, as follows: 'The Italians, who in this are more curious than we are, have made a summary which is incorporated in a Latin volume entitled *Novus Orbis*, which includes some of our navigations, written not as they merit and as they happened.' (*Asia*, Dec. I, bk. v, ch. viii.)

[2] The 14th of September in the second edition.

with seven caravels.[1] Four of them had been lost in a storm and one went to Zaffal. They remained in that place of Calichut for three months, but finally, because of certain differences, they came to blows with those of the land. And after some of the men from the caravels and also many of the aforesaid place were killed, they departed on the 24th day of November of the same year and the aforesaid ships and caravels reached Cuchin, a place one hundred and ten miles distant from Calichut. That place of Cuchin is situated on the sea, and its lord is an idolatrous king who belongs to the sect of the King of Calichut.[2] The caravels above mentioned were received by the king of that place and they were made welcome. While they were in the aforesaid place, contracting various merchandise, as appears in the third book, seventy-eighth chapter of the voyage previously written,[3] there came from a city called Caranganor, about twenty miles distant from the aforesaid place of Cuchin, two Christian brothers, who boarded the caravels wishing to come to Western parts in order to be able to go to Rome and to Jerusalem. Since about eighty sails came from the region of Calichut to intercept the aforesaid caravels, these departed and together with them the said two Christians and others of the kingdom of Cuchin who had been given as hostages by agreement. Leaving on land an equal number of their own Portuguese, they took their route towards Portugal. Of those two brothers, one died on the way;[4] the other, named Joseph, lived. Later, at the end of June 1501, they arrived at Lisbon. When they had reached the aforesaid place, the aforesaid Joseph remained until the month of January. And when he departed from the said place there was given to him by the majesty of the Most Serene King, one as a companion who should accompany him to Rome, Venice, and Jerusalem. And thus, having been at Rome, he then came to Venice in the year 1502, in the month of June, and remained there for many days.

[1] A Venetian would naturally think of a Portuguese ship as a caravel. Prior to the voyage of da Gama the Portuguese had usually used caravels on their voyages and had established a justifiable reputation for them on the Atlantic. The Venetians used galleys both in the Mediterranean and in their fleet to Flanders, and square-rigged ships for heavy cargo. Their small lateen-rigged vessels were used for fishing.

[2] This was not strictly true. The Zamorin was a nair, while the King of Cochin was a brahmin.

[3] The Anonymous Narrative in *Paesi*.

[4] De Barros states that Priest Mathias reached Portugal and died there.

During that time the aforesaid Joseph gave news of the things written below.[1]

THE QUALITY OF JOSEPH, WITH HIS COUNTRY, AND THE GENTILES

Joseph, mentioned above, is a man forty years of age,[2] slender, dark by nature, and of ordinary stature. According to the judgement of those who have seen him and spoken with him he is an ingenuous man, truthful, and of the highest integrity; and in so far as could be understood by them, he is of exemplary life and may be said to be a man of very great faith. This has been learned from him; in the first place, that he is from Caranganor, which is ninety miles distant from Calichut on a certain bay called Milibar and fifteen miles distant from the sea; and as for its area, the city is said to be without walls and to be very long, a length of thirty miles, but inhabited only here and there in the manner of villas. Through that city run many rivers. Almost all the houses face the water. Two sorts of people live in the said city: namely, Christians and Gentiles [*Zentili*]. And in order that this name of Gentiles may be known to every one, those are called Gentiles, who in ancient times worshipped idols and various kinds of animals, as will be narrated later. The king of the above-mentioned city is an idolater. A small number of Jews are also found there, but they are much scorned, and a considerable number of Moors, mostly merchants, who voyage here from Cairo, Syria, Persia, and other places, to trade, for this place is the source of diverse sorts of merchandise.

THE INHABITANTS OF CARANGANOR AND THEIR CHURCHES AND SACRIFICES

The country, in so far as concerns the Gentiles, is divided into three parts: first, the gentlemen, who in their language are

[1] Fracanzano, who evidently wrote the introduction to this account, here states that he had not seen Priest Joseph. The information regarding Cabral's fleet was probably taken from the letter of Il Cretico and the Anonymous Narrative. The remarks regarding Joseph are from reports made at the time of his visit to Venice and the balance of the account seems to be from a written or more probably a printed statement not now known to exist.

[2] *Paesi* was printed five years after Joseph was in Venice. This evidently means that he was forty years of age at the time of his visit.

called *naires*; second, the farmers, who are called *canes*; third, the fishermen, who are called *nuirinan*. And this class of fishermen is the lowest, and they are molested by every one when they go through the country. And if they should meet any gentleman, it is necessary for them to flee before him; otherwise they would be ill treated. Each has separate temples. The women also have their own temples separate from the men. They offer in their temples the first-fruits of the land such as roses, figs, and other things. These Gentiles worship one single god, creator of all things, and they say that he is one and three, and in his likeness they have made a statue with three heads.[1] It stands with the hands joined and they call it *Tambran*.[2] A curtain is drawn before that statue and it is opened at the time of their sacrifices, as we shall relate here. They have various other statues of animals, but they do not worship them. And when they enter their churches some take earth and put it on their foreheads, and some take water. And they go to church three times a day, in the morning, at noon, and in the evening. They then make certain general sacrifices in this manner. They have certain of their men appointed with trumpets, horns, and tambors, who call them to church at the right hour. And after they have assembled, the priest, dressed in a certain large vestment, stands near the altar and begins to chant various prayers, and another replies to him. Then the people answer in a loud voice and this they do three times. Then out of one door goes a nude priest with a large crown of roses on his head, with large eyes, and with false horns. He carries in his hand two bare swords, and runs towards his god, and drawing the curtain entirely before it, he puts one of the swords into the hand of the priest standing at the altar. Then, with the other bare sword, he inflicts on himself many wounds, and thus, bleeding, he runs to a fire burning there in the temple and he leaps back and forth through it. Finally, with his eyes closed, he claims that he has spoken with his idol, who orders that certain things be done and instructs the people how they are to govern themselves. There are many other kinds of sacrifices which Joseph, because he did not understand the

[1] Representing Brahma, Vishnu, and Siva.

[2] See Dames's *Barbosa*, vol. i, p. 218 and note.

language and because he had not had many dealings with Gentiles, has not been able to explain entirely. Concerning their temples and religion enough has been said.

CUSTOMS OF THE KING AND THE INHABITANTS, AND WHERE THERE ARE MANY CHRISTIANS

The Gentile or idolatrous king has many wives, as do all the other Gentiles. Nor in their chastity is there modesty among them. When the king himself dies or any of the other Gentiles, their bodies are burned. The wives, in perfect possession of their faculties, voluntarily burn themselves alive eight days after the death of their husbands. And this, the aforesaid Joseph says, he has seen with his own eyes. The true sons of the king, after the death of the father, do not inherit the kingdom, but the nearest relatives other than the sons. The reason is this, that the wives of the king have this custom, they have relations with various persons, and on this account their sons are not considered worthy of the kingdom. And in the burial of their king they use the greatest ceremony. The Gentiles go dressed after this fashion: on their heads they wear a cap, that is, the king a cap of gold, and the other important men of velvet or brocade; the others go without. They are nude; they cover only their privy parts with linen cloths. They wear bracelets on their arms with various precious stones, finely worked. Likewise, they wear bracelets on their legs and rings on their toes, set with very fine precious stones. These, in their opinion, are of great price. They bathe their bodies two and three times a day, and they have many places assigned for bathing. The people, both men and women, are very handsome. They have their heads dressed in a careful manner, and on their heads they wear many jewels. When the Gentiles above mentioned write, they scratch on the leaves of trees with an iron point. Their language is the Indian, or Malanar [Malayālam]. And enough concerning this. As we have said above there are many Christians in this place of Caranganor, of whom some mention has been made in this chapter. Concerning each more will be said. And therefore it should be known to all that the Indus river is the beginning of India.

Towards the west is the Island of Ornus [Ormuz], which is at the beginning of the Persian Gulf. No other Christians are to be found except in the aforesaid place of Caranganor, but in India there are very powerful Christian kings of Caranganor like those of Cataio [Cathay]. These Christians of Caranganor are of very great number.[1] They obtain their houses at a certain price from the Gentile king, whom we have mentioned above, and they pay their rent each year, and in this manner they live there.

THEIR HOUSES AND HOW THEIR PONTIFFS GOVERN THE CHURCH

Their houses are made of board walls in different floors. Like those of the Gentiles, they are covered with boards of other kinds of wood. The temples of the Christians themselves are made like ours, except that their churches have only the cross, and on the top of the temples there is also a cross. They have no bells and when they call to worship they use the Greek rite. These aforesaid Christians in divine matters have as their head a pontiff, twelve cardinals, two patriarchs, bishops, and archbishops. The aforesaid Joseph referred to having departed with his superior, bishop of the aforesaid city of Caranganor, they boarded a ship and went towards the island of Ormus, which is 1500 miles distant from the aforesaid place of Caranganor. And from there they went by land a three months' journey. He came in company with the aforesaid bishop as far as Armenia,[2] to find his pontiff. This bishop was consecrated by him, and Priest Joseph aforesaid was ordained for mass. All the Christians of India and of Cataio do likewise. His pontiff calls himself Catolicha[3] and he has his head

[1] An estimate made in 1933 by Father Placid of the Syro-Malabar Church gives the adherents to that rite as 550,000, with Ernakulam as metropolis and Changanacherry, Trichur, and Kuttayam as suffragan sees. The Jacobites using the West Syriac Rite he estimates at 9,000. Their metropolis is Trivandrum, with Thiruvalla a suffragan see. There are also a few Nestorians at Trichur. (G. Schurhammer, *The Malabar Church and Rome*, Trichinopoly, 1934, p. v.)

[2] The Portuguese used Armenia to designate Upper Mesopotamia, where the Aramean languages were spoken. It is here used in this sense, and not the present country so named.

[3] Catholica is used elsewhere throughout the text for this office, but hereafter Catholicos will be given in the translation.

shaven in the form of a cross. He nominates his patriarchs,[1] as has been said above; that is, one in India, the other in Cataio; he sends the other bishops and archbishops, as has been said above, to their provinces as seems best to him. Of this Catholicos mention is made in Marco Polo where he treats of Armenia. In that place he says that there are two kinds of Christians, one of which is called *Jacopiti* [Jacobites], the other *Nestorni* [Nestorians]. And he says that they have a Pope who is called Jacolita, who is this Catholicos, as the above-mentioned Priest Joseph relates. He says in addition that the said Pope creates bishops, archbishops, and patriarchs, and sends them to India. There may be some who will ask what authority this Pontiff has. Our Pontiff Alexander asked Priest Joseph, when he was in Rome and speaking with His Holiness concerning the parts of India, who had given this authority to his Catholicos. And Priest Joseph replied to him that at the time of Simon Magus,[2] Saint Peter was Pontiff in Antiochia, and the Christians in the region of Rome, being molested by the art of this Simon Magus, because there was no one who could oppose him, sent to supplicate Saint Peter to allow him to be transferred to Rome. Leaving his vicar he came to Rome. And this vicar is the one who now calls himself Catholicos and he rules in the name of Saint Peter. As for the making of the said Pontiff or Catholicos, the twelve cardinals above mentioned gather in the province of Armenia, where they elect their Pontiff. The authority for this, they say, they have from the Roman Pontiff.

HOW THEY CONSECRATE AND BURY THE DEAD; FEASTS AND THEIR FESTIVALS

They have, in addition, priests, deacons, and subdeacons. The priests in truth have no tonsures, but on the tops of their heads thay have a few hairs. Children are baptized forty days after birth, if a case of necessity does not occur. They confess themselves, and take communion as we do, but they do not

[1] Patriarch is here metropolitan, archbishop.

[2] Simon Magus was a Samaritan sorcerer, whom Philip, Peter, and John convinced of the power of God. Simon attempted to buy this power, and Peter rebuked him for it. The practice of simony is named from him. He was the reputed founder of a gnostic sect.

have extreme unction. In place of this they bless the body. They have holy water at the entrance to the churches. They consecrate the Body and the Blood of Our Lord, as we do, with unleaven bread. And he says that, since they have no wine, for in those parts grapes do not grow, they take raisins, of which a very large quantity comes from Cataio, and they put them in water, and they strain it and obtain a certain juice, and with this they consecrate. They bury their dead as we do. And they have this custom, that when any one dies, many Christians assemble together and eat for eight days, and then they pray for the dead. They make wills, and in case they do not make them, their property goes to the nearest relatives. After the death of the husbands the wives are paid their dowers, and then they leave, and after a year they have the right to marry. They have four evangelists and four Gospels of the Passion. They observe Lent and Advent. On Good Friday and Holy Saturday they fast until Easter Day. They preach on the night of Good Friday. And during the year they have the feasts mentioned below: the Resurrection, with two holy days following; the Octave of Easter, on which they have a greater festival than all the others of the year, for they say that on that day Saint Thomas put his hand in the side of Christ and recognized that He was not a spirit; the feasts of Saint Thomas, of the Trinity, of the Assumption of the Blessed Virgin Mary, of the Nativity, and of the Purification, the feast of the Nativity of Our Lord, and Epiphany. They celebrate the feasts of the Apostles, and Sundays, and have two feasts the first day of July in honour of Saint Thomas, for Christians as well as Gentiles hold him in the greatest veneration. They have monks clothed in black who live in the greatest poverty and chastity, likewise nuns. The priests live in chastity, and if they are discovered in any infraction, they lose the right to say mass. The Christians cannot be divorced. All people have communion three times a year. They have most excellent doctors and students of letters. They have prophets as we do. Priest Joseph, mentioned above, says further that there are many books of learned men who have spoken concerning the Bible and the prophets. The Christians dress as Moors do, that is, in linen cloth. They have the year divided into twelve months, and they have even the intercalary day. Their day is really divided into sixty hours; they recognize these hours by day from the sun and by night from the stars.

CARANGANOR DURING THE WINTER, AND THEIR SHIPS

The people of Caranganor, mentioned above, are located between the equinoctial circle and the Tropic of Cancer, and according to what Priest Joseph told, they have thirteen and a half hours in the longest day of the year and ten hours in the shortest, speaking in terms of our hours and not theirs. When the sun is in the sign of Taurus, they have a perpendicular shadow and when in Cancer the shade is south; when the sun is in Virgo it makes a perpendicular shade, but when it is in Capricorn, the shade is north. The actual movement of the season is from the middle of May to the middle of August, and in that time they do not navigate those seas on account of the very heavy storms. In that part of India there are innumerable ships which sail to the west, to Persia, to Arabia, and to the Red Sea; to the east, to India, Cataio, Taprobana [here Sumatra], Faillan [Ceylon], and many other islands. These ships are very large. Some have twelve sails and countless sailors, and others less, according to their burden. There are some which have sails of matting; these come from the islands;[1] others have sails of cotton and of good fustian like ours. The ships are made with iron nails. This I say because there are some who say that they are fastened together with wooden pegs. And concerning this, wishing to have exact information from the aforesaid Priest Joseph, he was shown the construction of our ships. He laughed and said that theirs were like ours. The pitch is made of incense and other mixture. Formerly, on launching the ships into the water, they were accustomed to use two elephants, one at each side, and because sometimes the aforesaid elephants caused the death of their men, they no longer use this method, but have a great number of people come, who launch them. They have bombards, one kind of iron and another of wood,[2] but they are not like ours and are less powerful. And more concerning this.

[1] i. e. the Laccadive Islands.

[2] *ligno de focho.*

CONCERNING THEIR MONEY, AND THE THINGS WHICH GROW PLENTIFULLY THERE

There are three kinds of money:[1] one they call the *sarapho* of gold, which is of the weight of our ducat; the second, of silver, which they call *parante*, is worth six soldi; the third is called *tare*, three of which make one of our soldi. All of these coins have letters of their king engraved on them. In the aforesaid parts no gold or metal of any kind is found, but it is found in certain mountains near there, at a distance of about two hundred and fifty to three hundred miles. The province in which the site of Caranganor is located is entirely level, and has mountains at a distance. It has a hot climate, and every one is dark. Those who are in the mountains are white,[2] and live for a very long time, as Priest Joseph says; there are men a hundred years old who have all their teeth. The land of Caranganor is very fertile, except that it does not produce grain or horses. And the grain, in fact, comes from some islands near there. And the same conditions exist in Calichut and Combait. This is due to their sandy soil. The horses come from Ormus and from their mountains.[3] They work them only in carrying merchandise from place to place. Nor do they use them in fighting; they fight on foot. Their weapons are bows and arrows, swords and bucklers like *rodelle*;[4] they have lances and they are great sword jugglers. There are some who make armour for themselves from the back of the skins of certain fish, which are very hard, and some make them of iron. They have many kinds of animals. oxen, cows, horses, buffaloes, sheep, and many other kinds, all of which they eat for food except the oxen, which the Gentiles worship. They have elephants in very great numbers; they have small animals such as hens and geese in very large numbers. They have no pigs. And because we wanted particularly to know the value of some things, Priest Joseph was shown hens and a ducat. He replied that a hundred hens could be had for a ducat.

[1] For a discussion of the values of these coins see articles 'Pardao', 'Xerafine', and 'Tara or Tare' in Yule and Burnell, *Hobson-Jobson*. The *serapho* here mentioned seems to be the Egyptian gold seraphin or *dinar* equivalent to the Hindu *pardao*, a gold ducat worth about 11*s*. 6*d*. The *tare* was a very small silver coin. The relative values between the *tare* and the gold seraphin given here do not agree with those of other authors.

[2] For a description of these hill tribes see Logan (*Malabar*).

[3] i. e. Persia.

[4] i. e. small round shields.

RICE BREAD, AND PALMS WHICH PRODUCE INDIA NUTS

This province produces a very large quantity of rice and likewise of sugar. This rice they use ground, grinding it with sugar and oil. And it makes the most perfect bread, and they eat this instead of [our] bread. They also have twenty kinds of herbs, and all are nutritious. These they eat, and especially some roots of herbs. They have no rosemary or boxwood, likewise no peaches or apples, or vines, because all the aforesaid things were shown to the said Joseph, who said that trees of that sort did not exist in his region. But they have countless others and especially fig trees, of which they have a very large number, and these have larger figs than ours, so much so that whatever might be written about them would seem a thing incredible rather than otherwise. They have another tree which they call palm. The tree, in our manner, produces the India nuts and, as we have understood from the aforesaid Priest Joseph, from this are obtained four things: namely, wine, vinegar, sugar, and oil. And because it would seem a strange thing to many how so many things come from one tree, I do not wish to pass over in this chapter the text of Strabo, in book sixteen, where he speaks concerning the palm, and which is similar to what Priest Joseph says. Later it will be related what methods they use in making the aforesaid things. But the chapter begins thus: 'Other things are furnished by the palm, for from it bread and honey and wine and vinegar are made and various textiles. Blacksmiths use the pith instead of charcoal; steeped in water, it is given to oxen and sheep for fodder.'[1]

HOW THEY MAKE WINE, VINEGAR, SUGAR, AND OIL FROM THE PALM

The making of the four things above mentioned is in this manner. The aforesaid person says that in the month of August those inhabitants go and cut the branches of the said palms, as

[1] The palm is of value in other ways. The fibre of the nut or *coir* is now used for making brushes, mats, carpets, &c., the dried leaves for thatching roofs on huts. The trees are valuable for shade. Having no lower branches the ground between them may be used for the cultivation of some crops. The fruit, moreover, produces almost continuously. A single tree may produce from eighty to one hundred nuts a year.

is done among us when we trim the vines, for this season is judged to be spring among them, because the trees are in sap and sprout like the vines with us. When these branches are cut from the trees they produce a certain white liquid. They put vessels under them and collect it. For the first three days after the aforesaid liquid is gathered, it is as wine to him who drinks of it; after the three days are passed, it changes to vinegar. In case they wish to make sugar or honey or boiled wine in our fashion, they take that liquid of the first three days and put it over the fire in some vessels, and by means of the fire, the water is reduced to a small quantity and becomes sweet, as has been said above, by force of fire.[1] And over it they put the water and mix it every day for twenty days; then they put it through a strainer and use it instead of wine. According to their report, it is of the greatest excellence. Of the fruit of the aforesaid tree, called palm, they use the inside of the nut to make oil. And thus the four things are clearly explained. And, furthermore, of the wood they make charcoal, and of the bark, ropes and baskets. In conclusion it is the most perfect tree that is found, to our knowledge. In that region there grows a very large quantity of pepper, which dries because of the great heat of the sun. And its trees are of mediocre quality. And more grows in that place than in all the other parts of India; likewise ginger, myrobalans, cassia, and other spices, which are bought and marketed by Moors who barter in that region. These carry them to Cairo and to Alexandria and to Damascus and to Persia, and even, as the aforesaid Priest Joseph says, a greater quantity thereof goes beyond the mountains and to Cataio than comes to our regions, as we shall presently relate. Since we have told about the city of Caranganor, its customs, religion, and manners, and its fertility, we shall now return to the city of Calichut.

CONCERNING CALICHUT AND ITS KING, WITH HIS USAGES AND MERCHANDISE

The city of Calichut is located ninety miles westward[2] from Caranganor on the shore of the sea, and has there a most per-

[1] Palm sugar or *jaggeri*.

[2] This indicates the current belief based on Ptolemy, that India extended east and west and was not a peninsula. This continued to be shown on many European maps

fect harbour. That city is larger than Caranganor, and its lord is an idolater of the same sect as the lord of Caranganor, who does not differ in anything from the customs of the aforesaid king. Because we have said enough above both concerning his religion and everything else, we shall not go into further detail. In this city a countless number of Moorish merchants trade. They deal in coral, *zanbeloti*, carpets, and other merchandise. There are also some merchants who are called *Guzerati*, who also trade in various commodities. In this city almost all of India comes together, and this was even more so formerly when those from Cataio used to trade there. These people from Cataio are Christians, and they are as white as we are, and they are very valiant men. About eighty or ninety years ago they had a factory in Calichut, and because the king of that place committed outrages against them they rebelled, and having gathered a very large armada, they came to the city of Calichut, which they destroyed. From that time up until the present, they have not come to trade in the aforesaid place, but have gone to a city of a King Narsindo, which is called Mailapet [Malacca],[1] about nine hundred miles towards the east by way of the Indus [Ganges] river. These people are called Malasines [Chinese]. They carry varied merchandise; that is, cloth of silk of five sorts, copper, lead, tin, porcelain, and musk; and these are the ones who take the coral, and a good quantity of spices. It is said to be six thousand miles from Calichut to their region. They wear on their heads fezzes of great value, and they are very rich merchants. To return to the city of Calichut: the king of the aforesaid city is named Baufer. He has a large palace in which he keeps seven thousand men for the safety of his person. By night he makes the guards go around among the houses because the city is not walled, and three hundred men are assigned to this guard. In addition, he has a very large palace in which he has four separate audience chambers: one for

during the sixteenth century, although it is given more correctly on the map of Diogo Ribeiro in 1529. The Hindu navigators had a more accurate knowledge of its true shape. This is indicated in the use of the *kamal*, the knots of which were so arranged as to show the location of the principal ports on either coast by their latitude.

[1] The information is here somewhat confused. Malacca, inhabited by Chinese, Malays, and Hindus, is evidently meant instead of Mailapur, then under the rule of King Narasimha of Vijayanagar. Mailapur also is confused with Negapatam, to which Chinese junks occasionally came at this period.

Gentiles, one for Moors, one for Jews, and one for Christians. And when it happens that any one of these four nations wishes an audience, he goes to the place assigned to him, and there they are heard by the king. But first they are obliged to wash themselves, for otherwise the king would not speak to them. Besides, the said Gentiles have a custom, that when they go upon the sea, they do not eat under any circumstance, for if they do, they would be deprived of ever again seeing their king. We shall not take time to relate again what we have said above, that the women, after the death of their husbands, according to custom, are burned alive. And because one might marvel thereat it is not a strange thing, for the Indians have always had this custom not only among the women but also the men. They seem in this manner to attain certain immortality, as Strabo says in the fifteenth book when he treats of the legates or ambassadors of India sent from Porro, the king of that country, to Caesar Augustus. The same thing is related by Nicholaus Damascenus of Antioch, &c. Furthermore, in the city of Calichut, above named, much merchandise is handled, as I have said above, and at certain times of the year certain fairs are held to which all the people of Cataio, India, Persia, and Syria come. And upon our asking Priest Joseph whether any mention of our regions is made in that place, he said that none are mentioned except Rome and France and Venice. And he reports that the money of Venice is very highly esteemed. The said Priest Joseph, having been ordered to appear before our Most Illustrious Signoria, showed some ducats of the Doge of the House of Sten,[1] which he had brought from those regions.

CONCERNING THE KINGDOM OF CAMBAIA, ORMUS, AND GUZERAT

Now that we have spoken concerning Calichut, we shall go towards the west to the kingdom of Combait, which is twelve thousand miles[2] distant from Calichut. And from Combait it is three hundred miles straight towards the west to the island of Ormus. It is located at the beginning of the Persian Gulf and twenty miles away from the mainland which is called the cape

[1] Michele Steno, Venetian Doge 1400–14.
[2] This is evidently a misprint in the text for twelve hundred miles.

of Mogolistam which is the beginning of the gulf. This island is one hundred and fifty miles around. Its lord is a Mohammedan. And it has a great city, very populous. And it produces countless things and merchandise. In this place glass like ours is made; pearls are gathered; horses are produced in large numbers. These they then take throughout India to carry the merchandise.[1] Between this cape of Mogolistam, which is opposite the island of Ormus, and the city of Combait, there are found many lands inhabited by Moors: the first is named Sobelch, the second Semanaht, the third Chesimii. Then inland is the city of Guzerat and on the shore of the sea is located Combait, which is, as we have already said, three hundred miles from the Cape of Mogolistam. This city of Combait is deeply engulfed. And the gulf on which the city is situated is called the gulf of Guzerat. And the province is now called Guzerat, but in ancient times it was called Bedrosia. And because in this place we have made mention of Guzerat, we shall explain concerning its conditions. This province has many cities and castles. They are a powerful people and great merchants. They are idolaters; they worship the sun and the moon and cows, and if any should kill a cow he would be killed for this. They do not eat anything which meets death. They do not drink wine. The men are whiter than the natives of Calichut. They are the greatest conjurers in the world. They wear their hair well oiled, and they have beards, and they arrange their hair as the women do. They take only one wife and they are very chaste. Their food is vegetables and herbs which the land produces, in accordance with the ideals of Pythagoras. We have spoken of Guzerat. Now we shall tell of the city of Cambaia.

THE SITE OF CAMBAIA, AND OTHER PLACES,[2] ALSO OF THE KING, AND ITS SPICES

The city of Cambaia is located in the Gulf of Guzerat. It is very large and very populous, and according to common opinion, it is the noblest city in all India. They call it the Cairo

[1] The island of Hormuz is 12 miles in circumference. There is no water except that which is stored from the rains, and therefore little vegetation. Horses were raised in Persia and shipped to India because of the scarcity of feed there.

[2] There were many ports on the western coast of India at this time which were important in trade. This was due to many causes; first, because of the division of territory

of India. It is walled and has very imposing dwellings within its walls. Formerly its lord was a Gentile and idolater; at present he is a Mohammedan. This is the reason: when the number of Mohammedans increased more than that of the Gentiles, the Mohammedans took over the government of the province, which is almost entirely of Gentiles, as also the land. In this place grows lac, and incense in greater abundance than in any other part of the world. They are very great merchants and have a considerable number of ships with which they sail to Ethiopia, to the Red Sea, the Persian strait, and India. From this city of Cambaia to the cape of the gulf which is called Diongul, it is three hundred miles. In this gulf are found many cities which it would require a long time to describe. Near this cape of Diongul is found an island called Maya, and from this cape of Diongul towards the east is found a cape called Ely, the two being two hundred and fifty miles distant from one another. And from there to Calichut it is more than six hundred miles.

CONCERNING KING NARSINDO[1] AND A CHURCH OF SAINT THOMAS

Up to this point we have told about all the country which is found along the sea, beginning at Ormus, as far as Caranganor and the kingdom of Cuchin. We shall now tell about the regions inland. Towards the mountains and about three hundred miles distant from the sea is to be found a very powerful king, who is named King Narsindo, and he has a great city with three circuits of walls. It is called Besenegal [Bisnagar].[2] This king, as Priest

between a large number of small sovereigns each of whom wished to take part in the general trade and, second, because of the bitter rivalry between the indigenous merchants and the Arab colonies. Furthermore, each province had its speciality of certain natural products, all of which were much sought for in commerce. At the north the chief products were the embroideries and woven goods which were shipped through the port of Cambay to nearly the whole Mussulman world; in the centre the province of Canara exported its famous rice and sugar; at the south, Malabar offered two much sought products, pepper and ginger; finally, from Ceylon came cinnamon. (Heyd, op. cit., vol. ii, pp. 497–8.)

[1] Narasimha Saluva and his son, Immadi Narasimha, were the rulers of the kingdom of Vijayanagar from 1486 to 1505. Because of their energetic rule the name Narsinga was used by the Portuguese not only to designate the ruler, but often the kingdom itself. See Robert Sewell, *A Forgotten Empire* (London, 1900); B. A. Saletore, *Social and Political Life in the Vijayanagara Empire*, 2 vols. (Madras, 1934); H. Krishna Sastri, *Annual Reports of the Archaeological Survey of India*, 1907–12; D. Lopes, *Chronica dos Reis de Bisnaga* (Lisbon, 1897).

[2] Another name used by the Portuguese for Vijayanagar.

Joseph told, he has seen with his own eyes. When he goes with an army against his enemies, he takes with him eight hundred elephants, four thousand horses, and innumerable foot soldiers, and he says that his camp from south to north is thirty miles long, and from west to east, of equal breadth. Consequently it may be supposed that his kingdom is very extensive, and furthermore, according to what Priest Joseph says, it is three thousand miles around. Its faith is idolatrous. Now we return to the regions next to the sea, and first begin from Cuchin towards the east and India. A hundred miles eastward from Cuchin is found a cape which is called Cumari [Comorin]. From this Cape of Cumari to the Indus [Ganges] river is a distance of five hundred miles. Within this space there is a huge gulf which is called the Gulf of Oriza [Orissa]. And there is a large city named Oriza near which the Indus [Ganges] river flows. On this same gulf is located a city on a promontory extending into the sea; it is called Milapar [Mailapur]. In that city is a church of Saint Thomas as large as that of Saint John and Saint Paul in Venice. In it is placed the body of Saint Thomas. There many miracles are performed, and Gentiles and Christians hold it in the greatest reverence. There are to be found above in this Indian Sea many islands, among which two are worthy of mention. The first is Saylam [Ceylon], two hundred miles distant from the Cape of Cumari [Comorin]. On it horses are raised. After this, towards the east is the Island of Samotra [Sumatra], or Taprobana,[1] which is a three months' journey from Calichut. Then farther on is found Cataio and other regions, concerning which we shall not write further, on account of not having been able to learn more from Priest Joseph, mentioned above. Many things might be said concerning the spices and the other merchandise pertaining to India and the parts about which we have written in this our progress, but because they are not pertinent things to the narrative of Priest Joseph but rather an addition, and because we do not wish to proceed further, but to tell the simple truth, we have decided to end the present subject.

[1] There was much confusion at this period concerning the location of the island of Taprobana. Ptolemy and early writers identify it with Ceylon. With the more definite knowledge of Ceylon this name was also applied to Sumatra.

THE LETTERS SENT TO VENICE

THE importance of the voyage of Cabral in the history of Venice has previously been referred to. The anxiety of the Venetians to retain the sole monopoly of the European trade in spices and drugs made them view with apprehension the growing power of the Osmanli in the East. To protect her threatened commerce Venice sought the aid of the Christian states of Europe. Spain, too, had reason to fear the Moslems because of the expulsion of the Moors. There was thus a common bond between the two nations. Domenico Pisani was appointed ambassador to Spain by the Venetian Senate on the 7th of September 1500,[1] and because of the friendly relations between Spain and Portugal and their proximity, he represented Venice in Portugal as well. His chief duties were to remind Ferdinand and Isabella of promised aid, and to seek the assistance of the Portuguese fleets against the Turks. At this time the Venetian diarist Marino Sanuto proposed that some one should be sent to Portugal to offer condolence to Dom Manuel because of the death of his infant son, and also to endeavour to obtain the naval aid which the Venetians desired. The name of Il Cretico[2] was suggested, 'a person of great learning in Latin and Greek', and it was agreed that he be sent as a secretary to Pisani because of his suitability and because in this capacity less expense would be incurred. Henceforward Il Cretico was usually in attendance at one court while Pisani was with the other, but early in 1501 they were both in Lisbon. Through their efforts Dom Manuel was induced to send an armada under João de Menezes to assist Venice against the Turks.[3] We know that Pisani was in Lisbon in March 1501, because he wrote a letter[4] from there on the 13th of that month

[1] *Archivio di Stato di Venezia, Senato, deliberazione Secreto R38.*

[2] Giovanni Camerino, who is also called Giovanni Matteo Cretico, was a reader of Greek rhetoric at Padua. Because he had spent seven years on the island of Crete, he was usually called 'Il Cretico'.

[3] This left Belem on the 15th of June 1501.

[4] This letter is given by Sanuto (*Diarii*, vol. iii, col. 1595). It describes in a picturesque manner the festivities which accompanied his arrival and the conversation which Pisani had with Dom Manuel. Pisani later went to Lisbon to attend and add dignity to the ceremonies which took place upon the arrival of Pietro Pasqualigo, who was made Ambassador Extraordinary to Portugal on the 12th of April 1501, succeeding Piero Contarini. Pisani returned to Venice on the 20th of September 1502.

addressed to Granada. He then returned to Spain leaving Il Cretico in his place. Il Cretico remained in Lisbon until September, and was therefore present when the *Anunciada* returned and also at the arrival of the flagship towards the end of July. When the first of Cabral's ships arrived from India on the 23rd of June 1501, he immediately wrote a letter to Venice, telling briefly what he could learn regarding the voyage. This letter sheds some additional light on the voyage of Cabral and the cargo which it brought back. It shows also the participation of Bartolomeo Marchioni in the expedition and the elation of Dom Manuel upon the return of the fleet. It was the first news which the Venetians received telling of the return of Cabral's expedition and of what had occurred in India, although they had heard vaguely through Egyptian sources of its arrival there. The dismay which this report caused in Venice is vividly told by the diarist Priuli. The letter of Il Cretico was also the first account of Cabral's voyage printed in Venice, and may have been the first one printed, but no copy is now in existence. According to Girolamo Priuli, it was published in 1501. The statement made by Il Cretico that the fleet proceeded for two thousand miles along the coast of Brazil after leaving Porto Seguro has caused discussion among some historians of this voyage. In considering this statement, it may be well to remember that the letter was written largely from hearsay and is inaccurate in many particulars. If we accept what Il Cretico states we must deny that of other authorities generally considered more trustworthy, who definitely affirm the contrary.

Il Cretico seems to have sent his letter to the Doge at Venice, then Agostino Barbarigo. A copy was evidently also sent to the Doge through Pietro Pasqualigo and a second copy through Pisani. The introduction to the letter sent by Pisani as given by Sanuto is as follows: 'Most Serene Prince, I believe that Your Serenity has learned through letters of the Magnificent Ambassador, Domino Piero Pasqualigo, Doctor, the chapter of the letter of Missier Cretico, Doctor, who is with the kingdom of Portugal, of the 27th of July in Lisbon.'[1] Then follows the

[1] 'Copia et sumario di una letera di sier Domenigo Pixani, el cavalier, orator nostro in Spagna, a la Signoria' (*Diarii*, vol. iv, cols. 99–101). Also published in *Arch. Veneto*, vol. xxii, pp. 156 ff.

letter which Il Cretico sent to Venice as given in *Paesi*. The letter as sent by Pisani, however, is dated the 27th of July 1501, instead of the 27th of June, as given in the version of Cretico's letter printed in *Paesi*. The former date is evidently an error.

Manuscript copies of the letter are to be found in the Marciana Library, Venice, in the collection entitled *Viaggiatori antichi* (MS. Ital. Cl. 6, No. 208), and in Codex Contarini A (vi. 277). Another manuscript is in the Museo Civico of that city. It is also given in the diaries of Marino Sanuto and Girolamo Priuli. It was included among the letters in book vi of the first edition of *Paesi novamente retrovati*, and in subsequent editions and translations. In recent times it has been republished by Romanin (*Storia docum.* iv. 457–60), who takes it from the Marciana codex, by Fulin, who uses the codex in the Museo Civico (*Archivio Veneto*, tomo xxiv, part 1), and by Berchet (*Raccolta Colombiana*, part iii, vol. i, p. 43), who inserts the text published in the *Diarii* of Marino Sanuto (vol. iv, cols. 99–102). The translation which follows has been made from the text given in *Paesi* (bk. vi, ch. cxxv). This has been compared with that in the Marciana codex and the texts of Rinaldo Fulin and Marino Sanuto. The variations have been inserted in parenthesis.

Another secretary who accompanied Pisani to Spain was Angelo Trevisan di Bernardino. Trevisan had been secretary of Domenico Malipiero, the Venetian annalist, in 1489 and in 1498 when the latter was purveyor to the Venetian armadas. Malipiero was interested in the recent Spanish and Portuguese voyages, and, taking advantage of this opportunity, he requested his former secretary to secure for him such information as he could regarding them. Trevisan used every effort to do so. He became personally acquainted with Columbus and with Peter Martyr, who had by this time accumulated many notes for his *Decades*. While Peter Martyr was in Egypt in 1501, obtaining a treaty from the Mameluke for the protection of the Holy Land, Trevisan had access to his papers, and sent to Italy a portion of his first *Decade*, which was published in Venice in 1504 and known as the *Libretto*. Trevisan asked Il Cretico, when he was in Lisbon, to obtain for him information concerning the Portuguese voyages, and particularly regarding the fleet of Cabral, which was then expected. Trevisan wrote several letters to Malipiero telling of what progress Il Cretico was making in response to his request. Upon his return to Spain Il Cretico brought back with him information regarding the voyage of Cabral. In one letter written from Exigia in September Trevisan states that Il Cretico had come well informed in regard to the voyage to Calicut and was at work composing a treatise which would be very fine and acceptable to those who are pleased with such things. This is the basis for the belief that Il Cretico compiled or at least translated a portion of the anonymous Portuguese narrative, which was sent to Malipiero and possibly also to others in Venice, and which was printed in the *Paesi* in 1507.

The letters of Trevisan, a text of the narrative of Cabral's voyage generally called that of 'The Anonymous Pilot', a translation of a letter written by Dom Manuel to the Spanish sovereigns in 1501, and others relating to the Spanish voyages have been preserved in Malipiero's papers. They were presented to the Venetian Senate, and then passed into the possession of the patrician Jacopo Soranzo, whose library was later dispersed. Part of it passed into the hands of a priest, the Abbé Canonici, and part into the library of Amadeo Sviger. The Canonici library, at the beginning of the last century, went to England, and is now incorporated in the Bodleian Library. The Sviger library was divided between the Marciana Library and the Archivio di Stato in Venice, the library of the Counts Mannin in Passeriano, and that of the Reverend Walter Sneyd of London.[1] It is in this last collection that the letters of Trevisan relating to the voyage of Cabral are now to be found. When Guglielmo Berchet was compiling his monumental work on Columbus he located these letters and published them together with the first part of the Anonymous Narrative. The portions of the Trevisan letters referring to the voyage of Cabral or to Il Cretico translated in this volume are from the texts as given by Berchet.

Another letter was sent to Venice at this time, written by

[1] Mr. Sneyd was a collector of *Relazioni*. In 1855 he made an inventory of his collection for the British Museum; eighty 'Relations' are mentioned, but not specifically described. Mr. Sneyd apparently never published any of them. At his death they passed to his son, and are now at Newcastle-upon-Tyne.

Giovanni Francesco de Affaitadi. The Affaitadi family had for many years held a high position in Cremona as bankers and merchants. At some time before the discovery of America they established a branch at Lisbon, as did other Italians, to secure a portion of the trade which the Portuguese were developing in their African and island possessions. Here the Affaitadi engaged at first in the sugar trade with Madeira,[1] but with the return of Cabral's fleet they became interested in that of spices. Giovanni Francesco de Affaitadi, the head of the house at Lisbon, held a position as a Venetian merchant similar to that of the Florentines, Bartolomeo Marchioni and Girolamo Sernigi. Affaitadi, because of his wealth and his commercial and banking connexions, occupied almost a diplomatic position at Lisbon, so that on the return of Cabral's fleet he wrote a letter to the Signoria concerning it. He was asked by Pietro Pasqualigo, the Venetian *oratore*, upon his leaving Lisbon, to keep the Venetian Republic informed of the results of later voyages to India.[2]

The spice trade with India was a monopoly of the King of Portugal. The Affaitadi tried to obtain it, but were unsuccessful.[3] They did obtain, however, the exclusive trade in these commodities with Flanders, for a time. In this they were later joined by other Italians and by the Fuggers and Welzers of Germany. The chief products received in Flanders in exchange for spices were copper and silver to be used in the Indian trade. The wealth of the Affaitadi developed rapidly, and they later had agents at Seville, Valencia, and at Medina del Campo, where the largest fair in Spain was held, at London, at Lyons, and in various cities in Italy and the Low Countries. The name of this family is well known because some of their books of accounting have been preserved in Antwerp.[4]

The translation of this letter, written on the 26th of June 1501, has been made from Sanuto (*Diarii*, vol. iv, cols. 66–7).

[1] Since 1479 much sugar was exported to Flanders; 40,000 arrobas were sent at one time. A refinery existed at Antwerp before 1500.

[2] Giovanni Francesco de Affaitadi continued to live at Lisbon, where he died in 1528.

[3] The Affaitadi had a representative, Matteo de Bergamo, in the fleet of da Gama in 1502, who on his return wrote a report.

[4] For the Affaitadi see A. Goris, *Les Colonies marchandes méridionales à Anvers de 1488 à 1567* (Louvain, 1925); and J. Denucé, *Inventaire des Affaitadi, banquiers italiens à Anvers de l'année 1568* (Antwerp, 1934).

COPY OF ONE CHAPTER OF THE LETTER OF D. CRETICO, NUNCIO OF THE MOST ILLUSTRIOUS SIGNORIA OF VENICE IN PORTUGAL

DATED THE 27TH OF JUNE 1501

MOST Serene Prince, &c. I believe that Your Serenity has learned through letters of the Magnificent Ambassador that this Most Serene King has sent ships on the voyage to India. These have now returned, but of thirteen which went, seven were lost on the voyage. In the first place, Most Serene Prince, along the coast of Mauritania and Getulia[1] towards the south as far as Cape Verde, which in ancient times was called Hesperia, where the Islands of the Hesperides are; here begins Ethiopia, and from here on it was unknown to the ancients; from here the shore of Ethiopia runs towards the east, so much so that it corresponds to the line of Sicily.[2] From the said coast there are nine degrees, five or six of them this side of the equinoctial line.[3] And in the middle of the said coast is *la mina* of this Most Serene King, and from there on a cape, extending nine degrees beyond the tropic of Capricorn, stretches towards the south. This cape is called that of Good Hope.[4] Then comes the breadth of Barbary. From this place more than five thousand miles of shore stretch inward towards us. From this cape it extends again towards a cape called *Prasim Promontorio*[5] by

[1] The Greek name for the country inhabited by the Gaetulians, a people of Northwestern Africa south of the Mauri and Numidae in Mauretania, the modern Morocco. They are referred to by Pliny.

[2] The African coast-line turns south about three degrees west of a line passing along the west coast of Sicily.

[3] Il Cretico means to say that from Cape Verde to the coast-line running east and west, north of the Gulf of Guinea, it is nine degrees, and that this line is five or six degrees north of the equator. This is approximately correct.

[4] The Cape of Good Hope is located 34° 24′ 18″ S. and the Tropic of Capricorn 23° 27′. The latter location would be known from the Tropic of Cancer, which had been determined by the early astronomers. The latitude roughly given here by Il Cretico is that computed from the determination at St. Helena Bay by da Gama with a large wooden astrolabe. The use of sun tables would hardly be more accurate. The true position is 10° 53′ south of the Tropic of Capricorn.

[5] This is the Prassum Promontorium of Ptolemy, the farthest point shown to the south in East Africa. From thence the imaginary coast-line extended to the east. It seems to correspond with the present location of Mozambique.

the ancients. The other side thus far was known to the ancients. From here again it runs almost directly east to the Trogloditia,[1] where there is another vein of gold which they call Zaffala. There the ancients affirm is a greater quantity of gold than anywhere else. From here they enter the *mar Barbarico*,[2] and then into that of India and then arrive at Colochut [Calicut]. This is their voyage and it is more than fifteen thousand miles but, by cutting across, they shorten it somewhat. Above the Cape of Good Hope towards the west they have discovered a new land. They call it that of the parrots [*papaga*],[3] because some are found there which are an arm and a half in length, of various colours. We saw two of these. They judged that this was mainland because they ran along the coast more than two thousand miles but did not find the end.[4] It is inhabited by nude and handsome men. On their voyage they lost four ships. Two, they sent to the new mine;[5] they judge that these are lost.[6] Seven went to Colochut, where at first they were well received; and a house was given them by that lord. Some of the ships remained; the others went to other places near by.[7] And afterward came the Sultan's merchants, who were angry because they had interfered with them and wanted to load first. The factor of this Most Serene King com-

[1] The land of cave-dwellers, or, more literally, of 'those who creep into holes'. As early as the twenty-second century B.C. Nubian troglodytes are referred to as working in the gold-mines in the Eastern Desert. The word troglodytes also means coarse, brutal people. It thus refers here to the negroes, particularly to those who brought gold to the seaport of Sofala.

[2] This is the Sinus Barbaricus of Ptolemy, the Golpho Barbarico of Berlinghieri, and corresponds roughly to the Azanian Gulf of the Arabian Sea on modern maps. There were then available some eleven printed editions of Ptolemy's *Geographia*. Of these, the 1490 Rome edition might be considered the most authoritative version, and this was probably the one which Il Cretico used.

[3] This is the first time that Brazil is so called. This name had thus originated on the voyage, when the discovery was evidently not considered of great value.

[4] Il Cretico must have misunderstood his informant. The fleet was on its way to India and riches, and had no time for a voyage of exploration along the coast, nor were they interested in doing so. Gaspar de Lemos returned with the news of the finding of Brazil so that further exploration could be made. In the letter of Dom Manuel, furthermore, the king states that Cabral did not delay the fleet to make discoveries, and a similar assertion is also made by Caminha. This statement in the letter cannot be taken seriously.

[6] That is, to Sofala.

[5] The writer endeavours in this manner to reconcile the number of ships. He had evidently not learned what had happened to those of Vasco de Ataíde, Gaspar de Lemos, and Diogo Dias. That of Bartholomeu Dias was lost in the storm, but Diogo Dias returned. He includes the ship of Diogo Dias among those which went to India.

[7] Evidently referring to the ship which went to obtain the elephant.

plained to the lord (of Colochut), who was of the opinion that he should come to an understanding with the Moors, and said that if they took on a cargo he should take the spices away from them. As a result of this they came to blows, and all the land favoured the Moors. They ran to the house assigned to the Portuguese, and they cut to pieces all who were (within and) on the land. Those were about forty. Among them was the factor who had thrown himself into the water to escape. When the other ships, which were ten,[1] learned this, they came and destroyed the people of the Sultan, and with their artillery they did great damage to the land and burned a number of houses, because they were covered with straw. On account of this uproar they departed from Colochut and were conducted by their guide, who was a baptized Jew,[2] to another land about forty miles farther on, called Cuzin [Cochin], belonging to another king, enemy of the King of Colochut. He made good company with them and has a greater supply of spices than there is at Colochut. They took on a heavy cargo (they loaded seven ships with spices)[3] at a price I fear to tell, because they declare they have obtained a cantara of cinnamon for a ducat and less. This lord of Cuzin sent his ambassadors with these ships to this Most Serene King and also two hostages, who returned in safety. On their return the Moors and people of Colochut made plans to capture them and armed more than one hundred and fifty small ships with more than fifteen thousand men. However, since they had cargoes, they did not wish to fight. Those could not attack them because these sailed with a side wind which they could not use. In coming they reached an island where is the body of Saint Thomas, the Apostle. The lord of this treated them very kindly, and, having given them relics of the aforesaid saint, asked them to take spices from him on credit until the return voyage.[4] They were laden and could not take more. They have been fourteen months on the voyage but only four on the return, and they say that in the future they can make it in eight months or ten at the

[1] This is another error. All of Cabral's ships were then at Calicut, and they destroyed ten Moorish ships.

[2] Gaspar da Gama.

[3] Two, at least, were loaded at Calicut, and the balance at Cochin and Cranganore.

[4] This refers to the visit at Cananore. The reference to Saint Thomas is in error.

most.[1] On the return voyage six of the seven ships came back safely; the other ran upon a shoal. Its people were saved. This one was of six hundred *botte* (and richly laden).[2] Up to this time there has arrived only one of three hundred *botte*;[3] the others are near, it is said. This one arrived on the eve of Saint John. I was with the Most Serene King, who called me and told me that I might congratulate him because his ships had arrived from India, loaded with spices; and so I rejoiced in due form with him. He had a feast held in the palace that evening and a ringing of bells throughout the land (city), and on the following day he had solemn procession made throughout the land. Afterward, when I found myself with His Majesty, he referred again to his ships and he told me that I should write to Your Serenity that from now on you should send your ships to carry spices from here. He would make them welcome and they could feel that they were at home. And he would forbid the Sultan to go for spices. He wishes to put forty ships in this trade, some going, some returning. In short, he feels that he has India at his command. This ship which has returned belongs to Bartholomio,[4] a Florentine, together with the cargo, which consists of: pepper, about three hundred cantaras; cinnamon, one hundred and twenty cantaras; lac, fifty or sixty cantaras; benzoin, fifteen cantaras; of cloves they have none because the Moors had carried it away,[5] nor ginger either because it does not grow in the place where they took their cargo,[6] but only at Colochut. There are no small spices of any sort. They say that they lost many jewels during the disturbance at Colochut. Also, this should not be omitted: that the ambassadors of a king of Ethiopia, named King of Ubenam, came here.[7] He has sent a present to this Most Serene King, of slaves and ivory teeth, although such

[1] This ship was fifteen and a half months on the voyage including the stay at Calicut and elsewhere, and the return from Cochin took over five months. The shorter time proposed for future voyages assumed the establishment of factories without lengthy stops in India.

[2] The Portuguese accounts give 200 tons, indicating that a *botte* was a third of a Portuguese ton.

[3] This ship of 100 tons was that in which Marchioni and other Italians participated.

[4] Bartolomeo Marchioni.

[5] The Moors had evidently not allowed the Portuguese to purchase cloves at Calicut, having previously done so.

[6] This cargo was taken on at Cochin or Cranganore.

[7] That is, a king on the coast of Guinea. This information does not refer to Cabral's voyage.

things have been coming here for some time. Near there also grows pepper,[1] but it cannot be compared with the other. Moreover, this ship, on its return, met two very large ships which had left the new mine and were going towards India.[2] They had a great amount of gold, and because they feared that our men desired to capture them they immediately offered fifteen thousand *dobras*.[3] Each (ship) was worth more than five hundred thousand. But our men did not wish to seize anything; instead, they offered them presents and good will, for they wished to be allowed to navigate those seas.

EXTRACTS FROM THE LETTERS OF ANGELO TREVISAN TO DOMENICO MALIPIERO

From Granada, the 21st of August 1501:

Furthermore: We are daily expecting our doctor from Lisbon, who left our magnificent ambassador there: who at my request has written a short account [*opereta*] of the voyage from Calicut, of which I will make a copy for Your Magnificence. It is impossible to procure the map [*carta*] of that voyage because the king has placed a death penalty on any one who gives it out. This is as much as I can do now for the service of Your Magnificence, and if it seems possible to do more, command me.

From Granada (without date, but probably in September 1501):

In regard to the desire of your magnificence to learn of the voyage to Calicut, I have written you at other times that from day to day I am expecting Messer Cretico, who writes me that he has composed a small work [*opereta*]. As soon as he arrives, I will see that Your Magnificence has part of it.

(*Rac. Col.*, op. cit., part iii vol. i, p. 54.)

[1] This is *prima* in the text, apparently a misprint for *pipper*. The last part of this sentence is omitted in the 1508 edition of *Paesi*.

[2] This refers to the ship from Cambay which the fleet encountered while on its return voyage, crossing from Cananore to East Africa.

[3] The *dobra* was a Castilian coin which also circulated in Portugal at this period, with a value of fifty to the mark, and was thus somewhat more valuable than the cruzado, then worth 9*s*. 8*d*. (M. B. L. Fernandes, *Memoria das Moedas correntes em Portugal*, Lisbon, 1856.)

From Exigia, the 3rd of December 1501:

Messer Cretico, also a loyal servitor of Your Magnificence, renders thanks that you have deigned to salute him so kindly in your letters, and commends himself to you greatly, congratulating you from his inmost heart on your good fortune. He comes from Portugal at the end of this September, well informed concerning the voyage to Calicut, and is continually working on a treatise [*tractato*] which will be very fine and acceptable to those who are pleased with such things.[1]

If we return to Venice alive, Your Magnificence will see maps [*carte*] both as far as Calicut and beyond there less than twice the distance from here to Flanders. I promise you that everything has come in order; but this, Your Magnificence may not care to divulge. One thing is certain, that you will learn upon our arrival as many particulars as though you had been at Calicut and farther, and Your Magnificence will be made a participant in everything, as perhaps others will not.

(Ibid., p. 62.)

LETTER OF GIOVANNI FRANCESCO DE AFFAITADI TO DOMENICO PISANI

LISBON, THE 26TH OF JUNE 1501

MAGNIFICENT Orator, &c.[2]

Several days ago I wrote through Zuan Vesiga, but to-day we have yours in which you instruct that we give an account of the expedition of the armada of this Most Serene King. Although Missier Cretico will have written also, I wish to give news of the departure of this armada, which left here the 17th

[1] This statement and the fact that a copy of the Anonymous Narrative has been preserved with these letters form the basis for the belief that Il Cretico was the author of that account of Cabral's voyage.

[2] Sanuto gives the following heading for this letter: 'This is a copy of a letter of Zuan Francesco de la Faitada, written in Lisbon, on the 26th day of June 1501, addressed in Spain to Sier Domenego Pixani, Cavalier, our orator: which he sent to this country with his of the 10th of July.'

of June, and on the 18th was at Lacus [Lagos] in the land of Algarius [Algarve], which is forty leagues from here. From that place, Lacus, we are advised that on Monday last the said armada was increased by many ships and many men, and as I was advised through a letter of last Sunday, more than two thousand men were added from the Kingdom of Algarius in addition to those who went from here with the ships which departed. The reason that this king sends this armada to this place of the Moors, is to capture it. And this was done on Saint John's Day, by an assault on land. This is as much as is known of the aforesaid armada to the present day. It is expected that they will then pursue the route to which they were assigned. May God grant them victory.[1]

Your Magnificence will know that in the afternoon there came one of the small ships [*navilij*] which in January arrived at Colocut, which place is that whence spices are expected. And because I know that you will be pleased to hear the news which they bring, I shall advise how this Most Serene King sent to the said Coloqut twelve ships, large and small, of which ten were his own, one of Signor don Alvaro[2] in partnership with Bortolo,[3] a Florentine, and Hironimo[4] and a Genoese,[5] and the other of Conte de Porta Alegra[6] and also certain other merchants.

[1] This was the expedition of João de Menezes which according to de Goes (part i, ch. li) set sail from Belem on the 15th of June 1501 to assist the Venetians against the Turks. It consisted of thirty ships and caravels with 3,500 men. There also went at this same time, and also under de Menezes, another fleet which was sent secretly to capture the castle of Mazalquibir near Ouram. A stop was made in Algarve for reinforcements. Unable to capture Mazalquibir, the fleet destined there returned to Portugal. The main fleet proceeded to Sardinia, near which a carraca and two galleons belonging to some Genoese were captured. The fleet then continued to Corfu and was there joined by a large fleet of Venetian galleys and galleons. Anticipating a delay in further operations against the Turks and because the Venetians had already captured the Negropont, which was their destination, the Portuguese were excused from further participation in the armada and returned, reaching Sagres at Christmas, on their way to Lisbon. Here the king received his fifth of the booty and Count de Menezes was well rewarded.

[2] Dom Álvaro de Bragança was the fourth son of Dom Fernando, Duke of Bragança.

[3] Bartolomeo Marchioni, a rich Florentine merchant and banker residing in Lisbon.

[4] Girolamo Sernigi, also a Florentine, but to whom Dom Manuel had granted citizenship of Lisbon.

[5] Antonio Salvago, according to the belief of Peragallo (*Cenni intorno alla colonia italiana in Portugal nel secoli XIV, XV, e XVI*).

[6] Conde de Portalegre, Dom Diogo da Silva de Menezes.

In all there were twelve ships,[1] large and small, of which, at the beginning, when at a distance of eighty leagues, one of the ships of this king was lost, of which there has never been any news. The other eleven pursued their voyage, arriving at a place called *Cavo de Bona Speranza.* One day in July, after dinner, there arose a great wind so that by this accident there were lost three other ships belonging to the king and the small ship of the Conte di Porta Alegra. Thus there remained only seven. These continued until they arrived at Coloqut. I may also say that before they arrived at Coloqut, they went along the coast a distance of one hundred leagues, arriving at a place where the king did them great honour and sent them supplies of meat, lambs, and other presents.[2] They then went to Coloqut. The captain had a talk with the king of that place, and in the name of this Most Serene King, made him presents of many things, so that they became great friends. And the captain returned to the ship and he instructed the chief factor, with the other designated officials, that they were to remain on land; and they began to contract and to exchange their merchandise. At that time there was to be found in the said place of Coloqut a fleet of ships of the Moors of Mecha,[3] who were there to load spices. One day the Moors and the factor of the king came to a misunderstanding, one saying that he wished to load before the other, and the Moors killed twenty-five or thirty of the principal Portuguese, among whom were the chief factor and writers and certain *frati de observantia*[4] whom the king sent in the said armada. Some of those who were on land threw themselves into the sea. They swam to the ships and gave notice of what had happened to the captain, who ordered all ships ready to sail. And he began to bombard the Moorish ships, resulting in sending about twelve ships to the bottom[5] and killing more than three hundred Moors. This done, he began to fire the bombards towards the shore and killed many people, burning

[1] The ship of Gaspar de Lemos is not included.

[2] That is, along the coast of Africa, where they were entertained at Malindi.

[3] The Moors of Mecca were so called because their ships sailed from Jidda, the port for Mecca, and because they carried pilgrims.

[4] A branch of the Franciscan Order who professed a strict observance of rules.

[5] That is, ten at Calicut, and two at Pandarani, near by.

many houses. And the next day they captured many of the men of Coloqut and took them to their ships. The captain deliberated as to returning here. A Jew, whom the other captain brought when the first voyage to Coloqut was made by this king, who was sent in this armada, but who all this time was never permitted to go on shore,[1] told the captain not to return, but to go some seventy or eighty leagues farther, which would bring him to the proper place where spices grew. This place belongs to another king. The captain, after considering the proposal of the Jew, determined to do what he said, and he ordered them to sail towards this place which this man told him of, so that he arrived at this land which is called Chuchi [Cochin], where the captain sent men on shore to talk to the king of this land and to relate to him what had happened in Coloqut. The king of this land is a great enemy of the King of Coloqut, and on learning this he sent four of his most important men to the ships, in exchange for four others whom the captain sent on shore. And they began to trade, so that in nine days all seven of the ships were loaded with spices, namely, cloves, cinnamon, nutmegs, pepper, and other kinds of spices. And after the ships were entirely laden, the king sent another fourteen small boats of spices, and they returned them because they could not carry them. This the king sent them as a gift, without money or anything else in exchange. The King of Coloqut, while this armada went to load at this place, because he was an enemy of that other king and doubting if the traffic of Coloqut would be of sufficient importance,[2] ordered a large armada to be sent to capture the ships of Portugal. In this armada went more than fifteen thousand men. The King of Chuchi, who learned the news of this armada, informed the Portuguese captain, making him a great offer to save him as much as he could. And the latter took his departure, while the four men from the ships who were on land remained there, and the four others of the land who were in the ships came here with the said ships. And this they did with great friendship. One day while the said ships were ready to leave, to start on their return

[1] Gaspar da Gama, whom Vasco da Gama had brought back with him from India. (See Ravenstein, *Vasco da Gama*, Hakluyt Soc., p. 179.)

[2] i.e. doubting whether the trade with the Portuguese would be of much value to the people of Calicut.

voyage, the armada of Coloqut appeared, and those of the ships spread sail and, having a favourable wind, left behind the armada of Coloqut because those ships did not sail unless they had the wind astern.

In Coloqut were gathered together a great value of things which had already been purchased. There always existed on the voyage thither a great sum in these ships of the king. The fame of the riches of this king is so great that a third part is a large thing. After they had left Chuchi, as has been said before, when a distance from the said place of two hundred leagues, they found another land called Lichinocho [Cananore], and there lived a very rich king, who sent presents to the captain and sent him two ambassadors who came to the King of Portugal. Leaving this king, they departed on their voyage and came to Zofala. In this place they say there is a great trade in gold. And of the twelve ships, the king ordered that two should go to this land. But when the four ships were lost they were obliged to go to this land of Zofala.[1] They continued and one day there was a great wind, so that one of the seven ships went aground; and the people were saved. The captain ordered the said ship to be burned with the merchandise. When they arrived at the Cape of Good Hope, the captain ordered all the other ships to join together and they went together for three or four days. He then ordered that this one which has come, because it was the best sailer, should leave the others and should come to give news of those ships to this King of Portugal. And so it was done. This ship which has come is the smallest of all, and it belongs to Signor Alvaro and the three other merchants named above. It is the poorest of all the others; it carries three hundred cantara of pepper and two hundred of cinnamon, nutmegs, lac, and benzoin; and bears news of these things, namely, that all come laden.

This discourse I have made to advise Your Magnificence of the success of this matter of Coloqut. The above news was obtained from a mariner of the small ship which has arrived, which ship is still at Restello and is daily expected here. It is

[1] That is, with the two ships missing which were to go to Sofala, it was necessary for the whole fleet to return that way because one of the objects of the expedition was to visit that place.

understood that another is expected who is advised of everything in particular, &c.[1]

This letter arrived in Venice the middle of the month of July 1501.

(Sanuto, *I Diarii*, vol. iv, cols. 66–7.)

[1] *Intendendose altro, ne sareti avisato del tutto particularmente*, &c., i.e. on Cabral's flagship; this may possibly refer to the source of the account given in the Anonymous Narrative.

THE VENETIAN DIARISTS

FOUR prominent Venetians, Domenico Malipiero, Marcantonio Michieli, Girolamo Priuli, and Marino Sanuto have left a record in the form of diaries which give us an intimate knowledge of what appeared to them of interest in their city, almost day by day, from 1457 to 1535. These diaries are the foundation for the history of Venice during this period, and it is in two of them that is found, to a large extent, the information which reached Venice regarding the voyage of Cabral.

The portions of the diaries of Malipiero and Michieli which now exist contain no references of importance to the Portuguese voyages. The diaries of Girolamo Priuli and Marino Sanuto, however, are storehouses of information regarding the commerce and the political relations of Venice, including those with Portugal. Priuli, whose family had always been merchants, views the events as they occur more from a commercial standpoint, while Sanuto, a statesman, looks at them also from their political aspect.

Girolamo Priuli was born in Venice on the 26th of January 1476. His father, Lorenzo Priuli (1446–1518), held the most important offices in the Republic, and was a man of considerable wealth. He died in 1547. Priuli was in intimate touch with the commercial situation in Venice from the time that Cabral's fleet returned from India. He knew her merchants, the commodities they dealt in, and his high position in the community enabled him also to know the relations of that city with foreign countries. He realized as well as any one in Venice the effects which would ensue from the discovery of the new sea route, and in the early letters in his diary he foretells them, and we can see, as years pass, how much of his anxiety for the future was well founded. His diary begins with April 1494 and extends to July 1512 and consists of eight books. The first book, which extends from the 1st of April 1494 to the 14th of June 1500, has been printed.[1] Professor Rinaldo Fulin has published such extracts from the diary from August 1499 to March 1512

[1] Muratori, *Rerum Italicarum Scriptores* (2nd ed., Città di Castello, 1911).

as pertain to the Portuguese in India and to the Venetians in Egypt (*Archivio Veneto*, vol. xxii, part 1; also as a separate volume entitled *Diarii e Diaristi Veneziani*, Venice, 1881). In this he gives sixty-eight extracts, twenty-five of which are prior to 1505. The translations here made are from this selection, and are the entries which refer to the voyage of Cabral.

Marino Sanuto was called the Younger (1466–1533) because of an earlier writer by the same name who lived in the twelfth and thirteenth centuries, who was also a Venetian and equally celebrated. Through his own exertions he became one of the most prominent men in Venice at this period, and occupied a position in all of the councils of the Republic. On the 1st of January 1496, Sanuto began to write his diary which was destined to be probably the largest, most comprehensive, and valuable ever written by one man. While Sanuto must have had assistance at times, much of the diary, which fills fifty-eight volumes, he did himself. In it he gives notes, extracts, or complete documents which passed through his hands concerning the relations of Venice with other parts of the world. The diary continues until September 1533. It was published between 1879 and 1903. In it are found many references to the voyages of the Portuguese and to the Venetian representatives who were present in Lisbon and who gathered whatever news they could to send to Venice, where it was received with intense interest. He tells of the voyage of da Gama, but gives, more particularly, notices of the return of Cabral's fleet. In it are found the letters of Il Cretico and of Francesco de Affaitadi, printed elsewhere in this volume. There are other shorter references to Cabral's voyage, some of which are felt to be of sufficient value for insertion.

EXTRACTS FROM THE DIARY OF GIROLAMO PRIULI

1501—July.

Previous to the 24th of this month letters had come from Portugal from a nuncio of the Venetian Signoria, sent to that place on purpose to learn minutely the truth of the voyage to India begun by that king . . . which event was of greater importance to the Venetian state than the Turkish war, or any other wars which might have affected her. This nuncio wrote to the Venetian state by his letter of the 6th of June last as follows.[1] This letter was printed, which is the same as that herewith.

[*Here follows in the text of Priuli the letter of Il Cretico. This is also given in* Paesi *and in the diary of Sanuto.*]

At this point is finished the copy written to the Venetian state as is stated above, from a person worthy of belief. However, I leave it to the most intelligent readers as to how it appears to them, for in this letter are many things of great wonder in our times and almost incredible, which give me something very instructive to consider; but time will better enable us to understand the truth. But if God will lend me life, I shall endeavour to note the result so far as it can be understood, for already so much has been found out that nothing more can be learned now than infinite time desires should be known. It is understood, further, how the above-mentioned King of Portugal sent with the aforesaid ships coral and cloths of every kind, and money to the value of 60,000 ducats [provided] by the aforesaid king and other merchants for this voyage to India. And how much profit was derived from it, it is not possible to judge, because the spices have been taken to Portugal. It is true that seven ships were lost; nevertheless the other six which have arrived home have carried so much spicery for so much value of treasure, that it is almost difficult to judge it. I can say for the profit, that from one ducat they can make more than one hundred. But every intelligent person should know there was not so much profit as is written, but at any event it was great. And if this voyage should continue, since it now seems to me easy to accomplish, the King of Portugal could call himself the King of Money because all would convene to that country to obtain spices, and the money would accumulate greatly in Portugal with such profit as would follow each year from similar voyages. When this news was truly learned in Venice, the whole city was much stirred by it, and every one was stupefied that in this our time there should have been found

[1] The letter of Il Cretico is dated the 27th of June 1501 in *Paesi*. This is correct, and not the 6th, as apparently given in the Priuli manuscript.

a new voyage which was never heard of or seen in the times of the ancients or of our ancestors. And this news was held by the learned to be the worst news which the Venetian Republic could have had, to lose the liberty abroad. And the wars and the travails which we now have and for some time may have, are of the smallest moment in comparison with this news. And for this reason I wish to tell the truth and not to deceive. There is no doubt whatever that the city of Venice came to such reputation and fame as it now enjoys only through the sea, namely by the continual traffic and navigations which it has made by the voyages, because they carry each year a large quantity of spices with their galleys and ships, so that very great damage would be done to deprive them of it. And as is said, the whole world flocked to Venice with ducats to buy spices and other needs, and also placed their goods there. Whence through the arrival of foreigners and through the traffic of selling and buying each year and in every trading season, the city of Venice has come to this excellence which it has attained, and only through these voyages and this maritime traffic. And this they have gained by the sea, and with this they have also been able to sustain the war and acquire the state on the mainland as is seen. The reason why the profit from the *terra firma* is very bad, as well in war as in forced service, is that they consume as much as they raise.

Therefore, now that this new voyage of Portugal is found, this King of Portugal will bring all the spices to Lisbon. And there is no doubt that the Hungarians, Germans, Flemish and French, and those beyond the mountains, who formerly came to Venice to buy spices with their money, will all turn towards Lisbon, for it is nearer to all the countries, and easier to reach. And for this reason they will have a better market because all of this is of importance. And this is because the spices which come to Venice pass through all of Syria and through all of the countries of the Sultan. And in each place they pay very large duties and similarly in the Venetian state they pay unsufferable duties, presents and excises [*gabelle*]. Therefore, through the countries of the Sultan, extending to the city of Venice, the presents, duties, and excises are so great that I might say this, that whatever costs a ducat would be multiplied in price by these to the amount of sixty or one hundred ducats. That is, I say, that which costs a ducat in Calicut with the duty, presents, and excises mounts as above said. Therefore the King of Portugal, having found this voyage the other way round, would alone have the spices of the caravels, which they would import for much less in comparison with the other spices mentioned above, and for this reason they could give the spices a much better market than can the Venetian merchants; furthermore, it is shorter to conduct the spices to Flanders, Hungary, England, France, and other places from Portugal than to carry them from Venice. It may be said in conclusion that assuming this voyage from Lisbon to Calicut has begun, the spices in the Venetian galleys must lessen and also the merchants. And when this traffic in merchandise is lessened in Venice, it can be considered that the milk and nutriment of Venice are lessened to a *putino*. And because of this I see clearly the ruin of the Venetian city, because as the traffic lessens, so lessens the money which has produced the Venetian glory and reputation. Many still believe that this news cannot be true; others say that the King of Portugal could not continue this navigation to Calicut because of the thirteen caravels sent on the voyage to India only six returned in safety, and that the loss is greater than the gain; and that furthermore he will not find people who, for fear of life, will wish to go. Others comfort themselves, saying that the Sultan will provide for all this, because when the spices do not arrive in Syria and Alexandria, that he will lose the great treasure and profit which flowed from this, and because of this he will be incited to make all provisions regarding it. Others, furthermore, say to their profit, that always in places and large cities both ingenious persons always find something to say in favour of their belief and ill-wishers have things to say about things which may do harm. This is the only thing that matters, and it is of greatest importance, because with this news spices of all sorts will descend in price greatly in Venice, for the usual customer on learning this news will be restrained and obstinate in buying, as would the prudent ones.

I know I have said and written too long regarding this matter. I beg the reader that he excuse me, and chiefly because I have written in a confused and poorly adapted manner. For of the new matter and its great importance to our country, I have made what little transport to the pen as was appropriate. I am tired.

1501—August.

On the 23rd of this month there departed from Venice three large galleys on the voyage to Flanders. The Captain was Sier Alvixe di Prioli. These galleys had about 150 bales of spices: namely, 33 bales of pepper, *beledi* ginger[1] 100 bales, cloves 12 bales, and other kinds of spices to complete the amount; still they had little spices. And this was because the Venetian merchants, hearing this news of the Portuguese caravels coming from India, judged that the spices which arrived in Lisbon must go to Flanders, as seems reasonable, and everything would be lower in the West, because of this news. And this was the reason why very little spices went with the present galleys, compared with similar galleys. From many sources it is learned in Venice how the caravels coming from Calicut to Portugal have not arrived, save one, as is related before, and that the others, not being with it, are believed to be lost. And the above-mentioned caravel, which has arrived, has not as much spices as is said. And much comment is made regarding this, particularly by those who would desire that this voyage should not be found. And it is said further, that the King of Portugal was poorly satisfied with this voyage, and through the loss of these caravels he will lose this year, with these caravels on this voyage, 50,000 ducats, and that he does not wish to send this voyage again. And every one has his own opinion. And they retain similar hopes which are all vain, because this voyage to Calicut, which the King of Portugal will make every year, will become frequent and cause the ruin of the Venetian state.

1501—September.

On the 9th of this month letters came from Lisbon of the 1st of August. And through letters from Genoa and Lyons and other parts, it is learned that the caravels which were expected loaded with spices are in Portugal.

[1] Two kinds of ginger were known in commerce, distinguished as *beledi* and *colombino*. The first came from several provinces, the second was a speciality of the district of Koulam. The word *beledi* is evidently derived from the Arabic *beled*—country.

Three of the said caravels came from Calicut and one from the gold-mine which had a large quantity of gold. And the above-mentioned caravels had such a quantity of spices as is related above. Still it is variously reported, some say more, and some less. One report is that there was a very great quantity of spices, chiefly pepper and cinnamon, and a little *beledi* ginger; others say that there were 3,000 cantara of spices in all. And one cantara is 150 lire in weight. Nevertheless, it matters little now what the quantity of spices is; but the importance is the finding of the voyage and the trade, which each year will carry a large quantity of spices. This news, as has been said above, was considered very bad news for the city of Venice, and some very wise people are inclined to believe that this thing may be the beginning of the ruin of the Venetian state, because there is no doubt that the traffic of the voyage and the merchandise and the navigation which the city of Venice made each year thence, are the nutriment and milk through which the said Republic sustained itself. And without doubt, from this traffic and voyages, because of the profit which each year is derived from them, the Venetian senators have risen to such honour and glory and fame and exaltation to which they find themselves. Whence it is that the King of Portugal has found this new voyage, and that the spices which should come from Calicut, Cochin, and other places in India to Alexandria or Beyrout, and later come to Venice, and in this place become monopolized, whence all the world comes to buy such spicery and carry gold, silver, and every other merchandise, with which money the war is sustained; to-day, with this new voyage by the King of Portugal, all the spices which came by way of Cairo will be controlled in Portugal, because of the caravels which will go to India, to Calicut, and other places to take them. And in this way the Venetians will not be able to take spices either in Alexandria or Beyrout. And when the spices lessen to the Venetians, then will also lessen the profit and the money. And, in consequence, when the money is less, they will not be able to do things which would be good; and little by little it will be consumed until it is exhausted. Still, this is a presumptuous prognostication, since the heavens may dispose otherwise. And truly the Venetian merchants are in a bad way, believing that the voyages should make them very poor, doubting whether spices would be obtainable in Syria because they would be taken in India. And later the German merchants and other nations who are accustomed to come to buy the spices in Venice, because they can have cheaper and better merchandise, will go to Portugal to secure the spices because each one seeks his own profit. At all events the results of this matter will demonstrate the effects.

1501—September.

On the 14th of the said month, letters came from Portugal, from Lisbon, from the Venetian secretary, of the 4th of last month, regarding the caravels come from India; through which confirmation is learned of the arrival of four caravels loaded with spices which have returned from Calicut with 3,000 cantara of spices: namely, 2,000 cantara of pepper, which is, in our method of loading, 800; 600 cantara of cinnamon; the rest to the total between ginger, sandalwood, and benzoin; and with one cantara equal to 150 of our lire. The King of Portugal did not, in truth, show much contentment with this voyage; and this because of the caravels which were lost and shipwrecked; and the death and drowning of the men; and he said that because of this voyage, he would lose 80,000 ducats. Still, the said king is preparing 24 caravels to send on the said Indian voyage anew, and he says that he wishes the said caravels to go farther beyond Calicut than on the past voyage; and this is because the King of Calicut did not make good company with his people who went with the ships. From which it can truly be held as certain that this King of Portugal should become a great lord of money discovered through this voyage, because he will find all the spices of India in such quantity that spices will no longer come into the hands of the Moors, either in Cairo, or in Syria; and the course of merchandise will become diverted to Lisbon, where the spices will be, and every one will go there to purchase, and all merchandise of all parts of the world, with the money, will flow to Lisbon to buy like spicery, because it is easy to go from Flanders and other places, as well as to have there a better market. The before-mentioned Venetian secretary also wrote how, in the equipment of the said caravels, there was no difficulty in finding men who wished to go on the voyage. And this, although they might perish, since last year, as appears above, many caravels were lost; still such was the great gain, that people put themselves in danger of life because of the gain. In fact, the king from Lisbon, to repair the loss received in the past voyage, as appears above, has made a requirement that on all the spices which with other things which should come with the aforesaid caravels in the Indian voyage, there should be paid, or rather given to the king, 29 per cent., and the remainder the merchants of the caravels could sell at his command. How much damage this voyage made to the Venetian city has been related above; nothing further need be said.

1501—September.

On the 19th day of the said month through letters of the Venetian orator, who arrived at Lisbon, in Portugal, to that Most Serene King, seen and honoured and accepted with all demonstrations and with very large words of that king of friendship and goodwill for the Venetian state, &c., all *pro forma*, it is learned of the arrival of the Portuguese caravels come from Calicut in India, regarding which so much has been said above. And many merchants and others in Venice in the past have not wished to believe it; until now that they see the letters of the orator, they are enlightened with the quantity of spices above mentioned. And on this day, also in consonance with this news, through letters from Bruges in Flanders, there is learned that two caravels have arrived in that part, come from Portugal with spices brought from Calicut, and that they have begun to sell. The pepper is somewhat green and small, but still good; the cinnamon is somewhat large. So that this can be considered the beginning of the damage which the Venetian state can receive from the voyage found by the King of Portugal.

(R. Fulin, *Diarii e Diaristi Veneziani*, pp. 155–64.)

EXTRACTS FROM THE DIARY OF MARINO SANUTO

On the 22nd of February 1501 Dom Manuel wrote a letter in Latin to the Venetian Doge,[1] Agostino Barbarigo, in which he offered an armada to aid the Venetians against the Turks. In this

[1] Sanuto, *Diarii*, vol. iii, cols. 1593–5.

he uses his new title, which was confirmed by the Pope in 1502, 'King of Portugal and of the Algarves on this side and beyond the sea in Africa, Lord of Guinea, and of the Conquest, Navigation and Commerce of Ethiopia, Arabia and India'. This letter was sent to the Doge by Domenico Pisani, with a letter written from Lisbon on the 13th of March. In it he tells of the ancient friendship between the two states and refers to the congratulations which the Doge had sent to Dom Manuel regarding the marriage of his majesty. On the 23rd of March he again writes of the preparations being made for the fleet of João de Menezes and makes the following reference to that of Cabral.

The 23rd of March 1501. He writes further that a year ago the King of Portugal sent thirteen caravels to Calicut for spices, and they say that they are expected shortly; and he is jubilant to have found the way to the spices. And the king told them that as a consequence of this he would derive great benefit. And there are now in port four other caravels with merchandise for Calicut, and they will depart in three or four days.[1] The way is very long; it is four thousand leagues, sixteen thousand of our miles; and he has talked with men who returned with the caravels which went as above.

(iii, col. 1597.)

From Spain, from Sier Domenego Pixani, the cavalier, our orator [*without date, but placed in July 1501*].

He writes of the progress of the armada of the King of Portugal which went to Calicut and of the caravels which returned with spices; and he sent the copy of a letter received from Lisbon of the 26th day of June of Zuan Francesco Afaitado which, because it is very long, will be noted later. And this news of the arrival in Portugal of spices from Coloqut gives to those of this land much to think of: especially considering that the other six ships which were in convoy with this caravel are daily expected, and the merchants are fearful of their ruin.

(iv, col. 87.)

[1] Those of João da Nova.

August 1501. From Alexandria, through letters of June in those of the Bragadini, of San Sovero and Sier Beneto Cabriel.

The news of the spices of India arrived in Portugal is verified: and that the Moors in Cairo have learned that ships and caravels have arrived in Coloqut and loaded with spices: and the Moors wishing to disperse them, forty Franks are dead.

(iv, col. 98.)

On the 30th of September [1501] there arrived here a royal orator of Spain going to the Sultan of Cairo who embarked on our Alexandria galleys.[1] It is said that he goes to pray the Sultan to release the brothers of Monte Syon and to treat them well; and that thirty thousand Moors of Granada are baptized of their own wish, and not by compulsion.

(iv, col. 146.)

Copy of a letter of Sier Filippo Contarini to Sier Vetor Querini, dated in Alexandria the 4th day of September 1501.

[This letter begins with a list of commodites both for import and export at Cairo with the current prices. It then gives a description of the disordered rule of the Mamelukes which necessitated the closing of the Moorish shops, and of the large sums of money given to the eleven thousand or twelve thousand slaves in Egypt who belonged to that class.]

Regarding the things of India and Calicut. In the first place: we have word of the arrival safely there of eight Portuguese caravels, with merchandise and money. And while engaged in buying and selling, Moorish merchants overcame them and drove them from there. And they told the said lord that these were corsairs and men of bad character and that he should not sell anything to them, and if they continued to come it would be the total ruin of his country. In this manner they convinced him with many other reasons. And they so knew how to say such things that the people became excited, and they gave them arms, and forty of those Portuguese who were on shore are dead, and in this manner they put them to flight. The boats took sail and all are departed. And according to what they write, they have loaded eight hundred *schibe* of spices in their

[1] Peter Martyr of Anghiera.

ships. And they almost departed without paying the said Indians or giving them anything in exchange. On the contrary. This is as much as I have been able to learn through a Moorish letter written by the nephew of Amath Bubacho who had gone to India, as a *canzelier*.

(iv, cols. 167–8.)

From Spain, from the Orator, given at Saragossa, the 12th day of October [*1502*].

How the princes had not yet arrived; and the Queen is in Castile, where it is said she will be to provide for the war against France. And through another letter of the 12th this orator writes that he has had letters from Lisbon, from Zuan Francesco Ascaitato, of Cremona, of the 10th of September. He advises that the four ships expected from India which left eighteen months ago have not arrived; and the caravels sent last year to discover *la terra di Papagà* or rather of *Santa Croce*, returned on the 22nd day of July; and the captain referred to having discovered more than 2,500 miles of new coast and never having found an end of the said coast. And the said caravels have come laden with brazil-wood and cassia, and they have brought other spices, &c. I note that as to the news from Calicut, on the 13th day there arrived at Lisbon the caravels with spices, which news is in the hands of Sier Alvise de Molin.

(iv, col. 485.)

THE REPORT OF CA' MASSER

UNDER the pretext of engaging in business in Lisbon, a Venetian named Leonardo Massari, better known as Ca' Masser,[1] arrived there on the 3rd of October 1504. Ca' Masser, in reality, was sent to Portugal by the Venetian senate to secure information regarding the fleets which were being sent to India, and to make a report concerning their cargoes and other matters of interest to that Republic.[2] Foreigners in Lisbon, and particularly Venetians, were suspected at this time, perhaps because so much information regarding the Portuguese voyages had been sent to other places. In spite of the secrecy which Ca' Masser maintained, his true mission was known to Dom Manuel through a Florentine, Benetto Londa, a nephew of Bartolomeo Marchioni. On the arrival of Ca' Masser in Lisbon he was immediately called to the royal palace. Here the king questioned him at length, and as a result had him sent to prison. Later, when he was able to convince the king that the story he had first told him was true, Ca' Masser was released and had no further difficulties.

Ca' Masser remained in Portugal for two years, and upon his return to Venice made a report concerning the first nine voyages to the East, in which he gave much information regarding the cargoes and trade conditions, as well as an interesting description of the court of Dom Manuel. A translation of his account of Cabral's voyage is here given.

The manuscript was found in 1845 (*Relazione di Leonardo da Ca' Masser*, Marciana Library, Cod. ital. 877, cl. vii), and was published in the next year by G. Scopoli ('Relazione di Leonardo da Ca' Masser alla Serenissima Republica di Venezia sopra il commercio dei Portoghese nell' India dopo la scoperta del capo di Buona Speranza', in *Arch. Stor. Ital.*, Append. tom. ii, Florence, 1845). Another edition was published by Prospero Peragallo (*Centenario do Descobrimento da America*, Lisbon, 1892).

[1] According to Heyd (*Histoire du Commerce du Levant*, Leipzig, 1886, vol. ii, p. 525), Ca' Masser is the abbreviation for *della casa dei Massari*.

[2] His instructions, dated the 3rd of July 1504, are given in *Archivio Veneto*, vol. ii, pp. 203–5. Here also are published two of his letters, one dated the 18th of September 1504, from Medina del Campo, and the other from Lisbon on the 16th of September 1506.

EXTRACT FROM THE REPORT OF CA' MASSER

On the 9th of March of the year 1500, His Highness sent 13 ships, large and small. The captain was Pedralloro and one Ali Scorer as his factor, with the said Gaspar. And he went on the voyage around the Cape of Good Hope. On the way there overcame him a sudden storm, through which seven ships were lost and there only remained six ships, which continued their voyage to India. The first stop where they had commerce was in Chuchim, and there they treated with that king, who showed that he was glad that they navigated in that part, and he became a good friend of this Most Serene King. And he put on shore the said factor, Ali Scorer. And thus for his security, the Portuguese made a fortress there on a point of the Chuchim river as an habitation for the said factor and security for his merchandise, so that the Portuguese enjoyed some security. And there he contracted with the King of Chuchim copper and other small merchandise and money, and took in exchange spices, strong pepper *K.*[1] 2,000. And he returned thence to Lisbon in 1501 on the 29th of July with six ships, which were on the voyage about 18 months. On this same voyage in returning from Chuchim, the said captain with the said factor, Ali Scorer, went to Colocut and had a talk with that king, and the factor went on shore with certain merchandise. And the King of Colocut made him a certain factory where the Portuguese could live and place their merchandise securely on land. And there being good harmony between the factor and the King of Colocut, the king showed a desire to trade with them in his land, and this was agreed to by the factor with about 47 men. After some days, three or four Portuguese came to words with certain Moors, of which many live in this land. And this was because certain Portuguese had done some violence to a certain Moor, so that the said Portuguese were wounded. These suddenly ran to their factory, and many of them came out armed against the Moors. And all the Moors who were found there committed many outrages. And because the captain took, the day before, a *sambuco* of 300 Moors, all the Moors united with great fury to go against the

[1] The abbreviation used by the Venetians for *cantara*, about one hundred pounds.

said Portuguese and entered within their factory and cut to pieces all the 47 men with the factor. And from this there grew a war between the King of Colocut and this Most Serene King of Portugal. And the King of Colocut had three Portuguese hostages in his house for security, who made the king understand how they had been inconvenienced by the Moors. It is certain the said king had the greatest displeasure at such inconvenience, and was very sorry for it, and tried to find some provision so that he might punish those who were malefactors. But there was such a large number (it was said there were 5,000 Moors), and all was turmoil in the land, that the king could not follow it farther. When the chief captain of the ship learned what had occurred on shore, he suddenly commenced to bombard the land and ruined many houses on the face of the shore. With this there was born the war with the King of Portugal.

LETTERS SENT BY BARTOLOMEO MARCHIONI TO FLORENCE

27TH OF JUNE 1501 AND JULY 1501

THE Florentines were the most numerous of any of the Italian people at Lisbon in 1500. They were there chiefly as merchants and bankers. For some years, however, these Florentines had been forced to ally themselves more closely with the commerce of Portugal, for in September 1494 their entire marine had been permanently destroyed by the Pisans.[1] They were thus quick to take advantage of the opening offered by the expulsion of the Jews from Portugal. When the sea route to India was established it was the Florentines more than any other outside nation who were permitted to benefit by it, because the Venetians could not be thoroughly trusted in voyages so detrimental to their Republic.[2]

The most prominent of the Florentine families was undoubtedly that of the Marchioni, of which Bartolomeo Marchioni was the head. It was from Bartolomeo Marchioni that John II secured for Pedro da Covilhan and Afonso de Paiva in 1487 a letter of credit for 400 cruzados addressed to his representative in Valencia, who in turn gave them one to the banking house of Cosimo de' Medici at Naples, so that they might continue their travels to India and Ethiopia.[3] Marchioni was also in communication with the Florentine banking house of Juanoto Berardi at Seville, and, on Berardi's death in 1495, with his successor, Amerigo Vespucci.

It must have been with some difficulty that Dom Manuel obtained ready money to secure and equip the thirteen vessels which constituted Cabral's fleet. The German houses of Welzer and Fugger were not, at that time, represented in Portugal,

[1] Florentine ships had formerly brought to Lisbon fine woollen cloths, and leather goods, and from the neighbouring city of Lucca came silks. They had taken, in return, preserved fish, cork, ivory from Guinea, and commodities from Morocco, among which leather and feathers took an important place.

[2] Conestrini, 'Relazioni commerciali di Fiorentini co' Portoghesi' (in *Arch. Stor. Ital.*, 1846, App. III), and A. de Gubernatis, *Storia dei viaggiatori italiani nelle Indie Orientali* (Leghorn, 1875).

[3] Conde de Ficalho, *Pedro da Covilhan* (Lisbon, 1898).

and what foreign capital was available was in the hands of the Italians, and chiefly of Marchioni, who was the largest banker there. He financed, in part, one small ship, the *Anunciada*, on Cabral's voyage, which was the first to return, and it is probable that Marchioni also furnished money to the king. He later lent large sums to finance the voyages to India, as is indicated by two receipts, one dated 1507, and the other 1514, for 71 and 36 contos respectively, large amounts at that time. It has been suggested that the expedition to Brazil made by Vespucci in 1501 was not sent by the King of Portugal although approved by him, but was a private enterprise financed by Marchioni. While preference was usually given by Dom Manuel to Portuguese merchants, Bartolomeo Marchioni and Girolamo Sernigi, both Florentines, seem to have been exceptions because of their commercial prominence. As an indication of their appreciation of these favours, Marchioni and Sernigi presented Dom Manuel with a very beautiful Bible, illuminated with Italian miniatures, which is now in the Torre do Tombo at Lisbon. Marchioni was the chief merchant trading in sugar from the island of Madeira, and also participated extensively in the voyages to Guinea, to Madeira, to Brazil, and to India. He was probably the richest man in Lisbon.[1] He sent a ship in the fleet of João da Nova in 1501, with Fernando Vinnetti as his representative; and Giovanni de Empoli went with Vasco da Gama on his second voyage to India in a ship commanded by Buenagrazia, also owned by Marchioni. He later sent ships in the fleets of Afonso de Albuquerque and Diogo Lopes de Sequeira.

When the first of Cabral's ships reached Lisbon, the Italians immediately sent information to their home cities. There are copies of two letters from Bartolomeo Marchioni which he sent to Florence, the first dated the 27th of June 1501, announcing the return of the *Anunciada*, and a second written after the arrival of Cabral. These letters are of particular interest because they were written by an Italian resident in Lisbon who had a financial interest in the expedition.

[1] 'Bartolomeu Marchioni, also a Florentine, who was a resident of Lisbon and the principal one in material substance at that time who had benefited through it' (de Barros, Dec. 1, bk. v, ch. iv).

He had, therefore, better sources for his information from his own representatives, who had gone on the voyage, than had the Venetians, who did not participate in it. Copies of these two letters of Marchioni are to be found in the Riccardiana Library at Florence (MS. 1910). They were copied by Piero Vagliente, and form part of a collection of accounts of voyages which he made prior to his death in 1514. The latest manuscript is dated 1513. The collection also includes copies of the accounts of Marco Polo, Vespucci, the Sernigi letters telling of the voyage of da Gama, and others. It is written in the commercial hand of the period.[1] The originals are not known to exist. These letters by Marchioni have not hitherto been published. They give some additional information and confirm other accounts of Cabral's voyage.

On the 23rd day of this month there arrived in Lisbon a small ship named the *Anunziata* which came from Calichut, and this related how the other caravels which came with it remained behind a few leagues, each league being 3½ of our miles; which ship gave an infinite amount of news, and here, by this, I give you that which is most important.

It is said that it is four months since the fleet left a land in the confines of Calichut, all loaded with spicery, and that five ships of their command were lost in this going. They went to the new gold-mine and to Calichut. There were eight when they arrived at Calichut. Great honour and good reception were given them; and they held mass on shore. Their merchants and factor then began to trade [*s'abazarare*] with them. And there in that part were thirty Moorish ships to load and carry spices over an ocean sea on this same voyage, whence they later went to Domascho. And wishing to load first, the Portuguese came to such a difference that the Moors raised a great tumult and killed all the Portuguese who were on land, including their factor. And when those in the Portuguese ships saw this, they withdrew the ships and began to burn the Moorish ships and to bombard the land; and they destroyed thus many houses and

[1] The eminent Florentine paleographer Uzielli believes that this manuscript was in a hand characteristic of the end of the fifteenth and the beginning of the sixteenth centuries ('Amerigo Vespucci davanti alla critica storica', in *Atti del Congresso geografico Italiano*, p. 482).

killed many people and burned fifteen of those Moorish ships. And through the counsel of an Indian they departed from there and went to another land where they found a king hostile to that of Calichut. And there they were made great honour and much and perfect reception. And there they traded all their merchandise and filled the ships with spices and other things. This king wished to give them much spicery and credit on their return, on their word. They did not wish to load because they had abundant cargo for their ships. And from there they departed friends, and he begged them that on their return they should not make any other port. And the said king sent an ambassador to our king with infinite presents; and promising that they would return to the said place, they departed. The Moors of Calichut had armed 150 sails with 15,000 Moors and came to attack our ships. And because our ships were laden and would have to fight, this was not to be considered, and putting themselves in order, they lost sight of them with the wind astern. And on their coming they found many kings and lords, and of all they had good reception and presents. And they have found the body of Saint Thomas, the Apostle, whose land they were not able to see, and many relics which they have brought here in quantity to the king. And with these ships come four ambassadors with two Christian gentlemen. And all wish to submit themselves to our king. And many other things they related which pages are not sufficient to write on, nor is there time; and this is the cargo carried:

300	*chantara*	of fine pepper
160	,,	of cinnamon
60	,,	of lac
14	,,	of benzoin

These are the things to make mention of, and many other small spices. And what each of the other seven ships which are behind is loaded with, will be learned on their arrival.

They brought back two parrots of different colours which are an arm [*gomito*] and a half long which are more than an arm and a half of ours. They are marvellous things. And they gave notice of many other and various birds and animals, so that where Pliny told untruths, these prove his history.

Bartolomeo Marchionni,
From Lisbon.

It was told in our last letter how only one of the caravels which went on the voyage to Calichut had returned, and in that is seen the cargo which it carried. Later, of the other five ships which were behind, three have returned. The others are lost.[1] And these have brought 3,000 cantara of pepper, 1,000 cantara of cinnamon, and ginger, and cloves and other spicery, so that from here they will be able to furnish by this route all the West, and also Italy, in time. They must give great trouble to the Venetians, and on the route more to the Sultan who enjoys the traffic from there, because by this route they come at rather small expense and more easily. This king is putting twenty ships in order, to depart from this port the middle of November, or at latest next December. May it please God to conduct them safely. They will derive great treasure in this manner, and of it make great riches and all good and necessary things.

The above-mentioned caravels went to the new gold-mine and have brought some back from the said mine, and this king puts ships in order to send to that place, so that he may see the merchandise recently found there, and of what nature it is, and what assortment, and how much is given for it. This king has newly discovered in this [voyage] a new world, but it is dangerous to navigate over the expanse of these seas.

They have brought back many kinds of birds and animals unknown to us, and more often such as are described by Pliny in his history. They were held as falsehoods, but in these days what he relates is seen to be true.

The two ships which went to the new gold-mine are believed to be lost because there has been no news of them, and they say that the gold has not before been known. They believe that at other times these seas have been navigated, but later abandoned because they are so large. They were

[1] It is hard to reconcile this statement with that of the king in his letter of 1501. Two instead of three ships apparently arrived first, the flagship and that of Simão de Miranda. It is uncertain to which Marchioni refers as the third. The other two were not lost. This statement indicates that the letter was written immediately after Cabral's arrival.

unknown to us in our times. This king believes that such a voyage is a beautiful thing.

They say that they have some news of the island of Taprobana and hope in a short time to go there. May God permit them to go and return in safety, because each year new and beautiful things are known.

They say that they found a very large city which they say has silk-shops which belong to the king, with a hundred looms, and its work is of as many kinds as in the city of Strava, whence comes the Strava silk which is understood to come from the East. The said city is called Zanzura [Zanzibar] and is within the Red Sea,[1] and they tell of an incredible thing when they say that for 40 reals, which are 40 of our *quatrini*, an arm's length of crimson silk may be had, which may be found in abundance.

The Moors are white and resemble men of the Sultan of Babilonia. They say that they have sold Paternoster beads of amber at a silver mark and a half a string, which are six or eight [beads] each, at their place, equal to ten to twelve of ours, a string, and that such have resold for 2,000 silver marks, which is a good way to make great riches.

[1] This refers to the Erythrean (or Red) Sea, the name applied by the Greeks and Romans to the Indian Ocean, including the Red Sea and Persian Gulf.

LETTER OF AMERIGO VESPUCCI TO LORENZO DE' MEDICI

GASPAR DE LEMOS had returned to Portugal from Brazil some time during the summer of 1500,[1] bringing with him letters to the king from members of Cabral's fleet and particularly one from Pedro Vaz de Caminha. In this letter Caminha states that Cabral and his council advised the king to send another fleet to make further discoveries, because Cabral could not delay his voyage to India to do so. In addition to these letters news had certainly been received from Spain that Vicente Yañez Pinzon had reached Palos in September of that year and reported that he had visited the South American shore and had brought back a cargo of brazil-wood. It was therefore decided by the Portuguese that an expedition should be sent to continue the discovery of Cabral and to claim this land as within their sphere.[2] The selection of the leader for this voyage was not an easy matter. Many of the navigators who had knowledge of the Atlantic Ocean and to whom this enterprise might be entrusted had gone with Cabral's fleet. There were others, but they probably wished to share in the profits of the voyage to India. It was undoubtedly at the suggestion of Bartolomeo Marchioni that the name of his fellow countryman, Amerigo Vespucci, was proposed. Vespucci may also have agreed to finance this expedition, at least in part, in the hope of securing brazil-wood.

While Dom Manuel had reason to believe that the land dis-

[1] The return of Gaspar de Lemos and the report of the discovery of Brazil evidently did not create great excitement in Portugal. There is no mention of his arrival in any existing document. De Lemos may not have brought back any of the parrots which seemed such novelties when Cabral's fleet returned, nor is there any indication in the letter of Caminha that brazil-wood had been found. Both of these appear very prominently on the Cantino map, where they seem to be associated with the voyage of Vespucci.

[2] According to Duarte Galvão an expedition under the command of Gonsalvo Coelho departed from Lisbon for Brazil in March 1501, and returned in September of the next year. This, he states, reached land at 5° S. and coasted along the shore as far as 32° before it returned. There seems to be no conflict between this voyage and that of Vespucci except as to the date, which Galvão may have mistaken. Amerigo Vespucci was not a navigator, but was a banker who was interested in cosmography. The command of this fleet might therefore have been under Gonçalo Coelho, and Vespucci might still have gone with it and represented the King of Portugal or the Italian merchants.

covered by Cabral was within the Portuguese sphere, he may also have believed, since it was not known to be mainland, that the coast began its westerly direction somewhat to the south and would thus reach the Spanish sphere. On this account Vespucci, who could go representing both Spain and Portugal, would be a desirable leader.

Vespucci was well fitted to accompany this expedition. He knew about the earlier Spanish voyages, as he had previously gone at least twice to America and was interested in cartography. He also had the confidence of the Catholic kings, so that there would be no controversy as to whom the land he discovered might belong to. Word was sent to Vespucci by Giuliano di Bartolomeo del Giocondo, a fellow Florentine, requesting him to come to Portugal. Vespucci accepted the charge, and during the early part of May departed from Lisbon with a fleet of three vessels. Since there was ample time, they spent a few days securing a supply of fish along the African coast and then continued to Beseguiche for water and wood. Here two ships of Cabral's fleet which were on their return voyage were encountered, probably the *Anunciada* and the ship of Diogo Dias. Before proceeding to Brazil, Vespucci took advantage of this encounter and sent a letter back to Lisbon to be transmitted to Florence. In this he gives an account of the voyage of Cabral as he learned it from the interpreter, Gaspar de India, and from others.

The authenticity of this letter has been questioned by some historians for two reasons: because of the belief that it was not in the handwriting of Vespucci, and because it was not, judging by the printed accounts of his voyage which were assumed to be authentic, the kind of letter that he would have written. It is true that the letter is not in Vespucci's hand and is a copy. The copy, however, was made by Piero Vagliente at Florence and forms part of a collection of thirty-two accounts which otherwise appear to be authentic. Vagliente was closely associated with Nicolò Sernigi of Florence and thus with Girolamo Sernigi of Lisbon and would be in a position to obtain copies of letters addressed to Lorenzo de' Medici which, because of their interest, he would naturally include in his collection. Vespucci had gone to Seville at the age of forty to represent the Medici, with whom he had previously been associated. His letters, therefore, would be in the Florentine dialect, as are those which Vagliente copied, and not in the mixture of Spanish and bad Italian found in the printed accounts of his voyages,[1] particularly in *Mundus Novus* and the letter to Soderini, which may have been first printed elsewhere for popular distribution.[2] The letter from Beseguiche is the sort of letter which Vespucci would write. He was interested in cartography. In it, therefore, many place-names are found. He seems, in fact, to have been more concerned with the geography of the East than with the voyage itself. On comparing this letter with other accounts of Cabral's voyage there seems to be little doubt that it is genuine. Vespucci evidently met some of the Florentines on the *Anunciada*, particularly the representatives of Marchioni, who showed him the jewels which they had obtained. He naturally would not mention them by name, because of the injunction of secrecy regarding the voyage which Dom Manuel had imposed.

The original of this letter is not known to exist. The copy, however, is prior to 1514. This is to be found in the Riccardiana Library (MS. 1910). It was first published by Conde Baldelli Boni in volume i of his *Il Milione di Marco Polo* in 1827, and subsequently reprinted by F. A. de Varnhagen in *Amerígo Vespucci* (Lima, 1865), pp. 78–82.

The translation which follows is from the published text.

BESEGUICHE, THE 4TH OF JUNE 1501

MY magnificent Patron. The 8th of May was the last time I wrote you, when I was in Lisbon ready to depart on this present voyage which now, with the aid of the Holy Spirit, I have commenced, and I thought that until my return I could not write more to you. And it appears that chance has given me

[1] By the publication in Europe during the first decade of the sixteenth century of twenty editions of the *Mundus Novus* of Vespucci, which tells of his voyage to Brazil, and of the various editions and translations of *Paesi*, in which the voyage of Cabral is emphasized, the voyage to Brazil was better known in Europe outside the Iberian peninsula during this period than any other voyage to America. It was because of his voyage to Brazil, to make further discoveries for Portugal following the voyage of Cabral, that the name of Amerigo Vespucci was associated with that country, and caused the name America to be given to it and later to both continents.

[2] For a discussion of the Vespucci documents, see Alberto Magnaghi, *Amerigo Vespucci* (Rome, 1924), 2 vols.

another opportunity which enables me to write not only of distant land but of the high sea.

You have learned, Lorenzo,[1] as well by my letter as through the letters of our Florentines of Lisbon, how I was called while I was in Sevilla by the King of Portugal; and he begged me that I should dispose myself to serve him for this voyage; in which I embarked at Lisbon on the 13th of the past month.[2] And we took our way to the south. And we so navigated that we passed in sight of the *Isole Fortunate,* which are to-day called the Canary Islands, and passing them at a distance, taking our navigation along the coast of Africa, we navigated so far that we arrived here at a cape which is called *el Cauo Verde*,[3] which is the beginning of the Province of Ethiopia, and it is on the meridian of the Fortunate Isles and has a latitude of fourteen degrees from the equinoctial line. Here by chance we found, riding at anchor, two ships of the King of Portugal, which were returning from the parts of East India,[4] which are of the same ones which went to Calichut fourteen months ago which were thirteen ships; with which I have had very great discourse, not so much of their voyage as of the coast of the land which they passed along, and of the riches which they found and of those things which they took, all of which I will give brief mention below to your Magnificence; but concerning cosmography, because there was not in this fleet a cosmographer or even a mathematician, which was a great error, I will tell it in the same disconnected manner as they told it to me, save that I have somewhat corrected it with the Cosmography of Ptolemy.

[1] This was Lorenzo (b. 1463, d. 1507) son of Pier Francesco (b. 1415, d. 1476) son of Lorenzo (b. 1395, d. 1440) son of Giovanni (di Ricci), the founder of the house. It was from another son of Giovanni, Cosimo (Pater Patriae), that the more important and better-known members of the Medici family descended. Lorenzo was a prominent Florentine merchant and the head of his branch of the family after the death of his brother Giovanni in 1498. He was the former patron of Vespucci. It was to him that Vespucci wrote the letter known as the *Mundus Novus* and another from Lisbon after his return from Brazil.

[2] In the *Mundus Novus* Vespucci says he left Lisbon on the 14th of May 1501. In his letter to Piero Soderini he says the 10th of May; and in his third letter to Lorenzo Pier Francesco de' Medici he writes the 13th, as in the one here given.

[3] At the south of Cape Verde is the harbour named Beseguiche or Bezeguiche by the Portuguese and Italians. It was near Goree of the Dutch and the modern French port of Dakar.

[4] This indicates that the two ships which Vespucci encountered when he arrived at Beseguiche were the *Anunciada* and that of Diogo Dias.

This fleet of the King of Portugal departed from Lisbon in the year 1499, in the month of April, and they navigated to the south as far as the islands of *Cavo Verde*, which is distant from the equinoctial line about fourteen degrees, and beyond every meridian towards the west, which would indicate that they were six degrees, a little more or less, farther to the west than the island of *Canaria*, since it is well known how Ptolemy and the greater part of the schools of cosmography place the end of the inhabited Western world at the Fortunate Islands. Here they took the latitude with the astrolabe and with the quadrant; and I have found it to be thus. The longitude is a more difficult matter because of the little which can be known about it except by much observation, and watching the conjunction of the moon with the planets. Because of this longitude I have lost much sleep and have shortened my life ten years, and I believe all was well spent, because I hope to come to fame at a distant time if I return in safety from this voyage; God will reward me to the greatest extent in that all my work will redound to His holy service.

Now I turn to my subject: as I say, these thirteen ships above mentioned navigated towards the south of the Cape Verde Islands with a wind which they say was between south and south-west. And after having navigated twenty days about seven hundred leagues (each league of which is four and one-half miles) they went ashore in a land where they found white and nude people of the same land which I discovered for the King of Castile, except that it is farther to the east, of which by my other [letters] I have written you. There they say they obtained every refreshment. And from there they departed and took their navigation towards the east, and they navigated by the south-east wind, taking a quarter to the east,[1] and when they were a distance from the said land, they had such a storm of the sea with south-west wind, and it was so rough, that it overcame five of their ships, and submerged them in the sea with all the people. May God have mercy on their souls. And the eight other ships, they say, went with bare masts, that is without sail, for forty-eight days and forty-eight nights with

[1] The text reads *pel vento dello scilacco, pigliando la quarta di levante.* This refers to the portion of the voyage before reaching the South Atlantic anticyclonic wind area.

a very great storm; and they went so far that they were with their navigation beyond the wind of the Cape of Good Hope which is shown on the coast of Ethiopia, and is located beyond the tropic of Capricorn ten degrees on the southern side. I say that it is in the height of the equinoctial line towards the south, thirty-three degrees. The aforesaid found the location of the parallel. They found the said cape to be sixty-two degrees from the inhabited West, a little more or less, so that I may say that it is situated in the meridian of Alexandria. And from here they then navigated towards the north to the north-east [*quarta del greco*], navigating continuously along the coast, which in my opinion is the beginning of Asia, and the province of Arabia Felix, and of the land of Prester John, because here they have news of the Nile, which is to the west of them, which you know separates the parts of Africa from Asia. And on this coast there is an infinite population and cities, and in some they made port, and the first was Zafale, which they say is a city of such greatness as is Cairo, and it has a mine of gold; and they say that they pay tribute to their king two hundred thousand *miccicalli* of gold every year, and that each *miccicalle* is worth a castellana of gold, or thereabouts. And from here they departed, and they came to Mezibinco, where it is said there is much aloes and an infinite amount of lac and much silken cloth. And it has as great a population as Cairo. And from Mezibinco they went to Chiloa, and to Mabaza[1] and from Mabaza to Dimodaza and to Melinde, then to Mogodasco and Camperuia, and to Zendach, then to Amaab, then to Adabul and Albarcon. All these cities are on the coast of the ocean sea. And they went as far as the strait of the Red Sea, which sea you must know is not red, and it is like ours but has only the name of red. And all these cities are very rich in gold, and in jewels and cloths and spicery and drugs and in things of their own production which they trade with the cargoes from the parts of India; this, as you will understand who know, is a thing long to relate.

From Albarcone they crossed the strait of the Red Sea and went to Meca, where went a ship of the said fleet, which at this

[1] The identifications of place-names given by Baldelli Boni are not sufficiently accurate to be included in this translation.

time has arrived here at this cape. And thus far is written concerning the coast of Arabia Felice. Now I will tell you of the coast of the Red Sea towards India, that is within the strait of this sea.

At the mouth of the strait is a port in the Red Sea which is called Haden, with a large city. Beyond, towards the north, is another port which is called Camarcan, and Ansuva: then there is another port which is named Odeinda and from Odeinda to Lamoia, and from Lamoia to Guda. This port of Guda is near Mount Sinai (which, as you know, is in the Arabian desert) which they say is the port of all the ships which come from India, and from Mecca. It is in this port, they say, that they unload all the spices and drugs and jewels, and everything which they bring here. The caravans of camels come later from Cairo and Alexandria and conduct them there, where they say they go eighty leagues through the desert of Arabia. And they say that in this Red Sea they do not navigate, because of the many rocks and the shoals which are there. And many other things were told me of this sea which, not to be too prolix, are omitted.

Now I will tell of the coast of the Red Sea from the parts of Africa. At the mouth of the strait of this sea is Zoiche, the lord of which is a Moor who is called Agidarcabi, and it is said that this is three days this side of the port of Guda, that it has much gold, many elephants, and infinite supplies. From Zoiche to Arbazui. From these, the two ports of Arboiam and Zala in which Prester John is lord. And opposite is a port which is named Tui and which belongs to the great Sultan of Babylonia. Then from Tui to Ardem, and from Ardem to Zeon. This is as much as I have been able to learn concerning the Red Sea: I refer to one who knows it better.

It remains for me to tell what I learned of the coast of Mecca, which is within the Persian Sea, which is as follows. They left Mecca and went along the coast of the sea to a city which is named Ormuz, which is a port in the mouth of the Persian Sea. And thence from Ormusa to Tus and from Tus to Tunas, then to Capan, then to Lechor, then to Dua, then to Torsis, then to Pares, then to Stacara, then to Ratar. All these ports, which are thickly populated, are on the coast of the Persian Sea. I believe there may be more in my mind to which truly I might refer,[1] concerning which a man worthy of trust who is called Guasparre, who had gone from Cairo as far as a province which is called Molecca, which is situated on the coast of the Indian Sea, told me. I believe that it is the province which Ptolemy called Gedrosica. They say that this Persian Sea is very rich: but all is not to be believed, therefore it is left to a pen better than mine to relate the truth.

Now it remains for me to tell of the coast, which goes from the strait of the Persian Sea along the Indian Sea, according to what many who were in that armada told me; and chiefly the said Guasparre, who knew many languages and the names of many provinces and cities. As I say, he is a very authentic man, because he has twice made the voyage from Portugal to the Indian Sea.

From the mouth of the Persian Sea one navigates to a city which is called Zabule; from Zabule to Goosa, and from Goosa to Zedeuba, and then to Nui, then to Bacanut, then to Salut, then to Mangalut, then to Batecala, then to Calnut, then to Dremepetam, then to Fandorana, then to Catat, then to Caligut. This city is very large; and the armada of the Portuguese went to remain there. Then from Caligut to Belfur, then to Stailat, then to Remond, then to Paravrangari, then to Tanui, then to Propornat, then to Cuninam, then to Lonam, then to Belingut, then to Palur, then to Glencoloi, then to Cochin, then to Caincolon, then to Cain, then to Coroncaram, then to Stomondel, then to Nagaitan, then to Delmatan, then to Carepatan, then to Conimat. As far as this the fleets of the Portuguese have navigated, although they cannot determine the longitude and latitude of the said navigation, which is an impossible thing to do for those who do not have much practice in maritime matters, through which understanding would be possible. And I have hope in this my navigation to revise and correct a great part of the above and to discover much more, and on my return I shall give of all a good and true relation. May the Holy Spirit go with me. This Guasparre, who told

[1] The names of places were taken down by Vespucci as Gaspar gave them. Vespucci was evidently not acquainted with the real names, so the fact that many of them can be identified, in spite of their spelling, is good evidence that the letter is genuine.

me the above-mentioned things, and many Christians agreed with him because they were in one of these,[1] told me later the following: he said that he had been inland in India to a kingdom which is called the kingdom of Perlicat, which is a very great kingdom, and rich in gold and in pearls and in jewels and in precious stones, and he told me that he had been inland to Mailepur and to Gapatan and to Melata and to Tanaser and to Pego and to Starnai and to Bencola and to Otezen and at Marchin. And this Marchin he said was near a large river called Enparlicat. And this Enparlicat is the city where is the body of Saint Mark, the apostle, and here there are many Christians. And he told me that he had been in many islands and chiefly in one which is called Ziban, which he said he had sailed three hundred leagues and that this much had been at sea, the river, another four hundred leagues. He told me that it is a very rich island in precious stones and pearls and spices of every sort, and of drugs and other riches, such as elephants and many horses; so that I believe that this is the island of Taprobana, according to what he represented it to me. And further, he told me that he had never heard Taprobana mentioned in those parts which, as you know, is wholly in front of the above-mentioned river.[2]

Furthermore, he told me that he had been in another island which is called Stamatara, which is of equal greatness with Ziban and Bencomarcano, as well as being as rich as they are; so that, Ziban not being the island, Taprobana may be Scamatarra. From these two islands there come to Persia and to Arabia an infinite number of ships laden with all sorts of spices and drugs and precious jewels. And they say that they have seen a large fleet of ships from those parts which are very large and of from forty thousand to fifty thousand cantara capacity and which they call *giunchi*, and they have the masts of very large ships and at each mast three or four cabins. The sails are those of junks. They are not made with iron but are interlaced with cords. It appears that this sea is not tempestuous. They have bombards, but they are not in the sailing ships, nor do they put to sea much, because they continually navigate in

[1] *e molti Cristiani le consentirono, perchè furono in alcuna d'esse.*
[2] Vespucci is here referring to the maps of India and Ceylon as given in Ptolemy.

sight of land. It happens that this fleet of Portugal, to comply with the request of the King of Calicut, took a ship which was loaded with elephants and rice and more than three hundred men. A caravel of seventy tons took it. And on another occasion they sank twelve ships. Then they came to islands called Arenbuche and Maluche and many other islands in the Indian Sea, which are those which Ptolemy tells of, and which are in the neighbourhood of Taprobana, and all are rich.

The said armada returned to Portugal, and on the return voyage, when there remained eight ships, one of them laden with many riches, which they say were valued at one hundred thousand ducats, was lost, and five were lost in storms.[1] As for the flagship, until to-day it has not arrived here, as I say above; I believe that another day it will come in safety.[2] May God grant it.

What the said ships carried is as follows.

They came loaded with an infinite amount of cinnamon, green and dry ginger, and much pepper, and cloves, nutmegs, mace, musk, *algabia*, *istorac*, benzoin, porcelain, cassia, mastic, incense, myrrh, rose and white sandalwood, aloe-wood, camphor, amber, *canne*, much lac, *mumia*,[3] *anib* and *tuzia*, opium, *aloe patico*, *folio indico*, and many other drugs which you know it would be a long thing to relate.[4] Of jewels I know only that I saw many diamonds and rubies and pearls, among which I saw a ruby of one piece, round, of the most beautiful colour, which weighed seven and one-half carats. I do not wish to relate more because the ship . . . it does not allow me to write. From Portugal you can learn the news. In conclusion, the King of Portugal has in his hands a very great traffic and great riches. May God grant prosperity. I believe that the

[1] The ship of Vasco de Ataíde is here given as among those lost.

[2] *Della capitana, del quale oggi n'é capitata una qui* [sic] *come di sopra dico.*

[3] Ar. *muniya*—mummy, bitumen. Portions of mummies were exported from Egypt, and when powdered were valued as a drug, probably on account of the bitumen used in embalming them.

[4] Some of these commodities cannot be identified with certainty. *Algabia* is probably *algalia*, mentioned by Garcia da Orta as a source of perfume. Linschoten speaks of '*algallia* or civet'. *Istorac* is probably storax, much used in India as a medicine. *Canne* may refer to bamboo. *Anib* is probably *anil* or indigo, while *folio indico* may refer to indigo leaves. *Tuzia* seems to be *tutia* or oxide of zinc, which was sublimated from the ore. *Aloe patico* is evidently another species of aloes.

spices come from these parts to Alexandria and to Italy, according to quality and demand. Thus goes the world.

Believe, Lorenzo, that what I have written thus far is the truth. And if the provinces and kingdoms and names of cities and islands do not agree with ancient writers, it is a sign that they are changed, as we find in our Europe when, through a marvel, one is known by an old name. And for the greater clearness of the truth, Gherardo Verdi, brother of Simon Verdi di Cadisi, was present, who comes in my company, and to you he sends his respects.

This voyage which I now make, I recognize is dangerous as to the frailty of this our human life. None the less I make it with a free mind, for the service of God and for the world. And if God is served through me, He will give me virtue to such an extent that I may be directed to His every wish, if only to give me eternal repose for my soul.

OFFICIAL DOCUMENTS

THE LETTER OF CHIEF CAPTAINCY AND POWERS WHICH PEDRO ALVAREZ DE GOUVEIA CARRIED WHEN HE WAS SENT TO INDIA AS CAPTAIN

We, Dom Manuel, &c., make known to you captains, nobles, knights, squires, masters, pilots, sailors, crew and officers and all other persons who go and whom we send in the fleet and armada which is to sail to India, that because of the great confidence which we have in Pedro Alvarez de Gouveia, a noble of our household, and because we know of him that in this and in all other things with which we may charge him, he will know very well how to serve us and will give a very good account of himself: it is ordered that we give and entrust him with the chief captaincy of the said fleet and armada. Furthermore, we notify and command you all and each one in particular, that in all things which he may demand of you, and order on our part, you shall fulfil and do according to his requirements and commands, as entirely and with that diligence and good care which we would expect from you, and that you would do as though we in person had so told and ordered you, for so we hold it good and for our service. And those who so do and accomplish will render us great service, and those who act to the contrary, which we do not expect, will do us great disservice, and we will give them those punishments which such cases merit.

Furthermore, in order that the affairs of our service may be attended to and carried on as they should be in such a fleet and armada, and so that those may be punished who commit some offence or crime against our service, and in this or in any other cases which may arise, we confer upon him by these presents our full power and jurisdiction, which he may make use of in all cases, until his natural death, and his decisions and mandates shall be carried out without any appeal or redress. However, this power and jurisdiction shall not extend to the persons of captains of large and small ships who go with him and to nobles and other persons whom we send in the said fleet and armada, when crimes are committed which should be punished, because in these cases there shall be trials, and they shall be brought before us, so that we may see them and according to their quality they will be punished and chastised in accordance with justice. And in testimony of all contained herein we order this letter to be written, by us signed and sealed with our seal, and we order that this be accomplished and guarded so that in it there shall be no mistakes of any sort.

Given in our city of Lisbon the 15th day of February. Antonio Carneiro executed it, in the year of Our Lord Jesus Christ 1500.

(Ayres de Sá, op. cit., pp. 283–5.)

THE INSTRUCTIONS

THE commanders of the caravels which the Portuguese sent for discovery along the African coast did not require written instructions other than those furnished to the pilots. Bartolomeu Dias and Vasco da Gama, however, whose fleets were destined for India, may have carried them, although none are known to exist. Cabral's fleet was the largest which the Portuguese had sent. It went on diplomatic missions and carried cargo for trade. Because of the danger that the ships might become separated, regulations were necessary for signals and ports named to which those which lost convoy could proceed. In dealing with the Mohammedan and Hindu rulers instructions were desirable for the safety of the members of the fleet, for obtaining treaties, and for commercial relations. When Arab ships were met at sea they were subject to seizure, and regulations were required for the distribution of booty. Directions were also necessary regarding discipline, the operation of the fleet, the succession of commanders, and other matters of a similar nature. Before Cabral's departure, therefore, comprehensive instructions were prepared with great care. All of these no longer exist, but fortunately the most important portion, that which was intended as a guide for Cabral on his arrival in India, has been preserved. There is also a memorandum supposed to have been furnished by da Gama, regarding the conduct of the fleet at sea before reaching the Cape of Good

Hope, and a letter in which the king gave Cabral additional directions for the return voyage.

On subsequent voyages similar instructions were provided, and from these it is possible to supply some portions of Cabral's instructions which are lost.[1]

Memorandum of Instructions attributed to Vasco da Gama

Since Vasco da Gama had sailed to the Cape of Good Hope by the direct route, his advice to Cabral, who was to follow a similar course, would have been of assistance. Such advice was evidently secured and incorporated in Cabral's instructions. Varnhagen, in his search for early documents in the Archives of Portugal, discovered the most important portion of Cabral's instructions. A short time later he found one leaf of a memorandum, apparently by da Gama, at a sale of old papers. This he inserted in facsimile in the first edition of his *Historia geral do Brasil*. He there claimed that the document had been sent to the Torre do Tombo for preservation. But there is no record that this was ever received, nor can it be found there. In spite of this cloud on its authenticity, the memorandum may still be accepted with some degree of confidence, for the instructions for later voyages resemble portions of it almost exactly. It does not seem to have been written by da Gama but more probably, as Dr. Antonio Baião suggests, by the Secretary of State, Alcaçova Carneiro, during an interview with da Gama. These notes were evidently those incorporated in the official instructions which Cabral probably issued to the captains of the various ships. Da Gama was impressed with the necessity for preventing the loss of convoy by the ships, since he probably had some difficulty in this respect during his voyage. The methods he suggested were not new. Whenever ships went

[1] Complete instructions exist for the voyage of Francisco de Almeida in 1505 (Albuquerque, *Cartas*, vol. ii, pp. 272–334) and for Fernão Soares in 1507 (*Alguns Documentos*, pp. 161–83). Here the signals and directions for a ship to regain the fleet when it had become separated are given almost word for word as in the memorandum attributed to Vasco da Gama. These are also given in the instructions for Diogo Lopes de Sequeira, dated the 13th of February 1508, when he went to discover the west coast of Madagascar (the east coast having already been visited) (*Alguns Documentos*, pp. 184–97). They are again to be found in the instructions given to Gonçalo de Sequeira, who sailed the 16th of March 1510 (*Annaes Maritimas e Coloniaes* (Lisbon, 1845), ser. 5, No. 12, pp. 492–8).

together out of sight of land similar methods must have been used, but these evidently varied, and the recommendations of da Gama were those to be adopted for this voyage.

This memorandum is important, for it shows that da Gama not only suggested that the fleet should proceed in a southerly direction from the Cape Verde Islands and then east to the Cape, but he also advised, if the winds were favourable, that it should continue to the south-west from those islands, a course which Cabral followed. Inasmuch as these directions were entirely for navigation, there are no indications that a divergence westward was intended for any other purpose.

The memorandum consisted of more than one page, as is indicated by the fact that the sentence at the end is incomplete. The text is written in the centre of the page with notes on either side. It is crossed with lines showing that the information had been used and embodied in a more carefully worded document. The translation given is from the text in the *História da Colonização Portuguesa do Brasil*, vol. i, pp. xvi–xix.

The Instructions for Cabral's Guidance in India

Cabral went to India as the representative of the King of Portugal on missions of the greatest importance to his country. Though he was a man of only thirty-three years of age who had had little previous experience, there went in the fleet some of the best pilots and navigators in Portugal, so that their duties were in capable hands. The commercial activities were in the charge of Ayres Correia, who was also able to negotiate commercial treaties. It was further arranged that important matters should be discussed at councils composed of the principal men of the fleet, at which Cabral presided. He was also provided with instructions for his guidance, which were intended to provide for every contingency which might arise. Among them were those for his conduct towards the native rulers, which provide a clue to his actions. These instructions reflect the knowledge which the Portuguese had of India and its rulers before Cabral sailed. Unfortunately for him, this was in many respects inaccurate. Cabral followed his orders as exactly as he could, and because he did so he has in some instances been blamed. From those, however, who were with him and who understood his limitations he received no censure. This portion of the instructions explains several doubtful points, because there is no question as to their authenticity. The statement by Gaspar Corrêa that Cabral did not have the command of his ship but that Simão de Miranda held this position and went as Cabral's successor is shown to be erroneous. It indicates that there existed a preceding portion in which a method for signalling was given, and shows also that Ayres Correia carried independent instructions and that Cochin was known to the Portuguese, although it had not previously been visited by them. The instructions were written in a spirit of friendship and conciliation towards the Zamorin, with no indication of hostility except as a last resort. The heading raises the question as to whether this portion was not designed for the particular guidance of Cabral.

This document was found by Varnhagen in the Archives at Lisbon (Torre do Tombo, maço 1 of Leis No. 21, without date), and was first published by him. It has subsequently been reprinted several times. There is a previous translation into English (M. Clymont, *Pedralvares Cabral*, London, 1914, pp. 41–59). The following version has been made somewhat more literally from the text given in *Alguns Documentos* (pp. 97–107).

Additional Instructions Given to Cabral[1]

These are in the form of a letter and were evidently an afterthought on the part of the king. They give some additional information regarding the voyage, and show that Bartolomeu Dias carried independent instructions. Unfortunately these have not been preserved; they would indicate what previous knowledge the Portuguese had of the East African coast and the duties of the Dias brothers.

The letter here translated was found by Varnhagen and offered by him to the Associação Maritima and published in *Annaes Maritimas e Coloniaes* (Lisbon, 1845) ser. 5, No. 5, pp. 286–7.

[1] Torre do Tombo (*Armario 26 do interior da casa da Corôa*, maço 4, No. 91).

MEMORANDUM ATTRIBUTED TO VASCO DA GAMA

THIS is the way which it appears to Vasco da Gama that Pedroalvarez should follow on his voyage, if it please Our Lord.

In the first place, before he departs from here, to make very good ordinance so that the ships will not be lost some from the others, in this manner: namely, whenever they are obliged to change their course, the chief captain shall make two fires, and all shall respond to him, each with two similar fires.[1] And after they thus respond to him they shall all turn. And he shall thus have given them the signals: that one fire will be to proceed, and three to draw the bonnet and four to lower sails. And none shall turn or lower sails or draw bonnet unless the chief captain shall first make the aforesaid fires, and all have replied. And after sails shall thus have been lowered, none will be hoisted until after the chief captain makes three fires, and all have replied [A]. And if any is missing they shall not hoist sail but only go with lowered sails until the coming of day, so that the ships cannot be carried so far that they are unable to see one another by day. And any ship that has its rigging down will make many fires to summon other ships so that it may be put in order.

After in good time they depart from here, they will make their course straight to the island of Samtiago, and if at the time that they arrive there, they have sufficient water for four months, they need not stop at the said island, nor make any delay, but when they have the wind behind them make their way towards the south [B, C]. And if they must vary their course let it be in the south-west direction. And as soon as they meet with a light wind they should take a circular course until they put the Cape of Good Hope directly east.[2] And from then on they are to navigate as the weather serves them, and they gain more, because when they are in the said parallel, with the aid of Our Lord, they will not lack weather with which they may round the aforesaid cape. And in this manner it appears

[1] These signals were probably made by firing guns.

[2] *não deuem pousar na dita ylha nem faser nemhuna demora soomente emquanto lhe o tempo servyr a popa faserem seu caminho pelo sul e se ouverem de gaynar seja sobre ha banda do sudoeste. E tanto que nelles deer a vento escasso deuem ir na volta do mar ate meterem o cabo de booa esperança em leste franco.*

to him that the navigation will be shortest and the ships more secure from worms, and in this way even the food will be kept better and the people will be healthier.

And if it happens, and may it please God that it will not, that any of these ships become separated from the captain, then it must sail as well as it can to make the Cape and go to the watering place of Sam Bras.[1] And if it gets here before the captain it should anchor in a good position and wait for him, because it is necessary for the chief captain to go there to take on water so that henceforth he may have nothing to do with the land, but keep away from it until Mozambique for the health of his men, and because he has nothing to do on it.[2] [D, E, F.]

And if it be the case that the chief captain comes first to this watering place, before the ship or ships which are lost from him . . .

[The following notes, which appear on either side of the text, are indicated where they seem most appropriate.]

A (*left*). Save that if one of the ships cannot stand the sail as well as the captain's ship, and the strength of the wind requires him to draw it.

B (*right*). If the ships on leaving this city, before they pass the Canaries, should encounter a storm so that they have to return, they shall do everything possible so that all may return to this city. And if any one of them cannot do so, every effort should be made to reach Setuuel [Setubal].[3] And wherever it may be, it will at once make known here where it is, so as to receive orders as to what it should do.

C (*left*). They will return before the island of Sam Nicalao in case this is necessary[; or] because of sickness[4] at the island of Samtiago.

[1] São Bras or Mossel Bay is located 60 leagues beyond the Cape of Good Hope. Bartolomeu Dias stopped there and named it *Bahia dos Vaqueiros*. Vasco da Gama had remained there for thirteen days on his voyage to India, securing beef and water from the natives. It was here that he broke up his store-ship. Cabral would probably have stopped at Mossel Bay for supplies and water had it not been for the storm which he encountered in the South Atlantic.

[2] These instructions were written soon after the return of da Gama, since there is no reference here to the selection of two of the ships to stop at Sofala.

[3] On the Bay of Setubal, a short distance south of Lisbon.

[4] Possibly referring to an epidemic, such as those which had been experienced in Portugal.

D (*left*). If these ships departing from this coast should become separated from each other in a storm, so that some make for one port and others for another, the manner in which they are to join each other: and if the signs of guidance are not made by some one of the ships and it cannot be seen you will, with all the rest, make your way straight to the watering place of Sam Bras.

E (*right*). And there, while you take on water, the aforesaid ship will be able to overtake you. And if it does not overtake you, you will depart when you are ready, and will leave there for it such signs that it may know upon arriving there that you have gone on, and will follow you.

F (*left*). And signs should be set up, where routes are to be taken for the ships which lose each other, and this will be done with the very good experience of all the pilots.

FRAGMENT OF INSTRUCTIONS TO PEDRO ÁLVARES CABRAL WHEN HE WENT TO INDIA AS COMMANDER OF A FLEET

JESUS. Furthermore, as soon as, God willing, you depart from Angadyva you shall go your way to anchor before Callecut with your ships close together and placed in good order, decorated with your banners and standards and as fine as you can make them; and you shall stop in that place where you know is the best anchorage and safest for the ships, and you shall do no injury to any of the ships which you may find there nor between the aforesaid Angadyva and Callecut, even though you know they are from Mecca, but rather salute them and show them a good front and the signal of peace and goodwill, giving food and drink and all other good treatment to all who shall come to our ships; taking heed, however, that so many of them do not come aboard together as to consume many provisions, or to be able to take possession of the ships. And after you have cast anchor and moored the ships and all is put in order, you shall send out in a boat Balltasar and those other Indians whom you carry, and with them a pair of men from those who appear to you to have aptitude and fitness for the purpose and order them to go with the aforesaid Indians to the Camorym,[1] King of Callecut, and to tell him how always in times past, desiring much to know of the things of that land of India and its people, chiefly for the service of Our Lord, since we have information that he and his subjects and the dwellers in his kingdom are Christians and of our faith and people with whom we should be glad to have every sort of true friendship and helpfulness, we resolved to send our ships to seek the way to India, since we know that the Indians are Christians and men of such faith, truthfulness, and fair dealings that they should be sought out, in order that they might more completely have instruction in our faith and might be indoctrinated and taught in matters pertaining to it, as befits the service of God and the salvation of their souls, and afterwards to lend ourselves to trade with them and they with us, carrying the merchandise of our kingdom necessary to them and likewise bringing back theirs. And it pleased God, in view of our good intentions, that a short time ago Vasco da Gama, our captain, went in three small ships and entering the Indian Ocean, reached their country, the city of Callecut, whence he brought the aforesaid Indians in order that we might have speech and dealings with them. And we now order them to be sent back, and from them he may learn what is in our country. And thus as we send them back to him, so he ought to pay for the merchandise which the said Vasco da Gama at his command put on shore, and which was taken from him, and who gave us information chiefly concerning himself and his Christianity and good intention in the service of God, and in the next place, concerning his good faith and the fair dealings of his land in which we took much pleasure; and we resolved to send you with these few ships loaded with the merchandise which we were informed was necessary and profitable to the country, in order that, in our name, you might conclude peace and establish friendship with him, if he is pleased so to have it with us, as we hope, according to what Vasco da Gama told us; and it appears to us that he ought to be glad to do so since he is a Christian and true king; for from peace and trade with us in his

[1] The title Zamorin is of Portuguese origin. The more proper title is Samuri, derived from the Malayālam *tāmātiri* or *tamūri*, meaning Sea King. (*Hobson-Jobson.*)

land he will obtain great advantages chiefly through being instructed and illumined in the faith, which is a matter which ought to be more highly esteemed than any other; and in the next place, because of the great profit which he will receive from the merchandise which we will send from our kingdoms and domains to his country and which our countrymen will bring him; for that which we send at present is only for a sample, since we do not know whether these or other things are those which they most wish for there. And because you will be pleased to have an interview with him to tell him at greater length those things that we on our part commanded you to speak to him, and to give him our letters and some things which we now send him as a present for a beginning and indication of friendship, and if it appears to you that even if all trust should be put in him and his word, yet you should not go ashore without his giving you hostages, because of what was done to the said Vasco da Gama, who was detained at Pandarane; and also because of certain merchandise of ours which he took as a sample and ordered to be placed on land, and which was taken from him; and we believe that this was not done by him or through his fault but at the request and by means of some people without faith, who neither desire to serve him nor to preserve his truth. And therefore you shall ask him to be pleased to give you the aforesaid hostages who shall remain in your ships until you return to them, and say that you would be pleased, from information you have concerning them, if they were people whom you specifically name. You shall take means as seems best to you so that they may be seen and known by one of our people whom you shall send back with the aforesaid Indians, so that if the King of Callecut sends them your man may recognize them, and they may not substitute for them others not of equal importance and standing, and in this matter you shall take very great precaution. And, if he gives them to you, you shall go ashore and give him what I have already mentioned, and shall tell him things which he will be much pleased to hear, and which will bring him much profit and honour, and you shall beg of him not to think it strange that you should require the aforesaid hostages, for it is the custom of these kingdoms that no chief captain shall land from his ships in a place where peace has not been concluded without hostages and security, and that you have always done so on this voyage; for although in some places you touched at and where you were well received and invited to land you were unwilling to do so, nor would you land even if they had given hostages, but that you will do so in his case, because he is a Christian and virtuous, and because we sent you to him, and [you shall tell him that] before sending you these hostages he may safely send his factors and *carranes* of the country to the aforesaid ships, and to them shall be shown all the ships and the coffers, and bales shall be opened, and they shall see that they are full of merchandise and that we are sending merchants to him for his profit, and that they are not robbers, as we were told they gave him to understand when the aforesaid Vasco went there.

And if he wishes to give them, then, leaving the aforesaid hostages in your ships and in your power, and very well treated but nevertheless with so much precaution that they shall not be able to leave, you shall go to land with ten or fifteen men, such as shall appear to you the best to take with you, the other captains being in their ships, and also a captain in your own ship, all for the sake of security, so that the ships shall receive no damage from sea or from land; and you shall leave orders that until you return to the ships no one is to go ashore or to remove anything unless you give orders by one of the men who goes with you that this is to be done. Then you shall go to speak to the said king and shall give him our messages and shall offer him what we send him by you, and you shall tell him on our behalf how we desire his friendship and concord, advantage and trade with his country, and that with this object we send you there with those merchant vessels, and that we pray him to give instructions how our merchandise may be sold in safety, and that cargo for our ships shall be given us, of spices and other merchandise of the country which may be profitable for this; and to give orders that you shall have these at those prices which are in the land and at which they are usually sold, in such manner that if any of the merchants who are there disapprove of our trading there, they shall not be able to raise the price of the merchandise of the country beyond what they paid. And if on your arrival the said merchandise is engrossed by those who are there, he shall see that you get at these prices what is necessary for the loading of the ships, or, if previously his factor should wish to obligate himself personally to give you all the cargo which you require for the ships, divided into such quantities and kinds of merchandise as you shall indicate to him, having decided the price of his goods, and for how much they will take ours, you will consent so to arrange it for the sake of quicker dispatch and to transact business more expeditiously . . .

. . . .

. . . to whichever of these methods you agree he shall give his promise, and, that being done, you shall commence to order the goods you are carrying to be sold, and likewise the purchase of those which you wish to bring away, and from the beginning of your sales and trading he will know who you are, and the profits which he is to obtain now and henceforth from our ships.

Likewise, before going to the king, take means, if it shall be possible for you to do so, to learn if the duties which are paid there on merchandise that enters, also on that which goes out, are the same as Gaspar told us, of which you have a note, and if you find it is so, you shall tell the aforesaid king that you were aware that there are high duties in his country, and that it appears to you that he ought not to levy such high duties upon us, because we have recently begun to send merchandise to his country, and in all places it is the custom at the beginning of trade to dispense with duties and to grant favourable terms to those who come with merchandise, and that such is the custom in our kingdoms, and therefore that it appears to you that he ought to act thus towards us and our merchandise, and suggest to him some reasonable basis as to what is to be given for purchase and sale, telling him that although it is less than the others pay him, the number of our ships and the amount of merchandise will be, if God please, so great that the duties will yield him much more than they do at present. And if it shall appear to you that the said King of Callecut objects to this proposal in some way, and it seems to you that he does not take it well enough for you to hope it will be profitable, in such a case you shall be careful not to insist nor to say more to him regarding it, for what you have already said will be enough, in order that it may not appear to him that you are bringing forward a predetermined matter and that he is losing some of the duties which the Moors are paying him.

And if, by chance, he shall refuse to give the hostages here named, or such other similar ones concerning whom you have reliable information that they are in every way safe for you to take and receive in order that you may land in person, in such case you shall not land, and thereupon you shall send to suggest to him that since he does not desire to give them, it seems that he does not wish to talk with you and to see and hear of our things as we supposed, and that because of this it appears to you that you ought not to land without them; but that in order that trade in merchandise may be made and that he may be told regarding the things pertaining to it and to bring him that which was sent to him by you, you request him to be so kind as to send to the ships three or four merchants and persons for this purpose in exchange for whom you will send an equal number, to deliver to him through them the things which you may send him and to talk with him on your behalf. Thereupon you shall send Ayres Correa and with him two of his writers, one for the receipt, the other for the expenses, and you shall deliver to him that which we send him; and they are to speak to him of the traffic and settlement of the merchandise and delivery of the cargo in the manner in which we have indicated above that you were to speak if you met him; and they shall say that it appears a great mistake on his part and little to his advantage not to give the hostages which you asked for in order that you might land, because if you visited him you would tell him many things to his advantage, and you would establish there a house for us in which to lodge the priests and friars whom we sent in order to instruct him in the faith, and how it is necessary to believe in it to be saved. And also merchandise would be left there and . . . from which he will derive much profit . . . honour . . . to go to his country . . . and supply his subjects with the things necessary for lands to grow richer. And if, notwithstanding, he still refuses to give you the aforesaid hostages in order that after receiving them you may land safely, then you shall request that those whom he sends to the ships for those who go to him, may remain with you in the ships until they load them.

When this has been agreed upon with the said king, and of this we think there can be no doubt, the aforesaid Ayres Correa shall begin to take the merchandise on shore, and to sell and to buy what may appear to him profitable for our service, but he shall not land all the merchandise together, but only what appears to him necessary to be sold, and he shall at once put to use the money received from it in other merchandise which should immediately come to the ships; in this manner the least possible risk will be incurred on shore.

In case the said king should say that he will not give hostages because he has not the custom of giving them to anyone, since his country is safe and secure for all those who wish to go to trade there and that it will be so for you if you wish to land in it to trade and to buy and sell and other words to this effect, so that he still excuses himself from giving hostages so that you may land with them as security, as has been said before, as well as others so that Ayres Correa may obtain goods for the cargo with them as surety, in that case you shall again send word to him that what he says may be perfectly true and that you do not believe that anything else is done there, nor that he permits it, but that although such is his custom and that of his country, and although this matter of your requesting the said hostages of him appears to him a new thing, yet he ought to do for you that which you suggest, not only because you are not a merchant like the others who come to his country from near by, as you yourself know, but because you are our captain, and that you are chiefly sent by us with a motive of much love, peace, and friendship, because he is a Christian king and one with whom we much desire these things, and that for many years and times we have followed this aim, with the object chiefly of serving Our Lord, in order that therefrom might proceed the salvation of both the said king and of those of his land. And for this purpose you are bringing all the equipment and things, which you can mention to him in detail in this message, both priests and friars and all else which is necessary for it, and afterwards an agreement and accord may be made regarding matters of trade, so that it may be safe and sure for the future and with every ease for those whom we may send hereafter, and that thus it may come to pass that our people may go to his country and his people come to ours without any fear, if they so desire.

And in case the said King of Calecut will not on any account whatsoever come to give thus the aforesaid hostages either so that you may land in person or so that the said Ayres Correa may because of them conduct the business of loading merchandise as I have indicated above, you will then send word to him that you are greatly displeased with him for so doing, because you did not expect him to have any objection to this, and that you are still more displeased on account of the displeasure which we shall feel because you did not agree to or make there with him the matters and negotiations of our peace, love, and agreement, as we hoped, for you did not come nor were sent by us for this purpose only, but also that, after taking on your cargo, you carried instruction to leave there our factor in his city, to set up a house for our merchandise and to have with him other persons who were to remain in the house; from which he would derive great profit and in addition much satisfaction, because his country would become richer and better provided in its necessities, but since he shows so much reluctance in so small a matter and one which so greatly carries with it love, service, and friendship, although it gives you great displeasure for the aforesaid reasons, you will go at once to Callemur and there establish your seat and peace and set up your factor and the house which you brought for his city, and with him [the King of Callemur] you will come to an agreement regarding all matters in order that all our service may be attended to which you know will be done as completely as in his city, and perhaps more perfectly and securely, and that he knows that this is truly so.

And after you have thus in the most detailed manner done all that it seemed to you that you could do in the matter to the best of your judgement, and perceive that he does not change to the end which we seek there, then after one day or several days, as best appears to you, although there should be few delays because of the embarrassment which you know must arise, you shall then send another message, saying that although you are assured that our affairs and our service would be very completely attended to in Callemur, and that there we could very safely have our factor and house, yet because of the dissatisfaction which you know we would experience hereby because of our chiefly sending you to him and because of our desiring peace, friendship, and cordial understanding with him rather than with any other king of India, you have resolved to disregard all blame which may attach to you in this case and to transact your business with him and to take on a cargo from his city; and having made this final decision, you shall send ashore Ayres Correa and his writers, who in all respects, as already indicated, shall endeavour to obtain and to buy the merchandise for your cargo with the greatest possible speed and dispatch, proceeding with every precaution that may appear good to you, and taking care that he buys to the greatest advantage of our service.

And while you are thus conducting these negotiations and parleys with the aforesaid King of Callecut, you will endeavour in whatever manner you best can to learn if it is possible to obtain a cargo at Callnur for your ships and also if in case you should desire to go there and establish your house, this can be done for our service, and if you would be well received there, and also if everything would in the future be safe there, if you should establish yourself there, both as regards the cargo at any future time, and as regards the residence of our factor and all other similar information, so that you may not only be well informed as to what you are to do there, but also that you may be able to bring full and certain information concerning this when in good time you return.

Likewise, although inconvenience must arise from this method, since the people are not to land to conduct their business, this is the method which must be followed, namely: the aforesaid Ayres Correa shall buy all the spicery which the said people wish him to buy who entrusted him their merchandise so as to obtain the spices through it, and he is to offer it at prices at which it can be bought without any change, as is set forth at greater length in his instructions, and if perchance it should appear that this will be a matter of great difficulty for the said Ayres Correa, and if he cannot suffer it because of what he is to do on our behalf, then you shall send with him and his writers, a factor, one who shall appear to you most apt and suitable for it, and a writer shall be assigned to him who will buy the spices on behalf of the said parties, for the merchandise which he may receive from them, proceeding in such order that everything is done in good faith, and so that no deceit shall be practised on the parties; at the same time the said factor shall always agree with Ayres Correa upon the price of the merchandise, both of ours to sell, and of that to be bought in the land. And as regards the other small merchandise, precious stones and other things, another factor shall be appointed for these, one in each ship who shall go on shore; to wit: every day one factor shall go ashore from each ship, and shall make the purchase of such merchandise and shall return every day to sleep on shipboard, and in this manner everything will be provided for to the safety of our service.

And if, perchance, the King of Callecut shall give you the hostages before mentioned on acceptance of whom you are to land in order to speak to him and to give him our present and to do the other things which I have already indicated, then, if you perceive that things are being so arranged that they are being done with all security, and that he can be trusted regarding them, and that no inconvenience can follow, which you should easily feel through the modes and means of conducting business, and all the other things which can well indicate it, you are to tell him that we send you to him on this first voyage not only to make our peace and friendship with him, and there to load our ships which you have brought, with the spices and the products of India and of his land, but also that you may leave there in his city our factor and establish a house in which our merchandise and other persons are to remain, and priests and friars, and the things of the Church in order that our faith may be thus completely shown and taught him, so that he may be indoctrinated in it as a faithful Christian, from which he will learn how great is the love we have for him, and that we all desire his friendship and advantage. And you shall request him to command and order that houses shall be assigned to you in which our factor may be lodged, and keep in all security his merchandise and the people who are to remain with him, and that he and all those who remain with him as well as the merchandise that you leave with him may remain and be secure at all times. In evidence whereof he shall order his letter to be given you, and any other security you may know is the usage and custom of the land. And if the said King of Callecut gives you these securities and such others as you think that you should require for the greater safety of the stay of the said factor, to the best of your knowledge in accord with the usage of that land, then shall the said factor remain in that city with the merchandise . . . should be left over of the cargo and also of all the rest of the spices . . . ordered by his . . . and you are to tell him that, since you are thus leaving behind the aforesaid factor and other persons and also our merchandise, to which we were chiefly moved by his knowing how great is our desire for his friendship and advantage, it is our pleasure that you should ask him to send some honourable persons with you, who shall come to visit us, not only to see us and our kingdoms, but also through the deeds, honours, and rewards which they will receive from us, they may know better the good will which we have towards him and his affairs, and you are to endeavour to bring them, and, if you bring them, they are to receive from you all the honour and good treatment that is possible.

And if it should so happen that no hostages should be given you in any of the ways above mentioned, and of necessity you have to labour to obtain cargo for the ships in the manner already described, from which you will clearly know and see that our factor and merchandise as well as the other persons who are ordered to go with him to remain, cannot remain in safety in the aforesaid city of Callecut, in that case after our ships are laden, you shall send word to him that you had the intention as well as our command to leave there our factor and a house for our merchandise, as is set forth in the previous chapter, together with the rest which you will see there.

And after providing for the stay of the said factor and when the matters with the King of Callecut are settled in this way to his entire pleasure and to our service, and you have loaded your ships, you shall finally tell him that he must have already known what great security he is always to have from peace and friendship with us, which will always be perfectly preserved by us and ours at all times and to his profit and the good of his kingdom and its people, but that, inasmuch as we have learned that Moors, enemies of our holy faith, trade in his city, and that their ships and merchandise go there, with whom we continually wage war, both on account of the obligation which every Catholic king must have, and because it comes to us as if by direct succession, and in this connexion you may acquaint him in detail with the events of the war beyond the sea; also that in order that all matters both great and small shall be clear and certain as is proper between us and him, you shall make known to him that if you encounter ships belonging to the aforesaid Moors of Mecca at sea, you must endeavour as much as you can to take possession of them, and of their merchandise and property and also of the Moors who are in the ships, to your profit as best you can, and to make war upon them and do them as much damage as possible as a people with whom we have so great and so ancient an enmity, and also because we comply with our obligations to God our Lord, nevertheless that he is to be sure that although you and other captains whom we may send in the future, may encounter them in his port and before his city, yet, in order to preserve, as we always gladly should, his pleasure and satisfaction in everything, you shall do them no harm or damage but shall only do all you can against them when you meet those ships at sea, as has been already said, where they will do what they can against you and against our people whom they henceforth may encounter. And that he may be certain to know that he and his property are to be respected as is due to a king with whom we delight always to maintain affection, peace, and friendship, that when you or any other of our captains capture the aforesaid ships, none of the Indians found in them nor any of their merchandise or property will be injured in any way, but on the contrary, they will receive every honour and all good treatment, and will be sure of this, that they and all which belongs to them will be left alone, for war will only be waged against the said Moors as our enemies, and that it would further please us if he could exclude these Moors from his land and from trading in it, since, please God, he will receive from us and ours all the profit which until now he has had from them, and much more, and that it would be well and for God's service, because in this he would comply with his duty as a Christian king, if he would expel them from his country and not allow them to come there nor to trade in it, since no other advantages result from them and their residence, arrival, and stay there than the profit he gets from them, and this he will draw from our people with God's help, and with so much greater increase, that he would be content, and that if such Moors and ships of Mecca should be captured by our people, that in this case he should give us security by letter, that although because of this the said Moors of Mecca who may at such time be in his city or lands and any others should request him to make reprisals on our factor and house and merchandise and people that might be in it, in order that they shall thus be indemnified for the injury done to them by our people, he will not do so, and that no compulsion nor injury will be inflicted on our people or our merchandise on this account, but rather that he will always protect them as he is obliged by the peace and friendship which he has with us.

Furthermore, you shall tell him that inasmuch as we have learned that it is the custom in his city and land when any merchant dies there, that his estate, merchandise, and property shall become the property of the said king and be collected for him, that it would not be reasonable that this should apply to our factor, because this rule should be observed only of persons who trade in their own merchandise and transact business on their own account, which our agent does not do, for everything is ours. In this he is to give assurance that if God our Lord should take away our aforesaid agent and he dies there, then all our merchandise and property and also all our storehouse shall be exempt and free from this custom, and that our factor who shall succeed to the other at his death, shall do freely and without impediment all that the deceased factor was doing without anything coming to the said king, or his interfering with what is ours, for, as we say, it would not be reasonable to apply the regulation or to do to our man what is done to the other merchants and people.

Furthermore, things may come to this state from the progress of the negotiations you conduct, that you encounter such hindrance from him in a matter in which there should be none, over his giving hostages, that you must leave him and put into Callemur, then you shall depart with your cargoes and go direct to Callemur, and shall give [the king] our letters which you take with you, and shall tell him how we are sending you to those parts of India in order to establish peace and friendship with its kings, as we have long desired to do and as ought to be done between Christian kings, and that, inasmuch as you were told that on this your first voyage you would not be able to obtain a cargo in his country for our ships, you therefore went first to Calecut, where you took cargo, and that, inasmuch as we have learned that he is a true king and known to be such above all others, and that he is very firm in matters which relate to our faith and refrains from intercourse with the Moors, its enemies, and because we greatly desire it for all these reasons and for others which we have known relating to his virtues, we therefore commanded you to go to him to conclude peace and establish friendship with him in our name, for the future . . . friends, we and ours may avail ourselves of his country and he and his of ours, as is reasonable and pleasing to us, and not only for this purpose . . . but also that if he receives our peace and amity, as we trust, that you may then leave in his city our factor and people and a house of our merchandise, so that in time to come our large and small ships may take their cargo at his city, and they may sell our merchandise and may buy there what merchandise they need, from which he and all his land will be assured of great honour and profit. And inasmuch as perhaps his city is the principal gateway of all the kings of India, you are therefore to request that, if he wishes to arrange with you to do so, he will be pleased and hold it desirable that the aforesaid factor shall remain, and that he shall give you all security according to the custom of the country, namely, his letters, and any other similar thing; and if he wishes to send some person or persons to come with you to our kingdoms to see what is in them, you can take them with all certainty, since you believe it will be pleasing to us, and we will have them sent back to him in our ships, and they will receive honours and a reward from us, and during the voyage they will be treated by you as you yourself are treated. And, if he gives this, then our aforesaid factor shall remain, together with all those who are ordered to remain with him, and the merchandise and things which he carries for his stay, and when all has been arranged you shall come to him at the proper time. And at this first talk which you will have with the said king, you will first try to ascertain whether a cargo of spices can be obtained in his city, and if other Indian merchandise comes there, and if he would engage in this, and also if the merchandise which you now bring is desired there, or others, and if others, of what sorts, so that you may inform us correctly of everything, and moreover it will be the chief care of the factor . . . to know and to give orders as to how the said king may send . . . by them and give instructions that they be brought there for sale, so that he may be able to buy and have cargoes ready against the arrival of our ships, and, if it please God, they may be certain to find their cargo with all other things which he is charged with, as is decreed in his instructions.

And as soon as you have in good time arranged matters here in Callemur and agreed upon the staying of the aforesaid factor, and he has landed with everything intended to remain with him in the manner ordered in the preceding paragraph, you shall depart in good time for these kingdoms, and if on the voyage you encounter any ships of Mecca and it appears to you that you are able to capture them, you are to try to take them, but you are not to come to close quarters with them if you can avoid it, but only with your artillery are you to compel them to strike sail and to launch their boats, and in them they shall send and shall come their pilots, captains, and merchants, so that this war may be waged with greater safety, and so that less loss may result to the people of your ships. And if their ships should be captured, with God's help, you shall take possession, as best you can, of all merchandise which you find in them, and convey it to our ships; and you shall bring to us all the pilots and captains and some chief merchants who can come here in our ships, and you shall liberate for a ransom the others and the people of the said ships which you capture, provided that you are able and in a position to do so, and the weather permits; and if you are unable to do this, then you shall put them all in one of the ships, the most dismantled that there is, and shall let them go in it and you shall sink or burn all the others, taking great care that if, should it please Our Lord, you capture the said ships, you take all the merchandise, large and small, which in them . . . with all our service.

And as soon as, should it please Our Lord, you shall have crossed and arrived at Melynde, because you will then have learned which of the vessels of the entire fleet are better sailers, and which worse and slow, you shall act thus when you reach the said Melynde; namely: you shall separate all the ships which were the best sailers from the others, and shall give orders that these shall continue their voyage to these kingdoms without waiting for the others, but you shall give orders, however, that those which are thus the best sailers shall wait for one another and shall observe all the other regulations which you have brought with you relating to waiting and signals from one to another so as not to become lost, and you shall separate those which are poor sailers and slow, and these are to continue their voyage independently of the others in the manner which we have prescribed and explained that the fast ships are to do; and if it should so happen that your own ship is one of the fast sailers you shall come in company and convoy with these, and shall appoint a separate commander of the slow sailers and those which are worse to sail; such a person you will select for this purpose as appears to you to be the most suitable and fit, and to him you will commit and give all the authority which you yourself possess: and we hereby order that all the other captains and company shall obey him and comply with his orders as they would to you yourself, and if you should be among . . . with the slow ones, you will remain with them and will appoint another chief captain for the others, in the aforesaid manner . . . of the faster sailers, but if Sanchor de Toar should be with the slow sailers, providing always that he is not in the same division of the fleet in which you yourself are, in this case he is to be chief captain of the division into which he falls.

And although we indicate so minutely in these instructions the things which you are to do and to observe, because, according to the time and manner of conducting affairs (and on this especially), concerning which up to now so little is known, and on account of the difference which perchance you will find in the customs of the country, if it should appear to you that you ought to alter and arrange matters otherwise, in order to conduct and conclude them in a fitting manner, and as we would desire for our service, in this case, we, because of the great confidence which we have in you, hold it for good and command you to do and follow all that which appears best to you, always taking counsel in everything with the captains and factor and any other persons whom you think you ought to consult in the matter: and, finally, that which you decide and agree upon you will follow out and perform.

Furthermore, the second captain . . .

PEDRO ALVAREZ, CHIEF OF THE OTHER CAPTAINS; CONCERNING YOUR INSTRUCTIONS, WE HOLD IT FOR GOOD AND OUR SERVICE THAT YOU SHOULD COMPLY AND KEEP THOSE WHICH ARE CONTINUED BELOW

Be furthermore advised that on your return in good time, after passing the Cape of Good Hope, you shall not make other port nor a stop in any part, but shall only come directly to this city, save that it is for some necessity, or because it may be appropriate for our service that you should do so, because you cannot avoid or be able to do otherwise, in which case you shall do that which seems necessary for greater safety of the matters of our service; but in whichever of the places in which you may do so, be well advised that in all the fleet great care shall also be taken that there shall not be taken out any merchandise or that anything should be done contrary to our service. And at the island of Sam Tomé or Cape Verde or of the Azores, in which we have officials, you shall always obey in these the regulations of our customs officer and the officials who look after the matters of our service, as well as those guarded and made in our instructions for the caravels of Mina, by which I hold it for good that you shall not send out your boats [*barcas*] if you can avoid it, and having in this all advice and good order; and thus we recommend and order that you do, and as soon as you arrive in good time at this city, you will be advised. And thus we order you that neither you nor any one of the ships and caravels of the fleet, whether they are ours or others who go apart, shall launch any boat or consent that any arrive to you, or go in a boat of any sort until there come to you and to the ships of all the said fleet our factors and officials, and they make and provide that which we order them for our service and as it appears to them that they should do; and thus you are to understand and do, for this we hold for good. And in this manner we order to each one of the captains of the fleet that they comply and as their chief you shall give your instructions that they shall so do.

Furthermore, because it might happen that, with the aid of Our Lord, you should arrive in Callecut or in Calemir, in which two places your cargo should be of such abundance that by chance other ships might carry it if they could load; in this case, if it appears to you that it is for our service that you should do so, we hold it for good that you should buy some ship or ships of those of the land, so that you may load them and bring them with you unto some place where you can come to anchor, to place in our ships what is therein loaded, so that they shall take the place of the supplies which are daily consumed; it appears to us that this would be a good thing to do. And if they can satisfactorily and with security come with the fleet, it would thus be well. If it cannot be accomplished in the manner which is said and which thus appears to us would be to our service, you can do as follows and can still do that which will please us greatly, to place thus in them by purchase such an abundant cargo as we have told you before; and we order that Ayres Correa, our factor, accomplish that which is required for our service and you should authorize and direct him thus as to the purchase of the said ships as well as their cargo.

And if some of those from these parts who go in the fleet should wish to buy such ships of those of the land so that they might load them with some sort of merchandise in addition to the quintals which are authorized by us which they might bring to these kingdoms, we hold it for good that they may do so, and they will be obliged to pay us all our dues of merchandise which thus in similar ships are loaded and carried.

And we command you that on them you shall not place in this matter any embargo whatever. And these chapters you shall join with all the others of your written instructions.

[*On the reverse it reads*] Which I entered in the instructions of the chief captain and of Bertolomeu Dias, to the *alvara* of the licence in the chapter for Bertolomeu Dias.

LETTER SENT BY KING MANUEL TO THE ZAMORIN OF CALICUT

GREAT and most powerful Prince Zamorin, by the Grace of God King of Calecut. We, Dom Manuel, by His Divine Grace King of Portugal and the Algarves on this side of and beyond the sea in Africa, Lord of Guinea, &c., send you many salutations as to one we greatly love and prize. God Almighty, the beginning, middle, and end of all things, and under whose ordinance the days and human acts and times run their course, as by His infinite goodness He created the world and the Kingdom of Christ, His Son, Our Saviour, so in His great and infinite power and knowledge He ordained for future time many things for the good and profit of the human race, inspiring through the Holy Spirit the hearts of men that they might be made manifest and accomplished in times more fitting for them and marked out by Him, and neither before nor after. And since this is a truth well known by experience, if with sound and true judgement you will reflect on the great novelty and mystery of the voyage of our men and vessels to you and to those your lands, you must do in those Eastern parts what all of us and we do in the West, where we give many praises to the Lord God because in our day and yours He has bestowed such favours on the world that we are able not only to know through hearing, but to see and know by sight and by intercourse to unite and also be neighbours [one to another]. And while from the beginning of the world until now the inhabitants of those lands were so far removed from these and ever beyond all hope or thought of this, the Lord God now willed to inspire sixty years ago our uncle and vassal called the Infant Dom Henry, a prince of very virtuous life and holy habits, who for God's service and by His inspiration resolved to open out this navigation; and it was continued by the kings our predecessors until now, and, it pleasing Our Lord, He willed to give it the end we desired and that those men who now arrived there in one voyage only should make so long a journey until they reached you, as in all past voyages was made in sixty years; and these were the first men we sent out as soon as, by the Grace of God, we assumed the rule of our realms and lordships. And although this thing is seen to have been done by men, it ought not to be judged as the work of men, for it is not possible for them but of God alone, by whose power what is impossible to men is possible to Him, for since the creation of the world there existed, in those parts and these, great powers and lordships of princes and kings and the Romans and other people who possess the greater part of the earth, of whom we read that they had great will and desire to make this navigation and that they worked at it, but it did not please God to grant them such a possibility in those times, just as we ourselves could [not] have accomplished it if we had not had it from His hand and will. And since as long as God did not wish it to take place all the men of past times were unable to accomplish it, no one should think that now that He desired it, men are strong enough to oppose and undo it, and it is now a much greater wrong and injury to God to wish to resist His manifest and known will than it was to be obdurate against it before it was known. And among the principal reasons why we render many thanks to the Lord God in this achievement is because we have been told that there are Christian people in those parts, and it will be our chief desire to hold converse with you and to profit and give in great conformity of love and brotherhood, as Christian kings ought to do between each other, for it may well be believed that God our Lord did not ordain such a marvellous deed as this of our navigation only to be served in traffic and temporal profits between you and us, but also in the spiritual of souls and their salvation to which we are more bound. And He holds it for His greater service, therefore, that His Holy Christian Faith should be communicated and united between you and us as it was by all in all the small universe for quite six hundred years after the coming of Jesus Christ, until by the sins of men there arose some sects and contrary beliefs, foretold by Christ that they would come after Him for the trial and manifestation of the righteous and for the deceit of wickedness of those who deserved condemnation and destruction because they would not receive the truth to be saved; and therefore God perverted their knowledge and understanding to do evil and believe lies and be condemned, since they would not believe the truth and consented to falsehood. These sects occupied a great part of the earth between your lands and ours, and therefore our communication with you by land was impeded, but is now again opened through our navigation and made free by God, to whom nothing is impossible. Therefore, knowing all this and wishing to follow up and fulfill, as we ought, that which the Most High God clearly shows us to be his will and service, we now send there our captain and ships and merchandise and our factor who, by your pleasure, will remain there and perform his duties. And we also send religious persons instructed in the Christian faith and religion, and also church ornaments for the celebration of the Divine offices and sacraments, so that you may be able to see the doctrine of the Christian faith which we hold, given and instituted by Christ Jesus our Lord and Saviour to the twelve apostles, His disciples, which after His Holy Resurrection was by them generally preached and received by all the world. And some of them, to wit, Saint Thomas and Saint Bartholomew, preached in your parts of India, performing many and great miracles, drawing those people from the paganism and idolatry in which all the world formerly lived, and some of the said apostles converted them to the truth of the holy belief and Christian faith. Our Lord ordained Saint Peter as his principal vicar among all his apostles and disciples, who preached in the great city of Rome, which was then the head of the people and idolatry, and suffered martyrdom for Him, and there lies buried. And from that time until now the holy fathers, his successors, set up there by the same ordinance of Christ the chief head and seat of the Christian faith and religion, the Lord God wishing, as is shown, that Rome, which was formerly the mother of error and falsehood, should be and remain the mother of truth, of whose obedience and true doctrine we and all Christian kings, princes, and seignories are. Wherefore, pondering these things, and reasons of the will and service of my High God for Himself, who was and is the cause of our navigation and journey to you, very affectionately and as a brother we ask you to conform to His will and wish and to make your profit and that of your land, both temporal and spiritual, and that you may be pleased to receive and join in our friendship, trade, and intercourse which we thus peacefully offer you for His holy service, and to receive and treat our captain and men with that sound and true love with which we send them to you; for in addition to the very dear reasons and mystery of the will of God as He has shown us, who could see and recognize as His work, there is every reason why you should rejoice that people should come from so far, and with so great a heart, to seek friendship and intercourse with you and bring you such profit as you may get from our lands more than from any others. And if it should happen that owing to ill will and minds obstructive of good, which are never lacking, we find in you the contrary of this, which for every reason we could hardly credit or expect from your virtue, our fixed purpose is to follow the will of God rather than that of men, and not fail through any contrarities to prosecute this affair and continue our navigation, trade, and intercourse in these lands which the Lord God wishes to be newly served by our hands, not wishing that our labour to serve Him should be in vain, as we no less hope from His piety that it may in purpose, because we firmly believe and hope that, as He created these lands and gave them to you and to His peoples to possess, He will ordain that in His own, His Will will be done, and that there will not fail to be some one in them who will welcome and receive our friendship and our people who go there so much by His will and wish, to whom He so wonderfully opened the way and gave the power to go to them, which thing He himself knows how greatly we desire should rather be through good peace and friendship to Him; and may He be pleased to give us His Grace to know what is His Will and holy service. And as regards this, may it please you to give full faith to Pero Alvares Cabral, noble of our household and our chief captain, in all that he says and requests you on our part and treats of with you. From Lisbon, the 1st of March 1500.

(*Cartas de Afonso de Albuquerque*, vol. iii, pp. 85–8.)

APPENDIX

SHIPS AND PERSONNEL

CABRAL'S fleet consisted of both ships and caravels. There is no official document which tells how many belonged to each class, and the only authors who give us exact statements are Castanheda, who says that there were three round ships, and the rest were ships, probably meaning caravels, and Gaspar Corrêa, who states there were ten large ships of 200 to 300 tons and three small ones. Castanheda, who gives the best narrative of the voyage and usually refers to the vessels as caravels, was probably right. Corrêa had the classes reversed. This uncertainty in the description of the vessels is due to the inexact way in which ships were then designated. The *Capitania*, or flagship, and the ships of Simão de Miranda and Sancho de Tovar were undoubtedly *naos redondos*, or round ships. The remaining vessels were probably small ships and caravels, with possibly a few *caravelas redondas*, which combined the two types.[1] The 'round ships' were so called because when viewed from the front or rear they appeared round on account of their wide beam and bulging sails and to distinguish them from the 'long ships' or galleys of the Venetians. These round ships were provided with castles fore and aft, which were used as living-quarters, and which were also of advantage for boarding in case of a naval engagement. They had three masts. The fore- and mainmasts were square-rigged, and the mizzen-mast had a lateen sail. There was also a square spritsail at the bow.[2] No sails were employed above the top sails, but in fair

[1] There is no description of any of the ships of Cabral's fleet. The illustration of the fleet shown in the *Livro das Armadas da India* which is preserved at the Academia das Sciencias de Lisboa was made long after the voyage, and was derived from references to the ships as given by the historians. It is, therefore, of little real value. Since the ships must have been similar to those in da Gama's fleet and to other vessels of the early sixteenth century, information regarding them may be found in the volumes of Prestage, Ravenstein, Whiteway, and in those describing the caravels of Columbus. The following may also be consulted: Quirino da Fonseca, *A Caravela Portuguesa* (Coimbra, 1934), 'Lembranças das cousas da India em 1525' in *Subsidios para a Hist. da India Port.* (Lisbon, 1868), and H. Lopes de Mendoça, *Estudos sobre Navios Portuguezes nos Seculos XV e XVI* (Lisbon, 1892).

[2] In Roman ships this spritsail was attached to the *artemon* which projected over the bows athwartships and sometimes took the place of the foremast and bowsprit. It exercised an important function, for it enabled a vessel to sail with a side wind. It disappeared after the decline of the Roman Empire and was not again found on square-rigged vessels until the end of the fifteenth century. See G. S. L. Clowes, *Sailing Ships* (London, 1931).

weather bonnets were used. The caravels had three or four lateen-rigged masts and were often provided only with an aft castle. With the *caravela redonda* the foremast was square-rigged and the others lateen-rigged. This type had the advantage of being steadier than the caravels and of permitting the use of two castles. It is doubtful if any of the ships in the fleet exceeded 300 tons, and the smallest was not over 100 tons.[1] The ships of Pedro Álvares Cabral and Simão de Miranda were the largest and may have had a capacity of 250 or 300 tons. Because Sancho de Tovar went as second in command, his ship of 200 tons would probably only be exceeded in size by these two. A comparison of the respective tonnages of the fleets of da Gama and Cabral shows that Cabral's fleet was about five times the size of da Gama's.[2] Six of Cabral's vessels were lost at sea. From a financial standpoint, that of Sancho de Tovar was the most serious. The loss of ships, particularly along the South African coast, continued. Falcão estimates that of the 620 ships which left Portugal for India during the period between 1497 and 1579, 256 stayed in India, 325 returned safely, leaving 39 to be accounted for.[3]

The participants in the voyage of da Gama had gone without an understanding regarding pay. It is probable that the king over-rewarded those who returned, because of the results of the voyage and the privations they had endured. There was no difficulty in securing men for Cabral's voyage. For this reason it was felt wise

[1] The capacity of ships at this period was approximated. The Portuguese indicated it in *toneladas* and the Venetians in *bote*. In neither case was it a measure of cubic contents but rather of carrying capacity in tuns or casks, so that it is difficult to compare the sizes of these ships with those of to-day. In the narratives one finds the Portuguese give the capacity of the *Anunciada* as 100 *toneladas* and the Venetians as 300 *bote*, and similarly that of the ship of Sancho de Tovar as 200 *toneladas* and as 600 *bote* respectively. Ca' Masser gives the sizes of the three large ships of the fleet of Francisco de Albuquerque as 800, 500, and from 400 to 500 *bote*, and of the thirty which went with Francisco de Almeida he states that the largest was 1,000 *bote*, the next 800 *bote*, and the other ships down to 300 *bote*, while the caravels were from 150 to 200 *bote*. With the 'large ship' of Sancho de Tovar given as 600 *bote*, the flagship would hardly have been over 750 *bote* or 250 *toneladas*.

[2] In comparing the fleet of Vasco da Gama with that of Cabral one is struck with the relative importance of the store-ship in the former. It constituted at least a quarter of the total tonnage of the fleet and was sent with the definite purpose of carrying supplies. When these were exhausted it was to be destroyed. In Cabral's fleet only the ship of Gaspar de Lemos is mentioned by any author as having been sent for this purpose. With this larger fleet it is probable that other ships were used to carry the bulky stores for the sustenance of the greater number of people during a voyage which it was estimated might take a year and a half. Nearly half of the members of da Gama's fleet died during the voyage, so that another ship was abandoned. Cabral carried a proportionally larger crew, which may have been sent partly on this account. The abandoning of ships would thus not be necessary and all could return fully laden.

[3] Luiz de Figueiredo Falcão, *Livro em que se contém toda a Fazenda* (Lisbon, 1859), pp. 194–6.

to determine their pay in advance. Gaspar Corrêa tells us that 'What was decided was that the chief captain of the armada should have for the voyage 10,000 cruzados[1] and 500 quintals of pepper, paid for from his salary of 10,000 cruzados at the price at which the king might purchase it, on which he should not pay taxes, except the tenth to God for the monastery of Nossa Senhora de Belem; and to the masters and pilots 500 cruzados for the voyage and thirty quintals of pepper and four chests free; and to the captains of the ships 1,000 cruzados for each 100 tons, and six chests free, and 50 quintals of pepper for the voyage; and to the mariners 10 cruzados per month and ten quintals of pepper for the voyage and a chest free; and to every two ordinary seamen, the same as one mariner; and to every three pages, the same as to one ordinary seaman; and to the mates and boatswains, as to a mariner and a half; and to the official men, that is, in each ship two caulkers, two carpenters and two rope makers, a steward, a bleeding barber, and two priests, the third of that of two mariners; and to the men at arms, five cruzados per month and three quintals of pepper for the voyage; and in each ship went a chief gunner and two bombardiers; to the chief gunner 200 cruzados and 10 quintals of pepper for the voyage and two chests free; and to the bombardiers the same as to mariners; and to each man at arms his free chest. And all the quintals of pepper loaded with their money with only the tenth to God; and the payment of this pepper to be made to them by the king in money, according to the price he might sell it for with a deduction, if any, because the pepper dried on the voyage, a *soldo* to a *liura*; and payment in advance to the men at arms, and one year in advance to those married, and to bachelors half, and the same to all officials of the ships, and to the chief captain, 5,000 cruzados, and to each captain 1,000 cruzados, and to the men at arms six months each, and in their chests white clothing' (*Lendas da India*, p. 147).

The chief officers and pilots occupied the aft castle. On Cabral's ship provision was also made for the meetings of the council and for entertainment. The chief factor with his principal aids evidently went with Cabral and they too would be quartered there. The crew, each provided with a bed roll and a chest, slept below decks. In the waist of the ship cannon could be placed on either side, and in the centre was a large hatchway into which the ship's boats were lowered. The caravels probably had a bombard at the bow. Sails were manipulated with winches or capstans, which were also used for

[1] The cruzado at this time was worth 9*s*. 8*d*. Cabral's salary in money therefore was £4,833.

handling the cargo. At the stern was hung the *farol*, an iron cage in which firewood was burned at night. The sombre pitch-covered hulls were relieved by the bright colours with which the superstructures were painted. The flagship determined the speed and the changes in the course of the fleet; the others followed. The food for the crew consisted of biscuit, dried or salted meat and fish, rice, sardines, dried vegetables and fruits, particularly figs. Oil, honey, sugar, salt, and mustard were provided. Wine was evidently furnished to the crew, because large quantities of it were carried on other fleets.[1] The officers naturally fared better. Caminha states in his letter that chickens and sheep were carried on the ships. The crew suffered greatly from scurvy, and oranges were obtained as a remedy whenever possible. In addition to large quantities of provisions and supplies the fleet had cargo for trade. Two of the caravels, those of Bartolomeu and Diogo Dias, were destined for the coast of Sofala. These carried copper and small wares, such as looking-glasses, bells, and coloured beads, which the Portuguese, in their trade on the Guinea coast, had learned were desired by the negroes. More valuable cargo may also have been taken for trade with the Arabs. The main fleet took copper, in bars or worked, vermilion, cinnabar, mercury, amber, coral of various grades, and cloths, particularly fine woollens, satins, and velvets in gay colours.[2] The latter were chiefly used by the rich for decorations, since the people of the East were satisfied with their scanty cotton garments. Silks could be obtained to better advantage from China and embroideries from Cambay. For their purchases in the East the Portuguese also carried gold. This was in currency. As this was desired because of its intrinsic value, coins of nations other than Portugal were also taken. Those of Venice were particularly esteemed, because they were better known. These coins were called 'trade money' and were those which had not been greatly debased. Most of the money was carried in the flagship,

[1] The first provision in the instructions given for a fleet which went to India about three years later states that the crew were to be provided each morning with three *quartilhas* of wine. Since four *quartilhas* equalled a *canada*, or three English pints, the daily allowance was 2¼ pints. On this basis Cabral's fleet would have carried about 800 English tuns of wine.

[2] Ca' Masser states that the fleet of thirty sails which went under the command of Francisco de Almeida in 1505 carried a cargo worth 250,000 ducats, of which 80,000 was in coin. The cargo consisted of 3,500–4,000 cantara of copper, 60 of cinnabar, 30 of quicksilver, 42 of coral, and from 150 to 200 of lead. The return cargo was chiefly pepper, but other spices were purchased in varying quantities. In addition to the cargo the large supplies of provisions and water which were required for the long voyage occupied much of the capacity. The ammunition, and particularly the stone balls for the larger cannon, were not an insignificant item.

since the factors made purchases for the king, and every care must be taken that his interests be protected. The representatives of the Italian merchants and Ayres Correia with his staff were probably also provided independently, as they evidently traded on their own account, with a percentage deducted for the Crown.

The Captains

Sancho de Tovar, or *Toar*, sent with the fleet as second in command with powers to succeed Cabral in case of the latter's death. He was a Castilian *fidalgo*, who, after killing the judge who had condemned his father to death for following the side of Afonso V against Ferdinand and Isabella, fled to Portugal. His appointment as a member of the fleet was evidently due to his loyalty to the Portuguese Crown. The choice, however, does not seem to have been a happy one. His ship, probably the *El Rei*, of 200 tons, ran ashore near Malindi and was lost with its cargo of spices. Tovar later took command of the caravel of Nicoláu Coelho and visited Sofala. He did not sail again to India.

Simão de Miranda, a nobleman and son-in-law of Ayres Correia. His name is placed third in lists of captains by all authorities except Castanheda. His ship was probably about the size of the flagship. Because it accompanied the flagship and was sent on no special missions, this ship and its commander are mentioned only incidentally by the historians. It may have contained merchandise belonging to Ayres Correia and other Portuguese officials which did not belong to the Crown. It evidently took on cargo at Calicut. Miranda died in 1512, when captain of Sofala.

Aires Gomes da Silva, a nobleman of highest rank. His caravel was lost during the storm in the South Atlantic.

Vasco de Ataíde, a nobleman. According to Caminha[1] and in the first edition of Castanheda he commanded the ship which lost company near the Cape Verde Islands. Other authors state that this was commanded by Luis Pires. Neither reached India, so the question is not of importance.

Pedro de Ataíde, a nobleman and probably related to Vasco de Ataíde. Vasco da Gama married Catarina de Ataíde after his return

[1] Since Caminha saw the captains often while in Brazil, his statement cannot be questioned. The author of the Anonymous Narrative, a contemporary document, states that Vasco de Ataíde did not return to Lisbon. Castanheda, and following him de Barros and de Goes, claim that he did, although later Castanheda says that six ships were lost, which evidently included this one. According to Corrêa his vessel was a poor sailer and had difficulty in keeping up with the rest of the fleet. There is also a divergence of opinion as to whether the ship was lost during a storm. Caminha, our best authority, says that it was during clear weather.

from India, and this may have influenced the selection of the two Ataídes as captains. It was the caravel of Pedro, the *São Pedro*, which was sent to secure the elephant for the Zamorin. His ship was loaded at Cranganore. On the return voyage it became separated, but rejoined the flagship at Beseguiche. Pedro de Ataíde went again to India with Vasco da Gama in the *São Pedro*. He accompanied the fleet of Sodré to the Straits and returning with Francisco de Almeida was shipwrecked and died at Mozambique. De Barros and de Goes give him the nickname of 'Inferno'.

Nicoláu Coelho, an experienced captain who had gone with da Gama as commander of the *Berrio* and took an active part in that voyage. He returned to Lisbon before da Gama.[1] He again sailed to India with Cabral, possibly in the same caravel. On the return voyage he replaced Nuno Leitão da Cunha as the commander of the *Anunciada* and reached home nearly a month before the rest of the fleet. He went to India a third time in 1503 under Francisco de Albuquerque and on the return voyage was shipwrecked and died with that commander in January 1504.

Bartolomeu Dias, also known by the name of *de Novaes*, a *fidalgo* and an able navigator. After returning from his memorable voyage around the Cape, he continued his interest in this voyage. He supervised the construction of da Gama's ships and gave him much advice. He had three brothers, Pero, Alvaro, and Diogo. Pero accompanied him on his first expedition, and Diogo was a captain of Cabral's fleet. Bartolomeu Dias was lost during the storm shortly after the fleet left Brazil.

Diogo Dias, a brother of Bartolomeu, who had gone with da Gama as a writer on the *São Gabriel*. On Cabral's voyage he was the captain of the caravel which, having become separated from the fleet in the South Atlantic, sailed too far east and discovered Madagascar. Caminha speaks of him in his letter as a jovial man who was well liked by his companions.

Nuno Leitão da Cunha, whom de Barros calls a *cavaleiro*. He commanded the *Anunciada*, which was financed by Marchioni and other

[1] 'Nicolão Coelho was a *fidalgo* of great valour to whom El-Rey, D. Manuel, gave the captaincy of a ship to go in company with the great Vasco da Gama to discover India, in which he acted with great distinction and prudence; and when he returned, he arrived first at Cascaes before Vasco da Gama. And through him the king learned of all that happened in that discovery. On this account, among other favours which the king showed him, he gave him as arms a lion rampant on a red field between two columns of silver, which were upon some green mountains, and over each one a shield with five coins [*dinheiros*], and the sea at the foot; which signified the *padroens* which they left in the new discovery of the sea, the land of the Orient, and the lion, the valour with which this heroic deed was accomplished.' M. Severim de Faria, *Noticias de Port.*, 3rd ed., Lisbon, 1791, vol. i, p. 233.

Italians. This was one of the smallest though the fastest of the caravels. It was this captain who saved the life of Antonio Correia, the son of Ayres Correia, at Calicut. Da Cunha filled an important position at Lisbon after his return.

Gaspar de Lemos, a *fidalgo* about whom little is known. He commanded the supply-ship which returned from Brazil carrying letters to the king. This was the vessel which could best be spared from the fleet. Nothing is known of its return voyage. No place-names are recorded on subsequent maps to indicate that it skirted the coast to the north for the purpose of further discovery. The credit for the discovery of this coast probably belongs to Vespucci, who after landing at Cape Saint Roque followed it to the south. De Lemos probably proceeded direct to Lisbon, in accordance with Cabral's instructions.

Luis Pires, who may have been the captain of the caravel financed by the Count of Porta Alegra. Nothing is known of his life, and his ship capsized during the storm.

Simão de Pina, a nobleman who was related to the chronicler Ruy de Pina. He commanded a caravel which was lost during the storm.

The Factors

Three factors were identified with Cabral's fleet, Ayres Correia, the chief factor, Afonso Furtado, who was factor of the two caravels destined for Sofala, and Gonçalo Gil Barbosa, who went out as a writer but was left in charge of the factory at Cochin. There evidently were other assistant factors, some of whom were lost on the voyage, because according to the Instructions one factor was to go with each ship. It is probable that the Italian merchants had one of their own on the *Anunciada*. Corrêa names Gonçalo Gomes Ferreira as a factor who was left at Cananore, but he is not mentioned by other historians. The duties of the factors were to make commercial treaties, to conduct trade with the natives, and to take charge of the cargo. The writers were under their supervision and to them their duties were sometimes delegated. While under the authority of the chief captain, the factors were largely independent and were governed by a special section of the Instructions. Their salary is not given by Corrêa and it seems probable that other arrangements were made for them, either in the form of commissions or permission to trade on their own account.

Ayres Correia was evidently an experienced merchant in Lisbon with a knowledge of Eastern commodities. According to Castanheda it was from him that the store-ship of two hundred tons in the fleet of da Gama was purchased. As chief factor he was an important member of the council but looked to Cabral as his superior officer. In addition to all matters connected with trade, he had in his charge the making of commercial treaties. On this account he may be considered almost on an equal footing with the chief captain. He spoke Arabic fluently and probably had previously traded in Morocco. Correia has been blamed for the massacre in Calicut. This was due largely to lack of knowledge of Malayālam and to over-reliance on the word of the Arab traders. He died fighting on the shore. His son, Antonio, a boy of twelve, who was saved, later became one of the most famous captains in the East.

Afonso Furtado is given by Castanheda as the factor who was to be left at Sofala. De Barros and de Goes state that he was to be left there as a writer. He probably filled both offices. Bartolomeu and Diogo Dias, with whom Furtado was to remain in Sofala, were to stay on the East African coast and carried cargo for that purpose. On this account Furtado was sent ashore at Kilwa, the capital of the coast of Sofala. He may have succeeded Ayres Correia after his death.

Gonçalo Gil Barbosa was a brother of Diogo Barbosa, who was in the service of the Duke of Bragança and in that of Dom Alvaro, who sent a ship with Cabral's fleet, but which was lost in the South Atlantic. It was probably through Dom Alvaro that Gonçalo Gil Barbosa was able to secure the position of writer under Ayres Correia. Diogo Barbosa had a son, Duarte Barbosa, the author of the *Book of Duarte Barbosa*,[1] who it has been claimed accompanied his uncle and remained with him at Cochin. Gonçalo Gil Barbosa was acting as factor at Cochin and was left there when Cabral's fleet hurriedly departed for its return voyage. When da Gama reached India on his second voyage, Barbosa was transferred to Cananore to take charge of a permanent factory which was established there. Corrêa gives him the name of Gil Fernandez. He seems to have learned Malayālam while at Cochin and was thus of great value in the development of commercial relations both there and at Cananore.

The Writers

The writer (*escrivão*) or clerk kept the records and accounts and made the reports for the factors. We do not know how many accompanied the fleet, but probably at least one for each ship. From the fact that two were left at Cochin there seem to have been more than those whose names have been recorded. Pedro Vaz de

[1] Hakluyt Society, vols. 44, 49, 1918–21.

Caminha, Gonçalo Gil Barbosa, and João de Sá may have ranked above the others, and may because of this have had the duty of writing the account of the voyage. We have previously mentioned the two former.

João de Sá had gone with da Gama on his first voyage as a clerk on the *São Raphael*. He was held in high esteem by da Gama and when da Gama left for Terceira with his dying brother, Paulo, he was given the command of the *São Gabriel*. His name is among those who went with Pedro de Ataíde to capture the ship from Cochin. De Sá was later treasurer of the India House.

Other writers mentioned are Lourenço Moreno and Sebastião Alvares, who were left at Cochin, and Diogo de Azevedo and Francisco Anriquez, who, Corrêa says, were selected for Calicut and Cananore. Corrêa gives Fernão Dinis in place of Sebastião Alvares.

The Pilots

Each of the ships seems to have had a pilot, though the office of pilot and master may have been combined in some of the smaller vessels. Six ships sailed independent courses during parts of the voyage. Only the flagship and that of Simão de Miranda remained continuously together. The pilots were evidently under one or more chief pilots who remained on Cabral's ship. With the chief pilots were associated the native pilots for the East African coast and the Indian Ocean.

Caminha gives the names of two pilots, Afonso Lopez and Pero Escolar, but none is mentioned by other writers. Afonso Lopez is referred to by Caminha as 'our pilot', which may indicate that he was one of those with Cabral on the flagship. Pero Escolar did good service with da Gama and was rewarded by the king on his return.[1] He, too, may have been on Cabral's ship. Pero Escolar

[1] 'Dom Manuel, &c. To whomsoever this our letter may come we make known that since we have respect for the service which Pero Escollar, our pilot, has done us as well in the parts of Guinea as in the discovery of the Indies where we sent him, and so that we may make him favour and reward, we hold it for good and we wish that from the first day of January now passed from the present year of fifteen hundred onward he may have and shall have from us an annuity of four thousand reis. And this is given for our reward. And we therefore command the Chancellors of our Exchequer that they shall make note of it in our books and send a letter yearly to the place where he may have good payment from them. And so that he may keep our remembrance we send him this our letter, signed by us and sealed with our pendant seal. Given in Lisbon, the 18th day of February, Vicente Carneiro did it in the year of Our Lord Jesus Christ of 1500.'

(Arc. Nac. da Torre do Tombo, liv. 13 de D. Manuel, f. 7 v.) A. C. Teixeira de Aragão, *Vasco da Gama e a Vidigueira* (Lisbon, 1898), Doc. 11.

continued to act as pilot in succeeding fleets. In November 1509 he was at Cochin in this capacity, and in 1515 he was the pilot of the ship *Conceyçam.*[1]

Besides the pilots there also went in the fleet an astronomer, Master John, who has previously been referred to. After the fleet left Brazil, Master John is not heard of again and he may have continued on one of the smaller vessels which was lost.

The Interpreters

Only two official interpreters are mentioned as being with the fleet, Gaspar da Gama[2] and Gonçalo Madeira of Tangiers, who Castanheda says was left at Cochin. There were others, however, who spoke Arabic. Ayres Correia seems to have had the best knowledge of that language. He probably knew the dialect spoken in Morocco and may have had some difficulty in speaking correctly the language used by the Arabs in India. In the relations of the Portuguese with the Indians, Arab interpreters were necessary. Because of the lack of Portuguese interpreters, many misunderstandings arose at Calicut. The native fishermen whom da Gama had brought to Portugal had been taught Portuguese, but these, because of their low caste, were nearly useless. While Gaspar da Gama is called an interpreter, he does not seem to have been of much assistance in that capacity during Cabral's voyage, and does not appear to have been ashore at Calicut at the time of the massacre. He was apparently treated with some distrust in spite of his conversion and marriage in Portugal as told by Ca' Masser.

Other Members of the Fleet

Sancho de Tovar, as has been said, was the captain who went to succeed Cabral in case of his being incapacitated. Apparently there were other noblemen who went with similar instructions to replace other captains, or who filled subordinate positions. Several of these are mentioned. Among them were Dom João Tello, who is referred to by Caminha, and the Spaniard, Pedro Lopez de Padilla, who is named in the letter of Dom Manuel written in 1501.

[1] Brito Rebello believes that João de Lisboa, one of the most notable pilots at this time, also went with Cabral's fleet. 'It is not possible to state definitely that João de Lisboa went with Cabral, but it may be assumed that with Nicoláu Coelho would go one who was with him on the first voyage as Pero d'Alemquer, who went with Dias, followed in that of Gama.' João de Lisboa, *Livro de Marinharia. Tratado da Agulha de Marear* (Lisbon, 1903).

[2] A great deal has been written about Gaspar da Gama. See the report of Ca' Masser, and Ravenstein, *Vasco da Gama*, p. 179.

Men of minor importance who have not been mentioned elsewhere are Vasco da Silveira (de Barros), Fernão Peixato and João Rois, who were saved by Coje Benquim at Calicut (Castanheda), Fernão Perez Pantaja (Corrêa), who accompanied Duarte Pacheco[1] and Vasco da Silveira on the caravel which attacked the ship from Cochin, and Francisco Correa (Osorio) and Diogo de Azevedo (Corrêa), who were sent by Cabral to the Zamorin. Gonçalo Peixato is also named as one who escaped after the attack at Calicut (Osorio).

The natives who went with the fleet were Baltasar and four Indian fishermen, whom Vasco da Gama had taken from Calicut by force, Moorish pilots who Corrêa says had returned with da Gama, and an ambassador from the King of Malindi.

On the homeward voyage there came the two Christians, Priest Joseph and Priest Mathias, two natives from Cochin, an ambassador from the King of Cananore, possibly the converted Indian yogi, Miguel, though this is not sure, and a hostage from Sofala.

Friars and Priests

Vasco da Gama had reported that the people of India were Christians though not using the rites of Rome. For their instruction in the Catholic Faith, Franciscan fathers, well educated in the doctrines of the Church and strict observers of its rites, were sent in Cabral's fleet. These have been identified as follows: Frei Henrique, of Coimbra, guardian, Frei Gaspar, Frei Francisco da Cruz, Frei Simão de Guimarães, Frei Luis do Salvador. All of these were preachers and theologians. There went in addition Frei Maffeu as organist, Frei Pedro Neto, a chorister, and Frei João da Vitoria, a lay brother.[2] Frei Henrique had formerly been a judge of the Casa da Supplicação. He took the Franciscan habit in the convent of Alemquer and became celebrated for his learning and eloquence. Frei Henrique officiated at the first religious services in Brazil. The Franciscan brothers were on shore at Calicut when the factory was attacked, endeavouring to attend to their religious duties although they did not understand the native language. Three were lost during the massacre, and Frei Henrique, who was wounded, narrowly escaped. He returned to Portugal. He was Bishop of Ceuta in

[1] Duarte Pacheco Pereira was not with Cabral's fleet. See Introduction, *supra*, p. li.

[2] See Frei Fernando da Soledade, *Historia Seraphica Chronologica de S. Francisco, Provincia de Portugal*, iii. 489–90. The Franciscans were thus the first religious order to reach India with the Portuguese. The first Dominicans went to Cochin with the Albuquerques. They were followed by others, but it was not until 1548 that they went to establish themselves in the East. Frei Luis Cacegas, *Historia de S. Domingos* (Lisbon, 1866, 3rd part, bk. 4, ch. i).

1505, confessor to Dom Manuel, and Inquisitor. In the last position he presided at the first burning of a Jew in Portugal, at Lisbon. Frei Henrique died at Olivença in 1532. No record remains of the religious efforts of these fathers during the voyage, except the mention of the conversion of the yogi christened Miguel. There were also in the fleet eight priests, in the charge of a vicar, whose names are not known. The vicar as representing a bishop had jurisdiction in his behalf.

BIBLIOGRAPHY

MANUSCRIPTS

Biblioteca Nazionale di San Marco:

Viaggi vi, 277. Contarini A. Tratado del viazo fato p. le nave del re di portogalo a Cholochut . . .; Copia del viazo de Lisbona a Cholocut de lengua portogallese in lengua taliana.

—— Contarini B. Viazo a Colochut.

Viaggiatori antichi. MS. Ital., Cl. 6, No. 208. Accounts as contained in *Paesi novamente retrovati* . . . Vicenza, 1507, but in condensed form.

Biblioteca Riccardiana:

Riccardiano, 1910. Chopia d'una altra letera venuta di Lisbona da Bartolomeo Marchionni, soto di 27 di giungno anno 1501. ff. 47–8.

—— Chopia d'una lettera schritta [da] Amerigho Vespuci de l'isola del Chapo Verde e nel mare oceano . . . iiii di giungno 1501. ff. 48–52.

British Museum:

Sloane MS. 197. Resende, Barreto de: Livro do estado da India Oriental. 1646. Also two copies in the Bibliothèque Nationale which are practically the same as above.

Vatican Library:

MS. Vat. lat. 7746. Trindade, Paulo da: Conquista spiritual do Oriente. 1638. 2 vols. 1,193 pp.

PRINTED WORKS

Albuquerque, Afonso de: Cartas . . . Edited by Raymundo Antonio de Bulhão Pato and Henrique Lopes de Mendoça. Lisbon, 1884–1915. 6 vols.

Alguns documentos do Archivo Nacional da Torre do Tombo. Lisbon, 1892. (This contains the most important documents pertaining to the early Portuguese voyages and the discovery period in Africa and Asia which exist in the Torre do Tombo.)

Almeida, Fortunato de: História de Portugal. Coimbra, 1922– . 4 vols.

Anthiaume, A.: Cartes marines. Constructions navales. Voyages de découverte chez les Normands, 1500–1650. Paris, 1916. 2 vols.

Avezac-Macaya, Armand d': Considérations géographiques sur l'histoire du Brésil. Paris, 1857.

AZEVEDO, Pedro de, e BAIÃO, Antonio: O archivo da Torre do Tombo. Lisbon, 1905.

BAIÃO, Antonio: O Comércio do Pau Brasil. In História da Colonização Portuguesa do Brasil, vol. ii, ch. xi.

BALDAQUE DA SILVA, A. A.: O descobrimento do Brazil por Pedro Alvares Cabral. Lisbon, 1892. In Centenario do descobrimento da America.

BARBOSA, António: Instrumentos náuticos da época dos descobrimentos marítimas. In *Revista militar*, Lisbon, 1925.

BARBOSA, DUARTE: The Book of Duarte Barbosa. Translated and edited by Mansel Longworth Dames. Hakluyt Soc., London, 1918–21, vols. xliv, xlix.

BARROS, João de: Da Asia . . . dos feitos, que os Portuguezes fizeram no descubrimento e conquista dos mares, e terras do Oriente. With continuation by Diogo de Couto. Lisbon, 1777. 24 vols.

—— Coimbra, 1932. (First Decade only.)

BATALHA-REIS, J.: The Supposed Discovery of South America before 1448, and the Critical Methods of the Historians of Geographical Discovery. In *Geographical Journal*, Feb. 1897, vol. ix, pp. 185–210.

BENSAUDE, Joaquim: L'Astronomie nautique au Portugal à l'époque des grandes découvertes. Berne, 1912.

—— Histoire de la science nautique portugaise. Geneva, 1914.

—— Lacunes et surprises de l'histoire des documents maritimes. Coimbra, 1930.

—— Les Légendes allemandes sur l'histoire des découvertes maritimes portugaises. Geneva, 1917–22.

BETTENCOURT, E. A. de: Descobrimentos, guerras e conquistas dos portuguezes em terras do ultramar nos seculos XV e XVI. Lisbon, 1881–2.

BRAZ DE OLIVEIRA, João: Os navios de Vasco da Gama. Lisbon, 1892. In Centenario de descobrimento da America.

BURNELL, A. C.: A Tentative List of Books and some Manuscripts relating to the History of the Portuguese in India proper. London, 1880.

CACEGAS, Luis: Historia de S. Domingos, particular do reino e conquistas de Portugal. Lisbon, 1866. 6 vols.

CADDEO, Rinaldo: Le navigazioni Atlantiche di Alvise da Ca da Mosto . . . Milan, 1928.

CANTERA, Francisco: Abraham Zacut. Madrid, 1935.

CAPISTRANO DE ABREU, João: O Brasil no seculo XVI. Rio de Janeiro, 1880.

—— O Descobrimento do Brasil pelos Portugueses. Rio de Janeiro, 1929.

—— Prolegomenos da Historia do Brasil do Fr. Vicente do Salvador. In *Annaes da Bibliotheca Nacional do Rio de Janeiro*, vol. xiii, 1889, pt. i.

—— Vaz de Caminha e sua carta. In *Revista do Instituto histórico e geográphico Brasileiro*, 1909, vol. lxxi, pp. 109–22.

CARDIM, Fernão: Tratados da terra, e gente do Brasil. Edited by B. Caetano, J. Capistrano de Abreu, and R. Garcia. Rio de Janeiro, 1925.

CARVALHO, Alberto de: Memoria a respeito da sepultura rasa do descobridor do Brasil Pedro Alvares Cabral. Lisbon, 1902.

—— Os restos mortaes de Pedro Álvares Cabral descobridor do Brasil. Lisbon, 1903.

Centenario do descobrimento da America. Lisbon, 1892.

CLAUDE D'ABBEVILLE: Histoire de la mission des Pères Capucins en l'Isle de Maragnan et terres circonvoisines. Paris, 1614.

CLOWES, Geoffrey Swinford Laird: Sailing Ships. London, 1931. 2 vols.

Collecção de noticias para a historia e geografia das nações ultramarinas, que vivem nos dominios portuguezes. Lisbon, 1812–29. 7 vols. (Vol. ii has a Portuguese translation of the Anonymous Narrative from Ramusio.)

CONESTRINI, Giuseppe: Relazioni commerciali di Fiorentini co' Portoghesi. *Arch. Stor. Ital.*, App. III, 1846.

CORDEIRO, Luciano: De como navegavam os portugueses no começo do século XVI. In *Bol. da Soc. de Geog.*, 1883, 4th ser., No. 4.

CORRÊA, Gaspar: Lendas da India. Edited by Rodrigo José de Lima Felner. Lisbon, 1859–64. 7 vols.

CORTESÃO, Armando: Cartografia e cartógrafos portugueses dos séculos XV e XVI. Lisbon, 1935. 2 vols.

CORTESÃO, Jaime: Colonização do Brasil. In Peres, História de Portugal, vol. iv, pt. 4, ch. iii.

—— A expedição de Pedro Álvares Cabral e o descobrimento do Brasil. In História da Colonização Portuguesa do Brasil, vol. ii, ch. v.

—— O Imperio Portugues no Oriente ate 1557. In Peres, História de Portugal, vol. iv, pt. 4, ch. i.

—— Influência dos descobrimentos dos portugueses na história da civilização. In Peres, História da Portugal, vol. iv, pt. 5, ch. i.

—— Do sigilo nacional sôbre os descobrimentos. In *Lusitania*, Lisbon, 1924, fasc. i.

COSTA, A. Fontoura da: A Marinharia dos Descobrimentos. Lisbon, 1934. Separate of the *Anais do Club Militar Naval*.

COSTA, Candido: O descobrimento da America e do Brazil. Para, 1896.

—— As duas Americas. 2nd ed. of above, Lisbon, 1900.

COSTA LOBO, A. de Sousa Silva: História da sociedade em Portugal no seculo XV. Lisbon, 1903.

DANTAS, Julio: A era Manuelina. In História da Colonização Portuguesa do Brasil, vol. i, ch. i.

DANVERS, Frederick Charles: The Portuguese in India, being a History of the Rise and the Decline of their Eastern Empire. London, 1894. 2 vols.

DENUCÉ, Jean: Inventaire des Affaitadi, banquiers italiens à Anvers de l'année 1568. Antwerp, 1934.

DESMARQUETS, Jean Antoine S.: Mémoires chronologiques pour servir à l'histoire de Dieppe et de la navigation française. Paris, 1785.

ERRERA, Carlo: Della carta di Andrea Bianco dal 1448 e di una supposta scoperta del Brasile nel 1447. *Memorie della Società Geografica italiana*, vol. v, pt. 1. Rome, 1893.

FARIA Y SOUSA, Manuel de: Asia Portuguesa. Lisbon, 1666–75. 3 vols.

FELICIANO, José: O descobrimento do Brasil. São Paulo, 1900.

FERNANDES, M. B. L.: Memoria das moedas correntes em Portugal. Lisbon, 1856.

FERRAND, Gabriel: Introduction à l'astronomie nautique Arabe. Paris, 1928.

—— Le K'ouen-louen. Les anciennes navigations interocéaniques dans les mers du sud. In *Journal Asiatique*, 1919, 11th ser., vol. xiii, pp. 239–333.

FICALHO, Francisco M. C. de Mello, Conde de: Viagen de Pedro da Covilhan. Lisbon, 1898.

—— Garcia da Orta e o seu tempo. Lisbon, 1886.

FONSECA, Faustino da: O descoberta do Brasil. Lisbon, 1900.

FONSECA, Ignacio Joachim da: Descobrimento do Brasil. Rio de Janeiro, 1895.

FONSECA, Quirino da: A caravela Portuguesa. Coimbra, 1934.

—— Os Portugueses no Mar. Lisbon, 1926.

[Fracanzano da Montalboddo:] Paesi Nouamente retrouati. Et Nouo Mondo da Alberico Vesputio Florentino intitulato. Vicenza, 1507.

For textual comparisons the following editions were also consulted: Milan, 1508 (first Latin translation); Nuremberg, 1508 (German translation); Milan, 1508 (2nd ed.); Milan, 1512; Paris, 1516 (French translation); Milan, 1519; Venice, 1521 (Spanish translation).

FREITAS, Jordão de: O descobrimento pre-colombino da America austral pelos Portugueses. In *Lusitania*, Lisbon, 1926, fasc. ix, pp. 315–28.

FULIN, Rinaldo: Diarii e diaristi Veneziani. Venice, 1881.

GAFFAREL, Paul Louis Jacques: Les Découvreurs français du XIV au XVI siècle. Paris, 1888.

—— Histoire du Brésil français au seizième siècle. Paris, 1878.

—— Histoire de la découverte de l'Amérique. Paris, 1892. 2 vols.

GANDAVO, Pero de Magalhaes: Tratado da terra do Brasil. Historia da Provincia Santa Cruz. Rio de Janeiro, 1924. (Latest edition.)

GOES, Damião de: Chronica do serenissimo senhor rei D. Manoel. Lisbon, 1749.

—— Coimbra, 1926. 4 vols.

GORIS, A.: Les Colonies marchandes méridionales à Anvers de 1488 à 1567. Louvain, 1925.

GRANDIDIER, Alfred: Histoire de la découverte de l'île de Madagascar par les portugais. Paris, 1902.

—— Histoire de la géographie de Madagascar. Paris, 1885.

Great Britain. State Papers. Calendar, Venetian, I, 1202–1509.

GRYNAEUS, Simon: Novus orbis regionum ac insularum . . . Paris, 1532; Basle, 1537; Basle, 1555.

GUBERNATIS, Angelo de, Conte: Storia dei viaggiatori italiani . . . Leghorn, 1875.

GUILLAIN, M.: Documents sur l'histoire, la géographie et le commerce de l'Afrique orientale. Paris, 1856. Vol. i.

HEULHARD, Arthur: Villegagnon, roi d'Amérique, un homme de mer au XVIe siècle, 1510–1572. Paris, 1897.

HEYD, Wilhelm: Geschichte des Levantehandels in Mittelalter. Stuttgart, 1879.

—— Histoire du commerce du Levant au moyen âge. Leipzig, 1885. 2 vols. (Rev. ed., with supplementary material.)

História da Colonização Portuguesa do Brasil. Oporto, 1921–4. 3 vols.

HUMBOLDT, Alexander von: Examen critique de l'histoire de la géographie du nouveau continent et des progrès de l'astronomie nautique aux quinzième et seizième siècles. Paris, 1836–9.

HÜMERICH, Franz: Quellen und Untersuchungen zur ersten Indienfahrt des Vasco da Gama. Munich, 1897.

—— Quellen und Untersuchungen zur Fahrt der ersten Deutschen nach dem portugiesischen Indien. Munich, 1918.

—— Studien zum 'Roteiro' der Entdeckungsfahrt Vascos da Gama, 1497–1499. In *Revista da Universidade de Coimbra*, 1927, vol. x, pp. 53–302.

—— Vasco da Gama und die Entdeckung des Seewegs nach Ostindien. Munich, 1898.

HUNTER, Sir William Wilson: A History of British India. London, 1899. 2 vols.

JAYNE, Kingsley Garland: Vasco da Gama and his Successors, 1460–1580. London, 1910.

KAMMERER, Albert: La Mer rouge, l'Abyssinie et l'Arabie depuis l'antiquité . . . Cairo, 1935.

LANE, F. C.: Venetian Shipping during the Commercial Revolution. In *American Historical Review*, Jan. 1933, vol. xxxviii, pp. 226–39.

LA RONCIÈRE, Charles G. M. B. de: La Découverte de l'Afrique au moyen âge, cartographes et explorateurs. Cairo, 1924–7. 3 vols.

—— Histoire de la marine française. Paris, 1909. 3 vols.

LEITE, Duarte: Descobridores do Brasil. Oporto, 1931.

—— A exploração do litoral do Brasil na cartografia da primeira década do seculo XVI. In História da Colonização Portuguesa do Brasil, vol. ii, ch. xiii.

LEITE, Duarte; Os falsos precurçores de Álvares Cabral. In História da Colonização Portuguesa do Brasil, vol. i, ch. iii.

—— O mais antigo mapa do Brasil. In História da Colonização Portuguesa do Brasil, vol. ii, ch. ix.

LÉRY, Jean de: Histoire d'un voyage faict en la terre du Bresil. Paris, 1880. (Reprint of La Rochelle, 1578 edition.)

LISBOA, João de: A Livro de Marinharia. Tratado da Agulha de marear. Roteiros, sondas e outros conhecimentos relativos a navegação. Edited by Brito Rebello. Lisbon, 1903.

Livro de centenario. Associação do Cuarto Centenario do Descobrimento do Brasil. Rio de Janeiro, 1900.

LOGAN, William: Malabar. Madras, 1887. 3 vols.

LOPES, David de Melo: Chronica dos reis de Bisnaga, manuscripto inedito do seculo XVI, publicado por David Lopes. Lisbon, 1897.

LOPES DE CASTANHEDA, Fernão: Historia do descobrimento e conquista da India pelos Portugueses. Lisbon, 1833.

—— Coimbra, 1924, 1928.

LOPES DE MENDOÇA, Henrique: Estudos sobre navios Portuguezes nos seculos XV e XVI. Lisbon, 1892. In Centenario do descobrimento da America.

—— Do Restelo a Vera Cruz. In História da Colonização Portuguesa do Brasil, vol. ii, ch. vi.

LOPES DE SOUSA, Pero: Diario da navegação de . . . Edited by Eugenio de Castro, preface by J. Capistrano de Abreu. Rio de Janeiro, 1927.

MCCLYMONT, James Roxburgh: Pedraluarez Cabral (Pedro Alluarez de Gouvea), his progenitors, his life and his voyage to America and India. London, 1914.

MAFFEI, Giovanni Pietro: Historiarum Indicarum Libri XVI. Venice, 1589.

MAGNAGHI, Alberto: Amerigo Vespucci. Rome, 1924. 2 vols.

MALHEIRO DIAS, C.: A Expedição de 1501. In História da Colonização Portuguesa do Brasil, vol. ii, ch. viii.

—— A Expedição de 1503. In História da Colonização Portuguesa do Brasil, vol. ii, ch. x.

—— A Semana de Vera Cruz. In História da Colonização Portuguesa do Brasil, vol. ii, ch. vii.

MANUEL I, King of Portugal: Carta de el-Rei D. Manuel ao Rei Catholico . . . Edited by Prospero Peragallo. In Centenario do descobrimento da America. Memorias da Commissão Portugueza. Lisbon, 1892.

MASSER, Leonardo da Ca': Relazione . . . In Centenario do descobrimento da America. Memorias da Commissão Portugueza. Lisbon, 1892.

MAUGHAM, G. C. F.: Portuguese East Africa. London, 1906.

Memorias sobre o descobrimento do Brasil. In *Revista do Instituto histórico e geográphico Brasileiro.* 1855, 3rd ser., vol. xviii, No. 19, pp. 335–405.

MÉTRAUX, Alfred: La Civilisation matérielle des tribus Tupi-Guaraní. Paris, 1928.

—— Migrations historiques des Tupi-Guaraní. In *Journal de la société des américanistes de Paris*, 1927, vol. xix, pp. 1–45.

—— La Religion des Tupinamba et ses rapports avec celle des autres tribus Tupi-Guaraní. Paris, 1928.

MORAIS E SOUSA, L. de: A sciência náutica dos pilotos portugueses nos séculos xv e xvi. Lisbon, 1924. 2 vols.

NAVARRETE, Martín Fernándes de: Colección de los viajes y descubrimientos que hicieron por mar los Españoles desde fines del siglo xv. Madrid, 1825–7. 5 vols.

NORDENSKIÖLD, Erland: Comparative Ethnological Studies. Göteberg, 1919–30, vol. ii, 1920; vol. iv, 1921; vol. viii, 1930.

NUNN, George E.: The Mappemonde of Juan de la Cosa. Jenkintown, 1934.

OLIVEIRA MARTINS, Joaquim Pedro: História de Portugal. Lisbon, 1894. 2 vols.

ORTA, Garcia da: Coloquios dos simples e drogas da India. Edited by Conde de Ficalho. Lisbon, 1891. 2 vols.

—— Translated into English by Sir Clements Markham. London, 1913.

OSORIO, Jeronimo: De rebus Emmanuelis gestis . . . Cologne, 1580.

—— French translation by S. G. S. in Histoire de Portugal. Geneva, 1581.

PACHECO PEREIRA, Duarte: Esmeraldo de situ orbis. Edited by Rafael Eduardo de Azevedo Basto. Lisbon, 1892.

—— Edited by Augusto Epiphanio de Silva Dias. Lisbon, 1905.

PANNIKKAR, K. M.: Malabar and the Portuguese. Bombay, 1929.

PAULMIER DE GONNEVILLE, Binot: Relation authentique du voyage du capitaine de Gonneville. Edited by M. d'Avezac. Paris, 1869.

PEREIRA DA SILVA, Luciano: A Arte de Navegar dos Portugueses desde o Infante a D. João de Castro. In História da Colonização Portuguesa do Brasil, vol. i, ch. ii.

—— A Astronomia dos Lusiadas. Coimbra, 1915.

—— Duarte Pacheco Pereira, precursor de Cabral. In História da Colonização Potuguesa do Brasil, vol. i, ch. iv.

—— Kamal, Tábuas da Índia e Tavoletas náuticas. In *Lusitania*, Lisbon, 1924, fasc. iii.

PERES, Damião: História de Portugal. Barcelos, 1932. Vol. iv.

PIERIS, Paulus Edward, and FITZLER, M. A. H.: Ceylon and Portugal. Leipzig, 1927.

PIRES, Salvador: Estudos sobre a bahia Cabralia e Vera-Cruz. Bahia, 1899.

POLO, Marco: Il milione di M. Polo . . . ora per la prima volta pubblicato ed illustrato dal Conte G. B. Baldelli Boni. Florence, 1827.

POLO, Marco: The Book of Sir Marco Polo. Translated and edited by Sir Henry Yule. 3rd ed., London, 1903. 2 vols.

PRESTAGE, Edgar: The Portuguese Pioneers. London, 1933.

PURCHAS, Samuel: Hakluytus Posthumus, or Purchas his Pilgrimes. Glasgow, 1906. Vol. xvi. (Containing a translation of the accounts of Fernão Cardim and of Anthony Knivet concerning Brazil.)

Raccolta di documenti e studi pubblicati dalla R. Commissione colombiana ... Rome, 1892–6. Pt. iii, vols. i, ii.

RAMUSIO, Giovanni Battista: Delle navigationi et viaggi ... Venice, 1554, 1606. Vol. i.

RAVENSTEIN, E. G.: The Journal of the First Voyage of Vasco da Gama, 1497–1499. Hakluyt Soc., London, 1898, vol. xcix.

—— Martin Behaim. His Life and Globe. London, 1908.

Retratos e Elegias dos Varões e Donas. Lisbon, 1817.

RIBEIRO, João: História de Portugal. Rio de Janeiro, 1928.

—— O Fabordão. Rio de Janeiro, 1910.

RICARD, Robert: Publications relatives à la découverte du Brésil et à l'expedition de Pedro Alvares Cabral. In *Revue de l'Amérique latine*, Sept. 1922, vol. iii, pp. 42–8.

ROCHA POMBO, José Francisco de: História do Brasil. Rio de Janeiro, 1906.

ROMANIN, S.: Storia documentata di Venezia. Venice, 1855.

SÁ, Ayres de: Frei Gonçalo Velho. Soc. de Geog. de Lisboa. Lisbon, 1899, 1900. 2 vols.

SANCHES DE BAÊNA, A. R. S., Visconde de: O descobridor do Brasil, Pedro Álvares Cabral. Lisbon, 1897.

SANUTO, Marino: I diarii ... Edited by Rinaldó Fulin and Nicolò Barozzi. Venice, 1880. Vols. iii and iv.

SCHOFF, Wilfred H.: The Periplus of the Erythrean Sea. London, 1912.

SCHÜCK, A.: Der Kompass. Hamburg, 1915.

SCHULLER, Rudolph: The Oldest Known Illustration of South American Indians. In *Journal de la société des américanistes de Paris*, 1924, New Ser., xvi, pp. 110–18.

SCHURHAMMER, Georg: The Malabar Church and Rome during the Early Portuguese Period and Before. Trichinopoly, 1934.

SCOPOLI, G.: Relazione di Leonardo da Ca' Masser alla Serenissima Republica di Venezia sopra il commercio dei Portoghesi nell' India dopo la scoperta del capo di Buona Speranza. In *Arch. Stor. Ital.*, App., vol. ii. Florence, 1846.

SEVERIM DE FARIA, Manoel: Noticias de Portugal. 3rd ed. Lisbon, 1791. 3 vols.

SEWELL, Robert: A Forgotten Empire. London, 1900.

SOARES DE SOUZA, Gabriel: Tratado descriptivo do Brazil em 1587. In *Revista do Instituto histórico e geográphico Brasileiro*, 1851, vol. xiv.

SOUSA PINTO, Manuel de: A carta de Pero Vaz de Caminha. Edições e leituras. Coimbra, 1930.

—— Pero Vaz de Caminha e a carta do 'achamento' do Brasil. Lisbon, 1934.

SOUZA SILVA, J. Norberto de: Refutação ás reflexões. (Memorias sobre o descobrimento do Brazil.) In *Revista do Instituto histórico e geográphico Brasileiro*, 1855, vol. xviii, pp. 335–405.

SOUSA VITERBO, Francisco, Marques de: Pero Vaz de Caminha e a primeira narrativa do descobrimento do Brasil. Noticia histórica e documental. Lisbon, 1902.

—— Trabalhos náuticos dos portugueses nos séculos XVI e XVII. Lisbon, 1898–1900. 2 vols.

STADEN, HANS: The True History of His Captivity, 1557. Translated and edited by Malcolm Letts. London, 1929.

—— Warhaftige Historia und Beschreibung eyner Landtschafft der Wilden Nacketen Grimmigen Menschfressen Leuthen in der Newenwelt America gelegen . . . Frankfurt-a.-M., 1927 (facsimile of the first ed. of 1557).

STRONG, S. Arthur: The History of Kilwa. Edited from an Arabic manuscript. In the *Journal of the Royal Asiatic Society of Great Britian and Ireland*, April 1895, New Ser., vol. xxvii, pp. 385–430.

Subsidios para a historia da India portugueza publicados de ordem da classe de sciencias moraes, politicas e bellas-lettras. Lisbon, 1868.

TEIXEIRA DE ARAGÃO, Augusto Carlos: Breve notícia sôbre o descobrimento da América. Lisbon, 1892. In Centenario do descobrimento da America.

—— Descripção geral e historica das moedas cunhada en nome dos reis, regentes e governadores de Portugal. Lisbon, 1880. 3 vols.

—— Vasco da Gama e a Vidigueira. Lisbon, 1898.

TENNANT, James: Ceylon. London, 1859. 2 vols.

TERNAUX-COMPANS, H.: Voyages, relations et mémoires originaux pour servir à l'histoire de la découverte de l'Amérique. Paris, 1837.

THACHER, John Boyd: Christopher Columbus: His Life, His Work, His Remains. New York, 1903–4. 3 vols.

THEAL, George McCall: History of Africa south of the Zambesi. London, 1896. vol. i.

TIELE, Pieter Anton: Het oosten voor de Komst der Portugeezen. In *De Gids*, Amsterdam, 1874, vol. xxxviii, pp. 193–242.

—— De vestiging der Portgeezen in Indië, 1498–1506. In *De Gids*, Amsterdam, 1875, vol. xxxix, pp. 177–238.

Die topographischen Capitel des Indischen Seespiegels Mohît, übersetzt von Dr. Maximilian Bittner, mit 39 Tafeln versehen von Dr. Wilhelm Tomaschek. Vienna, 1897.

VARNHAGEN, Francisco Adolpho de, Visconde de Porto Seguro: Amerígo Vespucci. Son caractère, ses écrits, &c., Lima, 1865.

—— Examen de quelques points de l'histoire géographique du Brésil. Paris, 1858.

—— Historia geral do Brasil antes da sua separação e independencia de Portugal. 3rd ed. Edited by J. Capistrano de Abreu and Rodolpho Garcia. São Paulo, 1927– .

—— Nota acerca de como não foi na-Coroa Vermelha-na enseada de Santa Cruz, que Cabral primeiro desembarcou e em que fez dizer a primeira missa. In *Revista trimensal do Instituto histórico, geográphico e ethnográphico Brasiliero*, 1877, vol. xl, pt. 2, p. 5.

WHITEWAY, Richard Stephen: The Rise of Portuguese Power in India, 1497–1550. London, 1899.

YULE, Sir Henry, and BURNELL, Arthur Coke: Hobson-Jobson: a Glossary of Colloquial Anglo-Indian Words and Phrases. London, 1903.

YVES D'ÉVREUX, Capuchin [SIMON MICHELET]: Voyage dans le nord du Brésil fait durant les années 1613 et 1614. Leipzig and Paris, 1864.

ZAIN AL-DĪN, al-Maʿbarī: Historia dos Portugueses no Malabar. Manuscripto arabe do seculo XVI. Publicado e traduzido por David Lopes. Lisbon, 1898.

—— Tohfut-ul-Mujahideen . . . Translated into English by Lieut. M. J. Rowlandson. London, 1833.

Although many articles concerning Cabral's voyage and the controversies connected with it have appeared in both Portuguese and Brazilian periodicals, only the most important have been cited. Those in the *Revista do Instituto Histórico e Geográphico Brasileiro*, 1839 to prevent date, should be particularly mentioned.

INDEX

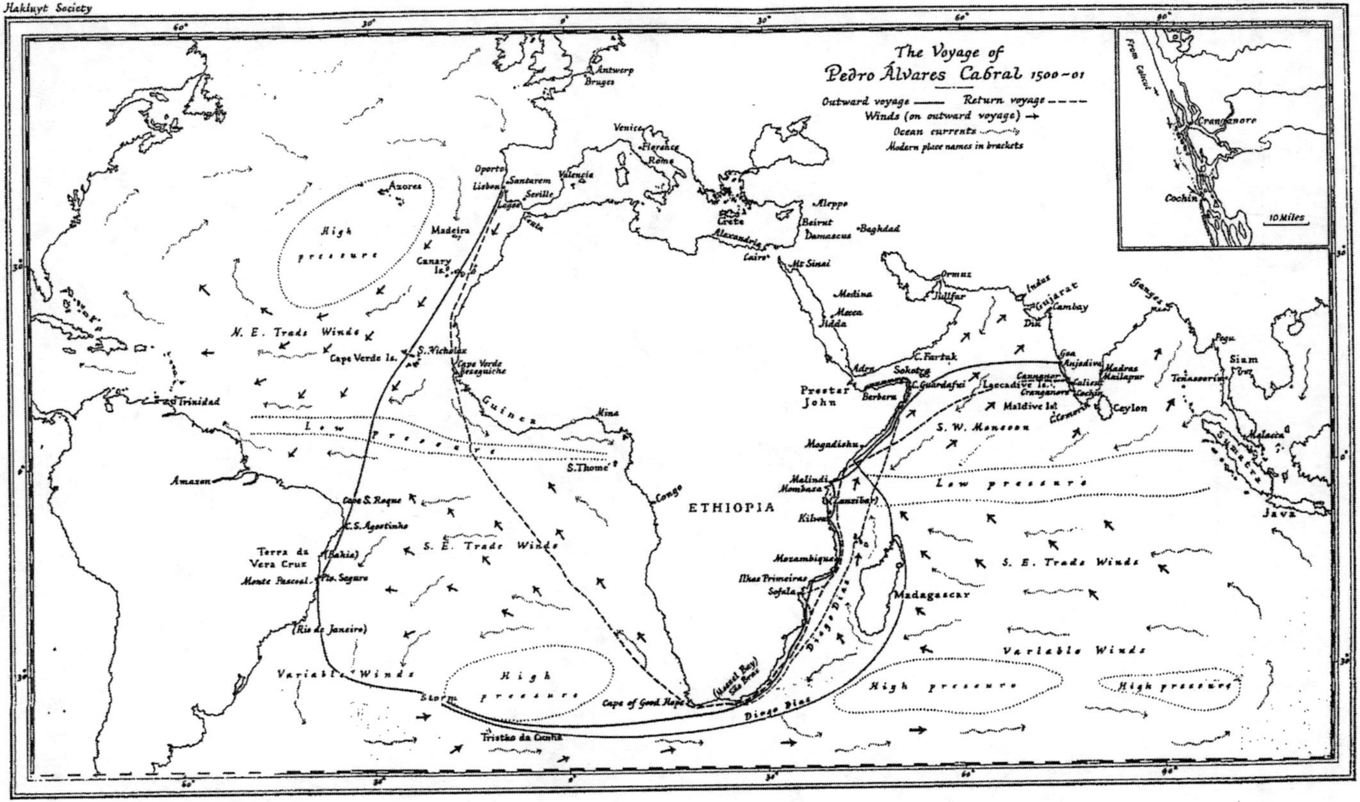
The Voyage of
Pedro Álvares Cabral 1500–01
Outward voyage
Return voyage
Winds (on outward voyage)
Ocean currents
Modern place names in brackets
Antwerp
Bruges
Venice
Florence
Rome
Valencia
Oporto
Lisbon
Santarem
Seville
Lagos
Ceuta
Azores
High pressure
Madeira
Canary Is.
N. E. Trade Winds
Cape Verde Is.
S. Nicholas
Cape Verde
Bezeguiche
Guinea
Mina
Trinidad
Low pressure
S. Thome
Amazon
Cape S. Roque
C. S. Agostinho
Terra da Vera Cruz
(Bahia)
Monte Pascoal
Pto. Seguro
(Rio de Janeiro)
S. E. Trade Winds
Variable Winds
Storm
High pressure
Tristão da Cunha
Cape of Good Hope
(Mossel Bay)
São Braz
Diogo Dias
Congo
ETHIOPIA
Crete
Alexandria
Cairo
Mt Sinai
Aleppo
Bairut
Damascus
Baghdad
Medina
Mecca
Jidda
Ormuz
Jullfar
Indus
Gujarat
Cambay
Diu
C. Fartak
Aden
Sokotra
C. Guardafui
Prester John
Berbera
Magadishu
Malindi
Mombasa
(Zanzibar)
Kilwa
Mozambique
Ilhas Primeiras
Sofala
Madagascar
Goa
Anjadiva
Cannanor
Calicut
Cranganore
Cochin
Laccadive Is.
Maldive Is.
(Comorin)
Madras
Mailapur
Ceylon
S. W. Monsoon
Ganges
Pegu
Siam
Tenasserim
Malacca
Sumatra
Java
High pressure
From Calicut
Cranganore
Cochin
10 Miles